Anglican Religious Life

2018-2019

**A Year Book of
Religious orders and communities in
the Anglican Communion,
and tertiaries, oblates, associates and companions**

Published by
Canterbury Press Norwich
a publishing imprint of The A & M Group Ltd *(a registered charity)*
Invicta House, 108-114 Golden Lane, London EC1Y 0TG
www.scm-canterburypress.co.uk

ARLYB 2018-2019 published September 2017

A catalogue record for this book is available from the British Library.

ISBN: 978-1-84825-962-1

Agents for Canterbury Press outside the UK:

Australia	Rainbow Book Agency	www.rainbowbooks.com.au
Canada	Novalis Books	www.novalis.ca
Europe (continental)	c/o marketing@hymnsam.co.uk	
Ireland	Columba Bookstores	www.columba.ie
New Zealand	Church Stores	christianbooksnz.com/churchstores
South Africa	Methodist Publishing House SA	http://methodist.org.za/work/publishing/methodist-publishing-house
USA	Westminster John Knox	www.wjkbooks.com
West Indies	c/o marketing@hymnsam.co.uk	

The Editorial committee of ARLYB and the publishers wish to thank **The St Andrew's Trust** and an anonymous source for supporting the publication of this *Year Book*.

The cover design is by Leigh Hurlock.
The nature photographs throughout the book are by Sister Mary Julian CHC, for which the editors express great thanks.

The photographs on the cover are from top left:
WSHS/WBHS, SSAP, TOM, BSG, OHP/CSC/CSF, Klaradals Kloster, CAH, CSM (Malawi), CHC, CSF, SLG, SSM (Duxbury)

Contents

Foreword
by The Rt Revd David Walker,
Bishop of Manchester
Chair of the Advisory Council of the Church of England

In over thirty years of ordained ministry within the Church of England, I have almost invariably followed the maxim of being ready to accept an invitation, but never volunteering. My work on the Advisory Council for Relations between Bishops and Religious Communities, usually known as the Advisory Council for short, is the one exception. When I heard, around twelve years ago, that one of its episcopal members had left, I wrote a letter asking to be considered for the vacancy. I have never for a moment regretted that departure from custom and practice. Working with Religious Orders in an era of immense change is both fascinating and uplifting. The contents of this *Year Book*, especially were one to compare it with a predecessor of no more than a decade ago, show that the Holy Spirit is up to something remarkable. What is now commonly referred to as New Monasticism was, back then, unheard of in Anglican circles. Now, much of the work of the Advisory Council of the Church of England is related to how we help such communities come to birth and grow healthy and strong.

The details of communities, old and new, share a common home within the pages of this *Year Boo---k*. It's a symbolic juxtaposition that reflects the way new and traditional forms of Religious Life are finding common ground in the wider Church. The practice of pairing up emerging communities with experienced Religious has both enabled hard-won wisdom to be passed on and also built up bonds of friendship and support that are precious to all. From these individual engagements has arisen a pattern of occasional larger gatherings where both can come together as we seek the will of God. Such events are becoming both more frequent and of longer duration; a sign that the sharing of worship, fellowship and purposeful conversation is highly valued and fruitful.

New communities that are coming to birth are different because of this engagement with their older brothers and sisters. And the more longstanding communities are emerging from these encounters different too, more confident of their own place and distinctiveness, as well as what they share. And, I would suggest, more ready to embark on new ventures, such as the growing groups of "alongsiders" to be found. Finally, my guess is that some of those who begin the exploration of community in a New Monastic setting will eventually find themselves on a different page of this *Year Book*. But that will be a story for a future edition.

A Prayer for Vocations to the Religious Life

Setting a particular Sunday each year as a Day of Prayer for Vocations to the Religious Life was begun in 1992. This is currently the **Fourth Sunday after Easter**. All are also invited to pray each Friday for the life and work of the Religious communities in the Church, using the following prayer, written by a Little Brother of Francis, originally for communities in Australia and New Zealand.

Lord Jesus Christ
in your great love you draw all people to yourself:
and in your wisdom you call us to your service.
We pray at this time you will kindle in the hearts of men and women
the desire to follow you in the Religious life.
Give to those whom you call, grace to accept their vocation readily
and thankfully, to make the whole-hearted surrender
which you ask of them, and for love of you, to persevere to the end.
This we ask in your name. Amen.

A NOVENA OF PRAYER FOR RELIGIOUS LIFE

Day 1: 2 Thessalonians 1: 3
We give thanks for Religious communities throughout the world.

Day 2: Romans 14: 7-9
We give thanks for members in our communities who have died.

Day 3: Acts 15: 36-40
We pray for those who have left our communities.

Day 4: Ephesians 4: 1-6
We give thanks for our own vocations.

Day 5: 1 Thessalonians 5: 12-14
We pray for our leaders and for all who make decisions.

Day 6: Titus 2: 7-9
We pray for novice guardians and all who teach in our way of life.

Day 7: 1 Corinthians 12: 27-31
We pray that we will be faithful to our vows.

Day 8: Acts 2: 44-47
We pray for all who seek to know and to do your will and that men and women will be led to join our communities.

Day 9: 2 Corinthians 4: 16-18
We recognize that the future is in God's hands. We pray that the Holy Spirit will help and support us as we live in the Light of Christ.

We give thanks for the Religious Life in all its forms in the Church, and today we pray especially for:

1 Community of All Hallows *in the UK*
All Saints Sisters of the Poor *in the UK*
Society of the Precious Blood *in southern Africa & the UK*

2 Community of the Holy Spirit *in the USA*
Holy Spirit Sisters (Alsike kloster) *in Sweden*
Community of St Mary *in Malawi, the Philippines & the USA*

3 Community of the Resurrection *in the UK*
Community of the Resurrection of Our Lord *in South Africa*
Communities in the Mar Thoma Church *in India*

4 Community of Saint Francis & Society of Saint Francis & the Third Order SSF *throughout the world*
Little Brothers of Francis *in Australia*
Sisters of St Francis *in Sweden*
Society of the Franciscan Servants of Jesus & Mary *in the UK*

5 Community of the Servants of the Will of God *in the UK*
Community of the Sisters of the Church *in Australia, Canada, Solomon Islands & UK*
Hopeweavers *in the UK*

6 Brotherhood of St Gregory *in the USA and elsewhere*
Sisters of St Gregory *in the USA*
Christa Sevika Sangha *in Bangladesh*
Church Mission Society *throughout the world*
The Order of Mission *throughout the world*

7 Community of Jesus' Compassion *in South Africa*
Order of Women in the Church of South India *in India*
Community of the Holy Name *in Lesotho, S.Africa, Swaziland & the UK*

8 Society of the Servants of Jesus Christ (FMJK) *in Madagascar*
Order of Julian of Norwich *in the USA*
Society of Our Lady of the Isles *in the UK*

9 Community of St Denys *in the UK*
Society of the Sacred Advent *in Australia*
Christian ashrams *in India*

10 Community of St Laurence *in the UK*
Chita che Zvipo Zve Moto (Community of the Gifts of the Holy Fire) *in Zimbabwe*
Chita che Zita Rinoyera (Holy Name Community) *in Zimbabwe*

We give thanks for the Religious Life in all its forms in the Church, and today we pray especially for:

11 Order of St Benedict *in independent Abbeys and Priories throughout the world*
Benedictine Community of Christ the King *in Australia*
Benedictine Community of the Holy Cross *in the UK*
Benedictine Community of Our Lady and St John *in the UK*
Congregation of the Companions of St Benedict *in Cameroon*

12 Community of the Holy Transfiguration *in Zimbabwe*
Community of the Transfiguration *in the USA*
Oratory of the Good Shepherd *throughout the world*

13 Community of the Glorious Ascension *in the UK*
Brotherhood of the Ascended Christ *in India*
Sisters of Jesus' Way *in the UK*

14 Order of the Holy Cross *in Canada, South Africa & the USA*
Society of the Holy Cross *in Korea*
Society of the Sacred Cross *in the UK*

15 Community of St Mary the Virgin *in the UK*
Society of Our Lady St Mary *in Canada*
Evangelical Daughters of Mary's Way *in Sweden*

16 Community of the Companions of Jesus the Good Shepherd *in the UK*
Community of the Good Shepherd *in Malaysia*
Society of St Anna the Prophet *in the USA*

17 Melanesian Brotherhood *throughout the Pacific region*
Community of the Sisters of Melanesia *in the Solomon Islands*
Devasevikaramaya *in Sri Lanka*

18 Companions of St Luke - OSB *in the USA*
Company of Mission Priests *in the UK*
Society of St Luke *in the UK*

19 Order of the Holy Paraclete *in Ghana & the UK*
Order of the Community of the Paraclete *in the USA*
Community of the Holy Name *in Australia*

20 Society of St Margaret *in Haiti, Sri Lanka, the UK & the USA*
Community of Nazareth *in Japan*
Single Consecrated Life *in the UK*

21 Community of St Anselm *in the UK*
Community of St Clare *in the UK*
Little Sisters of St Clare *in the USA*
Order of St Helena *in the USA*

We give thanks for the Religious Life in all its forms in the Church, and today we pray especially for:

22 Community of the Sacred Passion *in the UK*
Community of St Mary of Nazareth and Calvary *in Tanzania & Zambia*
Community of Ss Barnabas and Cecilia *in Australia*

23 Community of Celebration *in the UK & the USA*
Community of St John the Evangelist *in the Republic of Ireland*
Order of the Teachers of the Children of God *in the USA*

24 Community of St John Baptist *in the UK & the USA*
Contemplative Fire *in the UK*
Order of Anglican Cistercians *in the UK*
Worker Brothers & Sisters of the Holy Spirit *in Australia, Canada, Haiti & the USA*

25 Community of St Paul *in Mozambique*
Society of St Paul *in the USA*
Sisterhood of the Holy Nativity *in the USA*

26 Order of St Anne *in the USA*
Community of the Sisters of the Love of God *in the UK*
Church Army *in the UK*

27 Community of St John the Divine *in the UK*
Sisterhood of St John the Divine *in Canada*
Society of St John the Divine *in South Africa*
Brothers of St John the Evangelist *in the USA*
Society of St John the Evangelist *in north America & the UK*
Sisters of Charity *in the UK*

28 Society of the Sacred Mission *in Australia, Lesotho, South Africa & the UK*
Sisters of the Incarnation *in Australia*
Sisters of Jesus *in the UK*

29 Community of St Peter (Woking) *in the UK*
Community of St Peter, Horbury *in the UK*
Society of the Sisters of Bethany *in the UK*
Benedictine Sisters of Bethany *in Cameroon*

30 Community of St Andrew *in the UK*
Community of the Sacred Name *in Fiji, New Zealand & Tonga*
Community of the Gospel *in the USA*

31 Congregation of the Sisters of the Visitation of Our Lady *in PNG*
Community of the Blessed Lady Mary *in Zimbabwe*
Sisterhood of St Mary *in Bangladesh*

Worship resources for every season
magnet is a Christian resources magazine packed with:
• Creative ideas for worship
• Colourful meditation pages
• Bible studies and reflections
• Inspiring articles on faith and justice issues
• Bright ideas from local church and community projects
Just £12 a year – subscribe today
Ready…aim…shoot
Method and mastery
bible study
Adult Christianity: Paul's challenge to the Church
magnet
No. 113 Summer 2017
encouraging, enabling, equipping
www.ourmagnet.co.uk
Call: 01603 785911

News of Anglican Religious Life

Aspects of the life .... prayer and praise

The Order of Mission

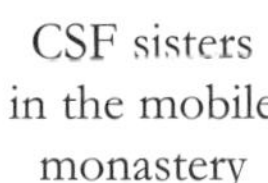

CSF sisters
in the mobile
monastery

News from Korea

Sister Catherine SHC writes:

Our three Burmese Novices, who came to Korea in June 2013, to test their vocation to the Religious community life with the Society of the Holy Cross in Korea, were clothed as Novices at Christmas 2015. The Novice Guardian has been guiding them carefully each day to build up a good harmony of prayer life, study and labour. Ignatian contemplative prayer has been taught so that they can keep praying at a deeper level each day in the Presence of God. They also learn the history of SHC and the spirit of the Religious community life.

They help weekly at the convalescent nursing home run by the Anglican Church. They also practise and have experience of mission work in different parishes on Sundays. Opportunities to share various experiences with the Vietnamese Novices of the Roman Catholic Church in Korea are strengthening solidarity between the two communities.

Celebrations

In November 2016, Sister Mary Luke CHC at Costock in the UK was given a surprise celebration by her community to mark her Silver Jubilee as Revd Mother. The Mass of the Holy Cross was sung by the Warden, the Venerable Gavin Kirk. The words of the long Blessing of a Benedictine Superior, sung during the Mass, were very moving and pointed to both the gifts and the cost of the leadership task. The mass was followed by a festive lunch, at which Sister Mary Cuthbert made an excellent speech before the toast, and then later came tea and cake in the afternoon.

At Edgware Abbey in 2016, the community's 150th anniversary was marked by a Eucharist on 11 June, followed by a celebration lunch; on 8 October came Sister Barbara's Diamond Jubilee of profession, another memorable occasion, during which she was presented with the St Mellitus Medal as seen in the photograph. The medal

is awarded to those with long and distinguished service in the diocese of London.

A Good Read!

In the early struggles to re-establish Religious Life among Anglicans, one personality has captured the imagination of many, that of Father Ignatius OSB (1837-1908). He was an enthusiastic evangelist for the Christian faith and stirred congregations with his ebullient preaching. Yet, he was an eccentric figure, mercurial and unpredictable. He longed to found a Benedictine community, but he was not stable enough to sustain the steady vision required of a founder. His attempts however took him to a string of locations until he finally settled in Wales at Cap-y-ffin. Here, he had constructed a gothic monastery, a new Llanthony Abbey, not too far from the medieval ruins of the original. On his death, he was buried there. His community did not last long after his demise, and the buildings eventually became a private house.

The story of Father Ignatius can be found in Hugh Allen's splendid book, *New Llanthony Abbey*, published by Peterscourt Press in 2016. Previous writings on Ignatius have either had a particular agenda or else played up the comic side of this monastic saga. The author here has assembled the facts with great attention to detail and introduces the reader to a host of other characters in the intricate story of Anglican monasticism. It is an exhaustive account that illustrates both Ignatius and his times and is a considerable achievement. The author also relates what happened to the community after the founder's death and the history of the house, whose most famous later occupant was the artist and sculptor, Eric Gill. Although the monastery is not accessible to the public, it is still possible to walk up the lane to the ruins of the monastic church and see Ignatius's grave.

Traditional and New in Canada

In June of 2013 the House of Bishops Committee of the Anglican Church of Canada on Religious Orders convened a conference of traditional monastic communities and the new and sometimes experimental monastic communities that had identified themselves in various ways within the Anglican Church of Canada. The conference began the exploration of the variety of understandings of Religious life: its rhythms, relationships and patterns of life and worship. It proved a congenial and creative gathering, and so a second conference was convened at St John's Convent, Toronto, in July 2016, again under the supportive auspices of the House of Bishops' Committee.

Both meetings concluded that making a formal division between 'Orders' and 'Communities', as used, for example, in the Episcopal Church of the United States, did not fit the Canadian experience. Instead, it was agreed 'to walk together as The Anglican Conference of Religious Communities in Canada'. It was realized that 'we are a community of communities even as we hold distinctive ways of living the Christian life.' The Office of the Primate would hold the list of participating communities. It was agreed that the Conference should convene again in 2018.

Love Fulfilled

The last sister of the Community of St Michael & All Angels in South Africa died on 14 May 2016. Sister Joan was 97 and had been professed 65 years.

The Community had been founded in 1874 by the then Bishop of Bloemfontein, Allen Becher Webb. The diocese was vast and he wanted sisters to be pioneers in all aspects of Christian ministry: education, health care and mission. The Community never grew to be large, yet its members achieved an impact that has lasted through the decades. The school the sisters founded in Bloemfontein still flourishes with a strong reputation. Even more significant was Sister Henrietta CSM&AA, who was one of the most iinfluential of those who founded the modern nursing profession in South Africa. It was CSM&AA who founded the first hospitals in Bloemfontein and Kimberly.

The Sisters also were keen to give opportunities for non-white women to enter the Religious life, no easy task in a part of the world where race was a controversial political issue even before the *apartheid* policies of the nationalist government that took office in 1948. The Basotho Community of St Mary of the Cross was guided by CSM&AA for thirty-five years and today it has become a province of the Community of the Holy Name.

The Sisters were familiar from their blue habits and copper crosses. After the Second World War, novices became fewer and by the 1980s it was clear the community was unlikely to continue for much longer. But the longevity of the last few sisters stretched its life well into the 21st century. Two lived to be over 100 years old and Sister Joan, the last survivor, was only a few years away from that milestone. With her death, the Community's direct pioneering work and witness has drawn to a close. But their legacy continues. Thanks be to God for CSM&AA!

Honorary degrees

Three former superiors of the Community of the Sisters of the Church were presented with honorary (B.Ed) degrees on 19 May 2017. All three had studied at Whitelands College in London, UK, before it became part of the University of Roehampton . The current leadership of the Institute decided as part of the celebrations to mark the 175th Anniversary of the founding of the first College in the group Whitelands, that all the former students, of all four colleges who completed their courses before the days of giving degrees, would now be awarded honorary degrees if they wished. This took place at the Royal Festival Hall on May 15th. The three CSC Sisters were presented with their awards at a special ceremony at the new CSC house at Gerrards Cross, UK, by the Dean of Westminster Abbey, The Very Revd Dr John Hall, Pro Chancellor and the Vice-Chancellor Professor Paul O'Prey.

Pictured are Sister Dorothea (superior 1962-78), Sister Judith (superior 1988-98) and Sister Anita (superior 1998-2009). Dorothea celebrated her 102nd birthday six months before this picture.

New entries

Each edition it is heartening to introduce new entries to the *Year Book*. There are two new acknowledged communities in the Church of England who now included. The **Community of St Anselm**, on which some information was given in the previous edition, now has its own entry. The community stems from the initiative of the Archbishop of Canterbury in 2015 and welcomes Christians aged 20-35 from all over the world, and any branch of the Christian family tree, for a year of living a shared life of prayer, theological study and service to the poor.

The other new entry is the **Community of Hopeweavers,** a 'dispersed fellowship of friends who seek God through stillness and silence, prayer, creativity, conversation and food, sharing the ups and downs of life wherever we are called to live and work.'

Both these entries can be found in Section 3.

Articles

Aspects of the life ... work at home

Making incense at Mucknell Abbey, UK

Gardening at SLG, Oxford, UK

Change is part of the rhythm of existence and it can cause alarm as well as bring hope. The articles in this edition look at change in different parts of the Religious life, its challenges and its blessings.

Change through moving
by Brother Thomas Quin OSB

In the first place, we changed just through the period of coming to the decision to move at all! It is easy for a Community, after living a long time in a beautiful, familiar setting, to assume that the life will just continue in that place and that the only things to change will be deaths and arrivals of Community members, the timetable and the name of the local electrician. The initial decision-making process introduced us to new ways of evaluating our Community life, learning to listen differently to our visitors and local supporters, and learning to communicate more honestly and reflectively with each other. In that period we changed from a divided Community – on this issue certainly, for or against – to a Community united in the realisation that it would be good for us to move. Also, our horizon was pushed back: the issue was no longer about where and how we lived but more about where and how the next generation of the Community lived.

We changed further in the period of imagining a new home and identifying some of our needs and wishes. We chose our architects before we even sold our old home and they – never having designed a monastery before – came to spend 48 hours with us, attending everything we did alongside us and asking us how we used the spaces we had. That made us articulate our Community life in a way we hadn't previously: what features of it were essential to our charism, which were determined by the place where we live and what we might like to do differently if we could. They then produced a symbolic structure of interrelated spaces which we refined with them. Finally they left with us a few inspirational books of glossy photographs of modern buildings, including churches, for us to look at and identify some styles we liked.

The third phase of change was the period of exploring and assessing properties on the market. We were sent mounds of paper and megabytes of brochures by the agents and these were checked against our needs and favoured styles. The agents justified this by saying that a lot of customers ended up buying something different from what they had originally said they hoped for – we found the same, with our architects sometimes reminding us, for example, "but you said you didn't wanted a listed building". There were two issues here. The first was the handling of expectations: when we were dreaming and hoping, we reached for the ideal; when we saw real properties, none was perfect. In the second place we had to face real trade-offs: the more we spent on the purchase, the less we would have in the bank to make alterations or additions. Community life can have a lulling, institutionalising, effect sometimes, and we had to re-learn how to be hard-headed, responsible adults.

The next group of changes was around the period of our specific design. We received details of about 100 properties. We visited (some of us) about eight and the architects sketched a rough idea of how to apply our symbolic structure to three. The final choice had to be a compromise between different parts of the ideal and different strands of practicality. Nothing in this life is perfect and our homeland is (only) in heaven. So some of our expectations were dashed and we had to handle that too. But, having decided on and purchased our new property – in our case this was more a less an empty shell – we had to work intensively with the architects on the specific design. Of course by now there were physical constraints on what was possible, actual Planning constraints and – from that earlier trade-off – actual financial constraints. All these constraints affected the final design and dashed some of our expectations. We had to think hard about our priorities and focus on what we needed for a viable Community life.

The fifth period of change was the on-site period, while demolition and then building work took place. It was a very steep learning curve and we discovered just how dependent we were on the professional competencies and management skills of others – not just the architects, but landscapers and various engineers. We kept reminding them that we wanted a monastery, not a hotel or a school or even a church. They kept reminding us of what we couldn't afford – or what we might want to do more cheaply so as to keep money in hand for some other features. Sometimes we were delighted by their inventiveness or thoroughness, and at other times we were appalled by their misunderstanding or carelessness. We kept having meetings with the architects, who supervised the building, and had hundreds of details or amendments to agree with us. While the abbot attended the monthly site meetings with the architects and quantity surveyors, the whole Community also visited the site several times and were shown round - and sometimes noticed things that were not on the plans! The Community gained a new appreciation of our vow of obedience: so many details came to us for decision, and so many of those were urgent matters of opinion or relative – rather than absolute – merit, that the abbot had to make a number of difficult decisions after inconclusive meetings.

Alongside much of this work we were saying 'goodbyes' and packing and clearing our home of sixty years. That in itself was demanding emotionally, pastorally and practically. It is all too easy, in a large community house, to keep things in case they're needed one day… We had a huge turn-out and had to try imagining what would be useful long-term and what would be unnecessary or inappropriate. Again we were facing the distinction between needs and wants, between imagined needs and uncertain actual needs…and mistakes were made: "If only we hadn't got rid of…"

And finally we moved into the new buildings and furniture arrived from store. Already then we were envisaging some changes of use even since the design! We were finding all the things that had been forgotten, or badly done, by the various contractors, and the twelve-month 'snagging period' was almost busier for us than the build-period! We were also discovering that some of our ideas were in fact reactions to the problems of our old home rather than necessary features of the new one; and, of course, there were some things we simply hadn't been able to visualise. We were surprised by the complexity of many of the 'sustainable' features we had asked for in the design and the expense of servicing them.

At the same time, we had lost our support network in terms of service and maintenance – that electrician whose name we all knew! And some of our local friends just thought the distance was too much for them to go on visiting or volunteering. But at the same time we were making new contacts and many people were welcoming us gladly – so we needed time and space to get to know them.

The whole exercise of moving, then, prompted and required considerable change in the Community, but of course the charism is the same and the life very much in continuity. The changes, while exciting, were also draining, and a certain number of Community 'treats' and rest periods were needed to get us through. We have also found that the change from venerable old buildings to sustainable new buildings has given us not only a new look but something of a new outlook, a new face towards outsiders which many find attractive, and a new openness to ways of welcoming those outsiders whether as guests or through our 'alongsider' programme. The entire project gave a boost to this Community.

A new monastic community within a traditional community

by Sister Constance Joanna SSJD

The Sisterhood of Saint John the Divine is a contemporary expression of Religious life within the Anglican Church of Canada, founded in 1884. The SSJD is a prayer and gospel-centered monastic community, open to the needs of the contemporary church and society, bound together by the call to live out their baptismal covenant through the vows of poverty, chastity, and obedience.

In this article, Sister Constance Joanna SSJD explores a new initiative at their Toronto Convent of inviting younger women to share the life of the community for a set time. "Companions on an Ancient Path is a unique expression of new monasticism within an established community that speaks to the next generation of Christians in an innovative way, and is critical for the life of the 'Ancient Future Church' we are called to renew."

The Birth of a Vision

SSJD launched their new "Companions on an Ancient Path" program with an invitation that went out in September 2015 across the church to "millennials" – women in their 20s and 30s – to consider a year's immersion experience in forming intentional Christian community within and with the support of a traditional monastic community.

This was a natural development of the values that have shaped the Sisterhood since 1884. We were founded as a pioneering community, with no single charism but rather a desire to be "open to the needs of the church and the contemporary world" and to adapt as the church and the surrounding society changed. The Sisters have long had a large extended "household of God", including Associates and Oblates (dispersed but often present in the houses of the Sisterhood) and Alongsiders (women who live alongside the Sisters and assist in their ministry).

Two major factors influenced the vision for Companions: first, the realization that young people long for a spiritual connection that they don't often find in church, and a desire to offer a "way in" to Christian spirituality and spiritual practices. Second, with an increased average age of Sisters entering the community, we started looking to the future and the necessity, if we were going to continue to thrive, of incorporating younger women into that sometimes-dispersed, sometimes-resident extended family, for a year or longer. Discussions began in 2012 when the Sisters' Chapter agreed a program for younger women who might want to spend a year "in God's rhythm." (This phrase was coined before we had heard of the St Anselm Community at Lambeth!) It would be a community-within-a-community, a new-monastic expression within a traditional community.

The Planning Journey

For various reasons the Sisterhood was not able to follow up on this idea immediately. But in the spring of 2015, the time seemed right to begin planning for "Companions on an Ancient Path" and a steering committee was formed including Sisters and some people associated with Wycliffe College in the Toronto School of Theology (University of Toronto). They included a former student, a current student, and the college registrar. In addition the Principal of Wycliffe offered encouragement, support, and ideas for courses. We decided on five participants as an ideal number for the first year. They would live in an extended part of the enclosure. A study and formation program, offered partly in-house and partly at Wycliffe College, with potential work assignments and volunteer opportunities was devised. To keep the program free, we applied for a grant from the diocese.

We developed a team to work with the Companions, made up of Sister Constance Joanna (Companions Coordinator), a Lutheran pastor and Alongsider, and a student intern, with additional assistance from a visiting Sister of the Chemin Neuf community. The Companions would have weekly individual mentoring meetings as well as facilitating various group sessions including *lectio divina*, theological reflection, and other group-formational gatherings. In addition to the team, other Sisters were to be involved in presentations and classes for the Companions on various forms of prayer, living a Rule of Life, and related topics.

Not everything was decided before our first cohort arrived! Once we learned more about the Companions' needs and interests, we planned other formational opportunities. We are fortunate in Toronto to be well-resourced in terms of theological education, psychological support, and spiritual support, and we can also provide opportunities for cultural exposure including art, music, and drama with the assistance of donated tickets!

The Companions are Launched

In September 2016, five women in their twenties and thirties arrived at St. John's Convent in Toronto, eager to begin. Their diversity was both a challenge as they formed community together and also a great blessing. They came from a wide variety of geographic, ethnic, and religious backgrounds (Dutch Reformed, Roman Catholic, Mennonite, Christian Missionary Alliance, and Anglican). Their educational and professional backgrounds were equally varied: some were launched on careers, some were students taking a gap year from university.

Commissioning of the first group of SSJD Companions of the Ancient Way

The Companions have been living "in God's rhythm," following the Sisterhood's rhythm of life with the daily office, Eucharist and private prayer. They join the Sisterhood for daily conference and share in Community Time most evenings either within their own circle or with the Sisters. They attend classes both at the Convent and at the Toronto School of theology in spiritual formation, monastic history and tradition, group dynamics and leadership, conflict management, and mission – how to share the love of Jesus in the emerging church of the 21st century. Those who desired have received academic credit for aspects of the program through Wycliffe College. Along with the Sisters, they have a weekly Grace (sabbath) Day, monthly and annual retreat time, and four weeks' holiday.

What do the Companions Think?

Here are a few quotations from the Companions' blog (www.ssjdcompanions.org):

In becoming a Companion, I find I am able to slow my pace of life. I am in the beginning of introducing myself to me, to find out who I am and what I need and want out of life. But most importantly being able to reintroduce myself to God and be able to understand God's needs, wants, and plans for me.

I am reminded of the words we use at baptism: "I sign you with the cross, and mark you as Christ's own for ever." Does it show in my interactions with others, in the choices I make, in the way I live my life, that I am Christ's? I might never know what mark I will leave here, and it is too early to tell what mark this place and the people with whom I share this life will leave on me. But already I feel that this daily rhythm of work and prayer, study and rest, time with others and time alone, is changing me.

It is safe to say that I am very new to this regular time of silent prayer together, but I am discovering more in the process and simultaneously feeling there is much to learn. I am eager to see how praying in silence can be a powerful experience. I am so grateful to be a Companion this year and learning about new ways of experiencing the love of Jesus in community.

After my bout of illness and being cared for in the Sisters' Infirmary I mentioned to one of the sisters how I tend to feel guilty when people do nice things for me. In response, she asked me, "Do you know what the opposite of feeling guilty is?" My mind drew a blank and I said, "No." She said, "It's gratitude." I smiled because I had achieved some enlightenment!

As a university student, I generally insisted upon a great deal of free time in my day and I've missed that here. However, God has reminded me that decadent amounts of leisure time haven't actually benefitted my relationship with God because of a lack of the very self-discipline I came to the convent to develop. Recalling this, I can breathe properly again, and am hopeful about the changes this year will bring about in myself and the other women on this journey with me.

The Sisters' Perspective

The Sisters (needless to say!) have loved having younger women living in our community, sharing their experiences, hopes and dreams with us. Their energy and willingness to help in our ministry and in our community life together has been inspiring. Their compassion for the poor, for social advocacy, and for creating a better world enlarges our vision. The Companions have provided us with an opportunity to reach out to young women who are serious about following Jesus. They will take monastic values of a balanced life back out into "the world" as they pursue their lives as students, professionals, and above all as followers of Jesus in an emerging church whose future shape we cannot easily predict.

We believe that the ancient practices of prayer and community, silence and solitude, work and study, rest and play, are still the most foundational for the church of the future. We trust that each of our Companions will continue as a Companion of Jesus after they leave the program, sharing the values of prayer, community, and service in whatever arena of life they find themselves.

Looking Forward to further Cohorts of Companions

Women in their 20s and 30s who might want to explore a year's immersion in deepening their prayer life, serving others, and finding inspiration for their future are invited to apply. For more information, please visit www.ssjdcompanions.org or contact the Revd Sister Constance Joanna Gefvert, program coordinator, at companions@ssjd.ca. The SSJD website is at www.ssjd.ca

New Monasticism: The Community of St Margaret the Queen: some theological reflections by Revd Father Dr Gareth Powell

On the first Sunday of Advent 2016, nine people took seasonal (yearly) vows to the Rule of the Community of St Margaret the Queen before Bishop Christopher of Southwark. In one sense this marked the end point of a process of discernment that has lasted just over a year and a half, asking what it was that God is calling us to, what our charisms are in this place at this time, and how might we faithfully bear witness to the Religious life? Yet in another sense it was the first fruits of a vision that emerged out of much prayer and discussion about all God might be calling forth in a beautiful, enormous, Victorian church in Streatham Hill in London, that of St Margaret the Queen. It had been closed early in 2014 before re-opening as a place of prayer, learning and hospitality in 2015. The vision that emerged in the year leading up to its closure as a parish church and in the lead up to my appointment in November 2014 was one in which the heart of any new community would lie in its commitment to a rule of life – a commitment to an intensity of Christian discipleship – alongside the considerable development work planned across the whole site to make this new life sustainable. This community would be made up of Christians already worshipping across Lambeth who desired to explore and deepen their faith.

So why this drawing together of a new monastic community? Why now? Why at all? Father Benson, one of the founding members of The Society of St John the Evangelist, said this, "religious life is not to be seen as over and above ordinary Christian life, it is ordinary Christian life developed under conditions where the church has fallen away from her true spiritual calling of conscious and habitual union with Christ." Father Benson thought that the re-emergence of the Religious life in 19th-century England said as much about the failure of the then contemporary church to teach and live the faith as it did about the revival of something more ancient. He talked of gathering up the truth of past ages and maintaining that which sustains. Might we also say the same thing today? Is the church in danger of decreasing our expectations of those we catechise, baptise and confirm? Are we accommodating ourselves to consumer culture and the idea of a choice based 'belief system', and by doing so lessening the demands of the Gospel? In such a context the rise of what is termed 'new monasticism' is perhaps therefore not surprising. It is one sign of the profound calling of God to His people to enter into the holy mystery of Christian community in an age when the church in England is struggling to provide places of intense Christian discipleship. This rekindling of Religious life says much about the potential for a renewal of our common religious life. We are seeing so many young people today who have an intense longing for the truths of Christian life, and a longing for that intensity of life which Father Benson vividly speaks about and lived. This intense longing emerges from the disappointments of so much of our contemporary communal life (or lack thereof) and the false promises of consumerism.

Father Benson was aware of the difficulties of his own age; a time of rapid urban expansion during the industrial revolution that overwhelmed the Church of England's capacity to minister effectively in so many cities across the country. The emergence of the sisters of charity serving in slum areas, supported by priests living together under a common rule, were one Christian response to that crisis. So we also must be open to the questions and directions of our society today, affirming, critiquing and enlivening them. As the Psalms and the Gospel of Matthew remind us, the Church is continually called to bring forth treasures old and treasures new, that which it holds dear and has guided it, and that which the Spirit stirs anew, both within and without the church. So what of our context today, what of possible treasures new?

The solid structures that have guided us since the enlightenment period are collapsing, becoming more and more difficult to describe and understand. The previous solidity of institutional life is no longer a reality: the state, the family, political parties, relationships, jobs, risk, security, freedom, are all fluid and continually changing. The main ideology driving this is consumer culture – the commodification of all things. Whereas previously we might understand consumer culture as to apply merely to goods, we now understand much of our social, political and economic life through this ideological lens. Relationships, jobs, where we live - all are commodified and disposable, and our legal system enshrines disposability and non-commitment. Often those in the lowest rungs of society bear the brunt of this utilitarian thinking. This has resulted in a society which is also aligned to fear: fear of the other, of the' strange'. In a commodified society you do not need to deal with difference as you can choose to be with those like you. Therefore the stranger and the strange can be cast as evil.

The church has not been isolated from this ideological shift. Several theologians have been alert at the way in which church polity itself has succumbed to this consumer impulse. Yet we desperately need to live the Gospel vision of all of creation flourishing, most especially in our cities, setting forth that wondrous vision of catholicity, that is, of the flourishing of difference, where those of much and those of little come and experience life together, not reconciled because of their common interest or culture but because of Christ.

This is why, emerging out of St Margaret's community life, we desire to use the vast spaces of the church to welcome and be hospitable to the local community by way of developing a café and kitchen, a bakery, entrepreneurial hot-desking space, and artist studios. Using the income from these activities to fund our youth work, work with the elderly and vulnerable, and expand our foodbank, civic and social advice, as well as provide an opportunity for the bakery, café and kitchen to have apprentices for former inmates of Brixton and Wandsworth prisons. Alongside this we are also planning on building a monastery for up to thirteen people to come and live, each taking seasonal (yearly vows) to our rule and living a life of prayer, learning and service together with the non-resident community.

In all this we are attending to that imperative of the Gospel, that the church be an icon to Divine love, imagining what the New Jerusalem might be like today in our own urban context. We are desiring to embody a vision of human flourishing, where people find dignity in work, where arts, culture and beauty are celebrated and encountered, where those who are considered least are not relegated to a side room but are as welcome as anyone else, and where the very fabric of the building speaks of the beauty and sanctity of God and of the material order.

Yet the heart of all these things is the praying, serving and learning Christian community living under a common rule, bound together in Divine love and charity. The daily offices and the mass are the orientating point for all this, and the origin of the Community of St Margaret's missiological sensibility. In many ways this vision it is a re-appropriation and re-imagining of certain forms of mediaeval monasticism, particularly that in Northern England and Ireland. In some monastic ruins you see many concentric circular walls expanding outward. In the centre the chapel, the rhythm of prayer and devotion, around this the brothers or sisters lived, around this the schools, artisans and guilds, around this the people, and finally even the livestock. All things caught up in Christ, the centre point of it all, whether recognised and acknowledged or not. It is this profound vision that Father Benson speaks of, and that I desperately pray that St Margaret's might offer people a taste of that they too may see and know and love Christ.

For further details see www.stmtq.com or email frgarethpowell@me.com

Renewing the Community Church
by Father George Guiver CR

God nudged us into doing something about our rather run-down church when the heating and the electrics collapsed in the same year. In the meantime our 100-seater choir stalls had become redundant, and the community moved to sitting between them, which had a hugely beneficial effect on the singing and on our sense of community – so we realised the stalls had to go. We were also beginning to use the church more with small groups, taking them round it to pray and reflect in different parts, and people would either be excluded or tripped up by the many steps. We looked for architects through a competitive process. Once chosen, we worked with them on exploring possibilities, and they pushed us towards imagining the church completely emptied, and its floor levelled throughout. This took quite a bit of imagination and to supplement what the architects produced, at least two of us learned to use an architectural programme that can create virtual interiors. We ended with a plan to gut the church completely and level the floor throughout. In this process the idea arose to create a pilgrimage route for groups, with an artistic focus at each station of salvation history. Much of the design was worked out in Chapter rather than on the architect's bench, every detail was fully discussed and we debated and voted over every inch.

We decided the building was to be flexible and adaptable, to open it up to occasional events such as concerts. But we also wanted to avoid being saddled with permanent arrangements that could not be altered or experimented with. At the same time certain items needed to express solidarity and permanence. This was true of the choir stalls, which, it was felt, needed to state to anyone coming in something about what was at the heart of our life – and so our new choir stalls are both monumental and movable. In an artistic culture such as ours we recognised the importance of the arts in winning people to the gospel and encouraging them into prayer. Working with artists has been good for us, discussing with them, proposing ideas and amendments, and beginning to live with what they have given to us and to all who come.

Once we had all the permissions, we took the risky decision of proceeding with the work before all the money was in, and worked hard to stay together in a process that produced its fair share of tension and heart-searching: there were one or two brethren who had misgivings about the project; in addition our own Community buildings were in need of repair and renewal, and some said we ought to put the Community's buildings straight first before refurbishing the church. In the end we decided God came first and the church was the priority. We were helped in that by the fact that our theological College and the regional training course needed a proper place for training students in worship, and could not manage for long without. For two years the Community refectory provided a very nice, intimate Chapel, and we certainly missed that a bit when we moved back into the church on 23 December 2011. But we also knew straight away that the church was going to be even better than we had hoped.

Two things immediately stand out from this story: one is that the hard slog of running an appeal was good for us, renewing many old friendships and revealing to us the large number of people who value our Community, more than we could possibly have imagined. It also pushed us sharply into catching up with the modern world in a variety of ways, administratively, artistically, and in discovering new ways to communicate with the world. The second fruit very quickly became apparent: the church started to be a magnet, and numbers coming to Mirfield began to soar, compounding our problems with our older buildings, which we now urgently need to refurbish and extend. We have learned how important it is to take great care over our place of worship – as one brother has joked about what we now have, "it makes you want to go to church". We also have many more people coming in just to sit and pray, and students are frequently there praying, in a way that wasn't the case before the renewal. It is also giving us a new engagement with people we wouldn't normally encounter: guests in our B&B who wander in or come to evensong, people who now get married in our crypt, people coming for concerts and organ recitals (we were given a fine Harrison organ). The local mayor asked to hold the civic service in it, and that was real fun.

If there are any downsides to the whole thing, they are at the administrative level. The huge amount of time involved over several years, which could have been devoted more directly to the gospel, and the problems that inevitably arise and cause work and worry. Our plans were challenged and had to go to a Consistory Court. The biggest overall problem was the floor, which was laid wrongly and must all come up and be re-laid, and that has involved lawyers and an adjudication process. But even that has been an education for us.

On the whole the project has done more for us as a community, and for many other people, than we could have imagined at the start. There is a strong message in this about: (a) the importance of place – the 1960s side-lining of church buildings needs to be reversed, as they are a part of the gospel message of the incarnation, and a key resource for experiencing and living out the spiritual journey;

(b) of the worshipping environment – in communities we need to take seriously all that has been learned in recent decades about liturgy, partly because so many in the wider Church today are pretty illiterate about principles of worship, much of it being more human-centred than we realize, rather than that waiting upon God which stands at the heart of Religious communities – our worshipping environment can help inspire people to; and

(c) engaging with the arts: we live in an artistically sensitive society, and if we become more artistic ourselves, we will be able to engage with the many people today who can connect with the gospel better through the imagination, than through concepts and words.

At Mirfield we have a sense that these three things draw people to come and share in the worship and the silence at the heart of our life, and go away encouraged, as I think we are ourselves.

Directory of traditional celibate Religious Orders and Communities

Aspects of the life ... celebrating

CSM sisters in Malawi

Section 1

Religious communities in this section are those whose members take the traditional vows, including celibacy. For many, these are the 'evangelical counsels' of chastity, poverty and obedience. In the Benedictine tradition, the three vows are stability, obedience and conversion of life, celibacy being an integral part of the third vow.

These celibate communities may be involved in apostolic works or be primarily enclosed and contemplative. They may wear traditional habits or contemporary dress. However, their members all take traditional Religious vows. In the Episcopal Church of the USA, these communities are referred to in the canons as 'Religious Orders'.

There are at least 1,743 celibate Religious in the Anglican Communion, (811 men and 932 women). There are no statistics currently available for some orders (so they are not included here) and therefore these figures are a minimum number.

The approximate regional totals are:

Africa:	316	(Men 49, Women 267)
Asia:	76	(Men 14, Women 62)
Australasia & Pacific:	762	(Men 561, Women 201)
Europe:	381	(Men 109, Women 272)
North & South America & Caribbean:	208	(Men 78, Women 130)

International telephoning

Telephone numbers in this directory are mainly listed as used within the country concerned. To use them internationally, first dial the international code (usually 00) followed by the country code (see list below).

Australia	+ 61	India	+ 91	Solomon Islands	+ 677
Bangladesh	+ 880	Republic of Ireland	+ 353	South Africa	+ 27
Brazil	+ 55	Japan	+ 81	Sri Lanka	+ 94
Canada	+ 1	Korea (South)	+ 82	Spain	+ 34
Fiji	+ 679	Lesotho	+ 266	Swaziland	+ 268
France	+ 33	Malaysia	+ 60	Tanzania	+ 255
Ghana	+ 233	New Zealand	+ 64	UK	+ 44
Haiti	+ 509	PNG	+ 675	USA	+ 1

Society of All Saints Sisters of the Poor

ASSP

Founded 1851

All Saints
15A Magdalen Road
Oxford OX4 1RW
UK

Tel: 01865 249127
(Voicemail is checked regularly.)

Email:
leaderassp @socallss.co.uk

Website:
www.allsaintssisters ofthepoor.org.uk

Mattins	6.30 am
Eucharist	Variable
Vespers	5.30 pm
Compline	8.00 pm

Variations on Sun, Sat, & major festivals

Office book
Own Office book, based on Anglican Office Book 1980

As a small Community, we have the God-given opportunity to recognise the very diverse gifts and callings of each individual. Returning to the charism of our Founder, we believe that God calls us to be channels of love to those in need, however the Spirit may lead us.

Sisters continue to be involved in Helen and Douglas House, hospices for children and young adults, and the Porch for adults who are homeless or vulnerably housed. St John's Home is now owned by Accurocare Limited as a separate business but our pastoral care for the frail and elderly residents continues. Our current refurbishment of the Comper Old School and extensions should provide an accessible resource with potential flexibility of use.

We now have the freedom to take an active part in the life of the parish and the wider church community. This includes preaching, ministry and spiritual accompaniment.

Our guest house welcomes those needing retreat or spiritual refreshment.

The heart of our Community life is the worship of God in the daily Office and Eucharist, and our commitment to prayer and spiritual reading.

God renews our calling day by day, both as a Community and as individuals and we welcome any who are discerning God's will for them.

SISTER JEAN RAPHAEL ASSP
(Community Leader, assumed office 18 October 2010)
SISTER FRANCES DOMINICA ASSP
(Assistant Community Leader)
Sister Helen Mary
Sister Margaret Anne *(priest)*
Sister Jane

Obituaries
31 Jan 2017 Sister Ann Frances, aged 77, prof. 36 years

Companions
Those who believe they are called to support the Community in prayer and fellowship may be invited to become Companions.

Guest and Retreat Facilities
Brownlow House, our guest house with six en-suite rooms. Self-catering.
Email: guestsister@socallss.co.uk

Bishop Visitor: Rt Revd Bill Ind

Registered Charity: No. 228383

St John's Home (for elderly people), St Mary's Road, Oxford OX4 1QE, UK Tel: 01865 247725 Fax: 01865 247920
Email: admin@st_johns_home.org Website: www.stjohnshome.org

Helen and Douglas House, 14a Magdalen Road, Oxford OX4 1RW, UK Tel: 01865 794749 Fax: 01865 202702
Email: admin@helenanddouglas.org.uk
Website: www.helenanddouglas.org.uk
Registered Charity No: 1085951

The Porch, 139 Magdalen Road, Oxford OX4 1RL, UK
Tel: 01865 728545
Email: info@theporch.fsbusiness.co.uk
Website: www.theporch.org.uk
Registered Charity No: 1089612

Community History & Books

Peter Mayhew, *All Saints: Birth & Growth of a Community,* ASSP, Oxford, 1987.

Kay Syrad, *A Breath of Heaven: All Saints Convalescent Hospital,* Rosewell, St Leonard's on Sea, 2002.
[This is the history of All Saints Convalescent Hospital, Eastbourne, started by our Mother Foundress in 1869 and run by the community until 1959.]

Sister Frances Dominica ASSP, *Just My Reflection: Helping families to do things their own way when their child dies,* Darton, Longman & Todd, London, 2nd ed 2007.
Available from Helen & Douglas House, £6.50.

Behind the big red door: the story of Helen House, Golden Cup, Oxford, 2006, £6.00.

All Saints Convent
PO Box 3127
Catonsville
MD 21228-0127
USA

Tel: 410 747 4104
Fax: 410 747 3321

Three All Saints Sisters went to Baltimore, Maryland, and the community house they began became an independent house in 1890.

In September 2009, the majority of the members of this American community of All Saints Sisters were received into the Roman Catholic Church.

Whilst still living at the Convent in Catonsville with the rest of the community, one sister remains in the Anglican Communion.

Sister Virginia of All Saints *(sometime Mother)*

Website: www.allsaintssisters.org

Benedictine Sisters of Bethany

Founded 2002

PO Box 975
Bamenda
North-West Region
CAMEROON

Email:
jmankaa@
hotmail.com

The Benedictine Sisters of Bethany were founded by Sister Jane Manka'a in June 2002. The sisters operate the Good Shepherd Home, an orphanage that is in two locations: Bamenda and Batibo North West Region. These two homes have over 150 orphan children ranging between the ages of 0 to 18 years. The Homes operate farms, bakery, agriculture, fish farming, chicken farm and crafts as a source of self-sustainability.

The Sisters follow the Benedictine Rule of life. Our Community has a companionship with the Community of St John the Baptist, an Episcopal sisterhood in the USA.

REVD SISTER JANE MANKA'A
(Mother superior and founder, assumed office 2002)

Sister Mary Lawrence
Sister Benedict Bih
Sister Rose Tah

Novices: 2 *Postulants:* 1

Other Address
Good Shepherd Home annex, Batibo, PO Box 975, Bamenda, North-West Region, CAMEROON

Morning Prayer
5.00 am

Midday Office
12.00 noon

Vespers
5.00 pm

Compline
8.00 pm

Eucharist
Every first Sunday of the month.

Community Wares
Chicken farm, bakery, agriculture, piggery, fish farming, African dolls and crafts.

Office Book: Book of Common Prayer

Bishop Visitor
Rt Revd Dibo Thomas Babyngton Elango,
Bishop of the Anglican Church of Cameroon

Brotherhood of the Ascended Christ

BAC

Founded 1877

Brotherhood House
7 Court Lane
(Rustmji Sehgal Marg)
Delhi 110054
INDIA
Tel: 11 2396 8515
or 11 2393 1432
Fax: 11 2398 1025

Email:
delhibrotherhood@gmail.com

Website: http://delhibrotherhood.org

Morning Worship & Eucharist 7.00 am

Forenoon Prayer (Terce) 10.00 am

Midday Prayer (Sext) 12.45 pm

Afternoon Prayer (None) 3.50 pm

Evening Worship 7.30 pm

Night Prayer (Compline) 8.30 pm

Today, the Brotherhood has one bishop (retired) and four presbyters, who belong to the Church of North India. Since the earliest days, the Brotherhood has had a concern for serving the poor and underprivileged. In 1973, the Delhi Brotherhood Society was set up to organise social development projects in the poorer parts of Delhi. The work and social outreach of the Brotherhood is with and not for the poor of Delhi. The Brotherhood has initiated programmes of community health, education, vocational training and programmes for street and working children.

MONODEEP DANIEL BAC
(Head, assumed office 27 November 2013)
RAJU GEORGE *(Deputy Head)*

Collin C. Theodore *(bishop)*
Solomon George
Jai Kumar
Probationers: 1

Associates and Companions
There are twenty-six Presbyter Associates and eight Lay Companions who follow a simple Rule of Life adapted to their individual conditions.

Community Publication
Annual Newsletter and Report (free of charge).

Community History
Constance M Millington, *"Whether we be many or few": A History of the Cambridge/Delhi Brotherhood,* Asian Trading Corporation, Bangalore, 1999.
Available from the Brotherhood House.

Guest and Retreat Facilities
The Brotherhood House at Court Lane has a large garden and well-stocked library. It is used as a centre for retreats, quiet days and conferences. The small Guest Wing receives visitors from all over the world. There are four rooms. Both men and women are welcome.
Most convenient time to telephone:
7.30 am - 8.30 am, 4 pm - 5 pm (Indian Standard Time)

Office Book: The Church of North India Book of Worship & Lesser Hours & Night Prayer (BAC)

Bishop Visitor: Most Revd Dr P P Marandih

Blog: http://delhibrotherhood.blogspot.in

Facebook: http://facebook.com/delhibrotherhood

Chama cha Mariamu Mtakatifu (Community of St Mary of Nazareth & Calvary)

CMM

Founded 1946

The Convent
Kilimani
PO Box 502
Masasi, Mtwara
TANZANIA
Tel (mobile):
0784 236656 or 0756 988635 (Mother)

Email:
masasi_cmmsisters @yahoo.com

Morning Prayer 5.30 am

Mass 6.30 am

Midday Prayer 12.30 pm

Evening Prayer 3.00 pm

Compline 8.30 pm

The Community was founded in 1946 by the Community of the Sacred Passion (CSP). Bishop Frank Weston is the Grandfather Founder of CMM, while Bishop William Vincent Lucas is the Father Founder of CMM. Both were Universities' Missionaries to Central Africa. The CMM Sisters are trying their best to keep the aims of the founders: to serve God, His Church and His people.

There are eleven Houses in Tanzania and one in Zambia.

SISTER DOROTHY CMM
(Mother Superior, assumed office 14 June 2014)
SISTER TABITHA CMM (*Sister Superior*)
SISTER REBECA CMM
(Sister-in-charge, Mother House)

Sister Magdalene
Sister Rehema
Sister Cesilia
Sister Ethel Mary
Sister Neema
Sister Esther
Sister Helena
Sister Martyha Brijita
Sister Eunice Mary
Sister Joy
Sister Franciska
Sister Anjela
Sister Gloria
Sister Anna
Sister Prisca
Sister Nesta
Sister Bertha
Sister Aneth
Sister Mary
Sister Agatha
Sister Lucy
Sister Berita
Sister Mercy Neema
Sister Lyidia
Sister Stella
Sister Agnes Margreth
Sister Merina Felistas
Sister Jane
Sister Anjelina
Sister Perpetua
Sister Julia Rehema
Sister Joyceline Florence
Sister Jane Rose
Sister Mariamu Upendo
Sister Josephine Joyce
Sister Skolastika Mercy
Sister Mary Prisca
Sister Paulina Anna
Sister Janet Margaret
Sister Theckla Elizabeth
Sister Janeth Elizabeth
Sister Edna Joan
Sister Josephine Brijita
Sister Dainess Charity
Sister Agnes Edna
Sister Jane Felistas
Sister Asnath Isabela
Sister Ethy Nyambeku
Sister Vumilia Imelda
Sister Anna Mariamu
Sister Foibe Edina
Sister Veronica Modesta
Sister Harriet Helena
Sister Hongera Mariamu
Sister Lulu Lois
Sister Lucy Lois
Sister Penina Skolastika
Sister Rhoda Rachel
Sister Judith Natalia
Sister Harriet
Sister Deborah Dorothy
Sister Nesta Sophia
Sister Hongera Elizabeth
Sister Bernadine Jane

Sister Phillipa Sapelo
Sister Antonia Thereza
Sister Violet Monica
Sister Beata
Sister Hope
Sister Erica Mary
Sister Mariamu Elizabeth
Sister Mariamu Stella
Sister Merina Maria
Sister Lizzy
Sister Veronica
Sister Juliana
Sister Merina Happy
Sister Rehema
Sister Hariet
Sister Valiet
Sister Cecilia
Sister Joyce

Novices: 11
Postulants: 4

Community Wares
Vestments, altar breads, agriculture products, cattle products, crafts, candles & poultry.

Office Book: Swahili Zanzibar Prayer Book & The Daily Office SSF

Bishop Visitor: Rt Revd Patrick P Mwachiko, retired Bishop of Masasi

Other addresses

P.O. Box 116
Newala, Mtwara Region
TANZANIA

P.O Box 162
Mtwara
TANZANIA

P.O. Box 45
Tanga Region
TANZANIA

P.O. Box 195
Korogwe, Tanga Region
TANZANIA

The Convent
P.O. Kwa Mkono
Handeni
Tanga Region
TANZANIA

P.O. Box 25068
Dar-es-Salaam
TANZANIA

P.O Box 150
Njombe
TANZANIA

P.O. Box 6
Liuli
Mbing Ruvuma Region
TANZANIA

Sayuni Msima
P.O. Box 150
Njombe
TANZANIA

Fiwila Mission
P.O. Box 840112
Mkushi
ZAMBIA

Mtandi
Private Bag
Masasi
Mtwara Region
TANZANIA

Chita Che Zita Rinoyera (Holy Name Community)

CZR

Founded 1935

St Augustine's Mission
PO Penhalonga
Mutare
Zimbabwe
Tel:
Penhalonga 22217

Bishop Visitor:
Rt Revd
Julius Makoni

Our Community was started by Father Baker of the CR Fathers at Penhalonga, with Mother Isabella as the founder. The CZR Sisters were helped by CR Sisters, and later by OHP Sisters. When they left, Sister Isabella was elected Mother. Today the CZR Sisters work at the clinic and at the primary and secondary schools. Some do visiting and help teach the catechism. We make wafers for several dioceses, including Harare. Some of the Sisters look after the church, seeing to cleaning and mending of the church linen. We have an orphanage that cares for thirty children, with an age range of eighteen months to eighteen years.

In 1982, half the Sisters and the novices left CZR and created another community at Bonda. Six months later, some of those Sisters in turn went to found Religious Life at Harare. So CZR has been the forerunner of other communities in Zimbabwe. Please pray that God may bless us.

MOTHER BETTY CZR
(Reverend Mother, assumed office 2006)

Sister Anna Maria
Sister Hilda Raphael
Sister Felicity
Sister Elizabeth
Sister Emelia
Sister Annamore
Sister Sibongile

Obituaries

Sister Stella Mary

Community Wares:
We sell chickens, eggs, milk, cattle (2 or 3 a year) and wafers.

Community of the Blessed Lady Mary

CBLM

Founded 1982

The Sisters care for orphans on St John's Mission, Chikwaka. One sister works for the diocese of Masvingo and one is working in Harare.

MOTHER SYLVIA CBLM
(Reverend Mother)

Sister Dorothy
Sister Anna
Sister Faustina
Sister Praxedes

**Address: Shearly Cripps Children's Home,
PO Box 121 Juru, ZIMBABWE**

Bishop Visitor: Rt Revd Chad Gandiya

Chita che Zvipo Zve Moto

(Community of the Gifts of the Holy Fire)

CZM

Founded 1977

Convent of Chita che Zvipo Zve Moto
PO Box 138
Gokwe South
ZIMBABWE
Telefax: 263 059 2566

House Prayer 5.00 am

Mattins followed by meditation 5.45 am

Holy Communion 6.00 am

Midday prayers 12 noon

Evensong followed by meditation 5.00 pm

Compline 8.30 pm

Office Book
BCP & CZM Office Book 2002

Bishop Visitor
Rt Revd Ishmael Mukuwanda, Bishop of Central Zimbabwe

The Community is a mixed community of nuns and friars, founded by the Revd Canon Lazarus Tashaya Muyambi in 1977. On a visit to St Augustine's Mission, Penhalonga, he was attracted by the life of the CR fathers and the CZR sisters. With the inspiration of the Spirit of the Lord, he believed it was of great value to start a Religious community. The first three sisters were attached to St Augustine's for three months, Sister Gladys being the first admission on 14 May 1978. The first convent was officially opened in 1979 and the initial work was caring for orphans at St Agnes Children's Home.

In January 2000, Canon Muyambi stepped down from leadership, believing the Community was mature enough to elect its own leaders, which it did in March 2000. The Community have a Rule, Constitution and are governed by a Chapter. They take vows of Love, Compassion and Spiritual Poverty. The Community is progressing well with young people joining every year.

SISTER TERESAH CZM *(Archsister, assumed office 2014)*
FRIAR JOSHUA CZM *(Archfriar, assumed office 2006)*
SISTER CYNTHIA CZM *(Deputy)*

Sister Gladys
Sister Eugenia
Sister Elizabeth
Sister Eustina
Sister Phoebe
Sister Lydia
Sister Anna Kudzai
Sister Vongai Patricia
Sister Alice
Sister Tendai A
Sister Itai
Sister Juliet
Sister Tirivatsva
Sister Lilian
Sister Precious
Sister Joyline
Sister Vongai
Friar Tapiwa Costa
Sister Violet
Sister Blessing

Novices: 2 *Postulants:* 7

Obituaries

8 Jul 2016 Sister Gladys Moyo, aged 52, prof. 26 years

Other addresses in Zimbabwe:

St Patrick's Mission Branch House, Bag 9030, Gweru

St James Nyamaohlovu, Bulawayo P. Bag, Matebeleland

No 9 Coltman Close, Mt. Pleasant, Harare

Community Wares

Sewing church vestments, school uniforms, wedding gowns; knitting jerseys; garden produce; poultry keeping.

Christa Sevika Sangha

(Handmaids of Christ)

CSS

Founded 1970

Oxford Mission
Barisal Division
Uz Agailjhara 8240
BANGLADESH

Email:
christasevikasangha@gmail.com

Oxford Mission,
Bogra Road
PO Box 21
Barisal 8200
BANGLADESH
Tel: 1715 211821

Morning Prayer

Holy Communion

Midday Prayer

Quiet Prayer together

Evening Prayer

Compline

The Community was founded in 1970 and was under the care of the Sisterhood of the Epiphany until 1986, when its own Constitution was passed and Sister Susila SE was elected as Superior. At Jobarpar, the Sevikas supervise a girls' hostel, a play-centre for small children and help in St Gabriel's Primary School. At Barisal, the Sevikas supervise St Mary's Asroi (Home) and St Agnes's Hostel. The Community also produces for sale a wide variety of goods and produce.

SISTER JHARNA CSS
(Sister superior, assumed office June 2011)
SISTER RUTH CSS *(House Sister, Jobarpar)*

Sister Sobha	Sister Shefali
Sister Agnes	Sister Shalomi
Sister Dorothy	Sister Shikha
Sister Margaret	
Sister Kalyani	*Novices:* 1 (Rebecca)

Community Wares

Vestments, children's clothes, embroidery work, wine, wafers, candles.
Farm produce: milk, fish.
Land produce: rice, fruit, coconuts & vegetables.

Community Publication

The Oxford Mission News, twice a year. Write to Oxford Mission, 18 Market Place, Romsey, Hampshire SO51 8NA. Tel & Fax: 01794 515004 Annual subscription: £5.00.

Community History

Brethren of the Epiphany, *A Hundred Years in Bengal,* ISPCK, Delhi, 1979.
Mother Susila CSS, *A Well Watered Garden,* (editor: Mabyn Pickering), Oxford Mission, Romsey, 2000 available from Oxford Mission address above, £5 including p & p.

Guest and Retreat Facilities

Two rooms for men outside the Community campus. One house (three beds) for women. Donations received.

Office Book

Church of Bangladesh BCP & Community Office Book (all Offices are in Bengali)

Bishop Visitor

Most Revd Paul S Sarker, Bishop of Dhaka

Community of All Hallows

CAH

Founded 1855

All Hallows Convent
Belsey Bridge Road
Ditchingham
Bungay, Suffolk
NR35 2DT
UK
Tel: 01986 892749 (office) Mon-Fri

01986 895749 (Sisters)

Email: allhallowsconvent@btinternet.com

Website
www.all-hallows.org

Morning Prayer
7.30 am

Eucharist
8.00 am (9.30 am Sat, 10.00 am Sun)

Midday Prayer
12.15 pm

Evening Prayer
5.30 pm

Compline 8.00 pm

God is central to the life of the Community as he is to the life of all his saints. This finds expression through regular celebration of the Eucharist, the praying of the Divine Office and each member's commitment to personal prayer and reflection on scripture and other spiritual reading; it also draws us into the impulse to serve Christ with the same love that he has for us. The active life which this feeds embraces hospitality in its widest sense towards groups and individuals, both on and offsite. This includes spiritual accompaniment, workshops including labyrinth-based events, retreats and quiet days as well as pastoral ministry at All Hallows Hospital and Nursing Home.

What is true of the Community's base in Ditchingham is also so of our house in Norwich which provides prayerful, loving hospitality and from which a significant amount of Community outreach is undertaken, particularly in regard to the Shrine of Julian of Norwich and the Centre which are adjacent to the house.

The past decade or so has seen the transfer of much of the C.A.H. site to become property held by lease to the Christian Conference Trust, a local Emmaus Community and the Benjamin Foundation who now run Ditchingham Day Nursery. This has brought new life and rhythm to the site without compromising the stillness and silence at the heart of our presence here. Change, and the accompanying decision-making, continues to be required, as of any living organisation if it is to go on living and being a source of life to the wider community. There is already an increasing sense of fellowship and unity with our extended family of oblates, associates and contact members and we continue to receive enquiries from those wishing to explore with us some facet of our calling for themselves. This is a big encouragement as we go on praying and discerning God's present call to us; and our dedication to All Hallows encourages us to keep our mind, heart and spirit open to all he shows us.

SISTER ELIZABETH CAH & SISTER SHEILA CAH
(Joint Leaders, assumed office June 2016)
SISTER RACHEL CAH (*Assistant Leader*)

Sister Violet
Sister Margaret
Sister Edith Margaret
Sister Pamela

Bishop Visitor:
Rt Revd Graham James, Bishop of Norwich

Companions, Oblates, Associates, Contact Members

COMPANIONS, OBLATES, ASSOCIATES and CONTACT MEMBERS offer themselves to God within the community context with a varying degree of 'hands-on' experience. Some experience of the Community 'alongside' can also be offered. Apply to the Convent for details.

Other addresses and telephone numbers

Lavinia House (address as All Hallows Convent above)
Tel: 01986 892840

All Hallows House, St Julian's Alley, Rouen Road, Norwich NR1 1QT, UK Tel: 01603 624738

Community Publication

A newsletter is circulated yearly at All Saints tide. To be included on the mailing list, please write to All Hallows Convent at the address above.

Community Wares

A wide selection of photography cards, as well as some others.

Community History and books

Sister Violet CAH, *All Hallows, Ditchingham,* Becket Publications, Oxford, 1983.

Mother Mary CAH, *Memories*, privately published 1998.
(A collection of memories and reflections primarily intended for friends and associates but available to all.)

Sister Winifred Mary CAH, *The Men in my Life,* privately published 2009.
(reminiscences of prison chaplaincy)

Sister Violet CAH, *A Book of Poems,* privately published 2011.

Sister Pamela CAH, *"Where am I?": a book exploring the labyrinth and its spirituality*, privately published, 2015.

Guest and Retreat Facilities

Suitable for individuals, couples or small groups. Other details available on request. Enquiries about staying at our guest houses should be addressed in the first instance to All Hallows Convent (address and telephone number as above).

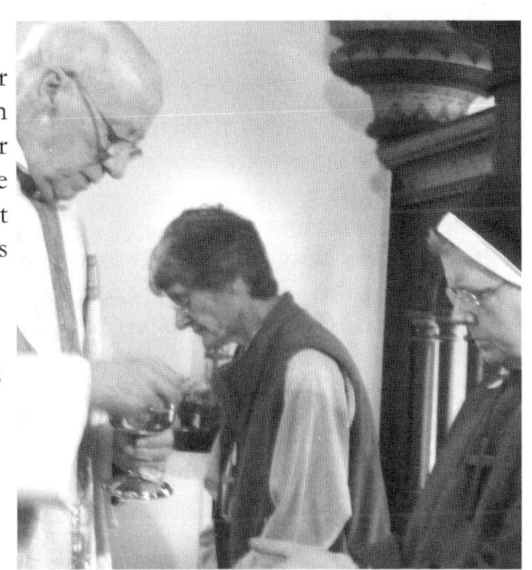

Most convenient time to telephone:
9.00 am - 12 noon; 2.15 pm - 4.30 pm; 7.00 pm - 7.45 pm (any day)

Office Books

Daily Prayer and Common Worship.

Registered charity : No 230143

Benedictine Community of Christ the King

CCK

Founded 1993

South Wangaratta
AUSTRALIA

BishopVisitor
Rt Revd John Ford

The Community of Christ the King is a Traditional Anglican Benedictine order, enclosed and contemplative. Its members have endeavoured to glorify God in a life of prayer under the threefold vow of Stability, Conversion of Life and Obedience. They follow a rhythm of life centred on the worship of God in the Daily Eucharist and sevenfold Office. Today, the remaining Sister of the community is in residential care.

Sister Patience CCK

Obituaries

15 Oct 2015 Mother Rita Mary, aged 90,
professed 58 years, Revd Mother 1997-2015

Oblates

The Community established an Order of Benedictine Oblates, open to women and men, clerical and lay.

Community History

Dr Lesley Preston, *Called to Pray: Short History of the Community of Christ the King*, Benedictine Press, Camperdown, Victoria, Australia, 2009. Available from Dr E. M. Crowther, 31 Hazlewood Close, Kidderminster, Worcs., DY11 6LW (for the price of the postage).

Community of the Glorious Ascension

CGA

Founded 1960

Brothers: **The Priory**
26 Helmers Way
Chillington
Kingsbridge
Devon TQ7 2EZ
UK

Tel: 01548 580127

Email: ascensioncga@fsmail.net

The Community seeks to live a common-life centred upon daily work, prayer and worship. The corporate pattern of the monastic life is at the heart of our life together; which aims to be informal and inclusive both in worship and hospitality. From its beginning, CGA has had a vibrant sense of mission which we try to maintain through our friendship with those who stay or visit, and also through involvement with people in the local area.

BROTHERS: BROTHER SIMON CGA
(Prior, assumed office 20 May 1993)
Brother David

SISTERS: SISTER JEAN CGA (*Prioress*)
Revd Sister Cécile

Obituaries

6 Mar 2016 Brother John, aged 87, professed 47 years

Sisters: **38 Green Park Way, Chillington, TQ7 2HY**
Tel: 01548 580939 Email:jean.pwll@gmail.com

Bishop Visitor: Rt Revd Robert Atwell, Bishop of Exeter

Registered Charity: No. 254524

Community of the Companions of Jesus the Good Shepherd

CJGS

Founded 1920

Harriet Monsell House
Ripon College
Cuddesdon
Oxfordshire
OX44 9EX
UK

Tel: 01865 877103

Email:
cjgs@csjb.org.uk

Morning Prayer
7.30 am

Eucharist 8.00 am
(9.30 am Sat & in College vacations)

Midday Office
12.30 pm

Evening Prayer
5.00 pm

Compline 8.30 pm

(all subject to variation in term time)

When the Community was founded, the first Sisters were all teachers living alone or in small groups but coming together during the school holidays. In 1943, West Ogwell House in South Devon became the Mother House and the more usual form of conventual life was established as well. The work of Christian education has always been of primary concern to the Community, whether in England or overseas, although not all the Sisters have been teachers.

In 1996, the Community moved to Windsor to live and work alongside the Community of St John Baptist, while retaining its own ethos. The Community aims 'to express in service for others, Christ's loving care for his flock.' At present, this service includes offering help and encouragement to those seeking to grow in the spiritual life through spiritual direction and prayer, and especially the befriending of the elderly, lonely, and those in need.

In 2012, the Community moved with CSJB to Ripon College, Cuddesdon.

MOTHER ANN VERENA CJGS
(Mother Superior, assumed office 20 March 1996)

Obituaries

15 Jul 2017 Sister Florence, aged 96, professed 69 years

Associates

Associates of the Community are members of the Fellowship of St Augustine. They follow a rule of life drawn up with the help of one of the Sisters. They give support to the Community through their prayer, interest and alms, and are remembered in prayer by the Community. They and the Community say the 'Common Devotion' daily. They are truly our extended family.

Community Publication

Newletter of CSJB & CJGS. Contact the Sister Jane Olive CSJB.

Office Book: Common Worship with additions from the old CSJB Office.

Bishop Visitor: Rt Revd Dominic Walker OGS

Registered Charity: No. 270317

Community of the Good Shepherd

CGS

Founded 1978

Christ Church Likas
PO Box 519
88856 Likas
Sabah
MALAYSIA

Tel: 088 383211

Residential address:
MQ8, Jalan Teluk Likas
Kota Kinabalu
88400 Likas
Sabah
MALAYSIA

Email:
sacgs8@gmail.com

Morning Prayer
6.30 am

Evening Prayer
4.30 pm

Compline
8.00 pm

Holy Communion
8.00 am
(1st & 3rd Thu of month)

The CGS Sisters in Malaysia were formerly a part of the Community of the Companions of Jesus the Good Shepherd in the UK *(see separate entry)*. They became an autonomous community in 1978. Their Rule is based on that of St Augustine and their ministry is mainly parish work.

In October 2000, the Sisters moved from Sandakan in the East Coast to Kota Kinabalu, the Capital in the West Coast. Here a new building was put up in the year 2007 to replace the temporary one. With the kind assistance of Associates, the Community continues to serve the Diocese through sewing, making a range of items from altar cloths to palls. Another group makes and supplies altar bread for the whole diocese. Our present chaplain is Revd Canon Chak Sen Fen, Dean of All Saints Cathedral. He is a great support to the Community.

SISTER MARGARET LIN-DIN CGS
(Sister-in-charge, assumed office 1978)

Associates
In Kota Kinabalu, some committed Christian women from the three Anglican Churches join in fellowship with the Community and have become associate members. They follow a simple rule of life to support the Community through prayer and to share in the life and work of the Community. Whenever they can, they come to join the annual retreat.

Community Wares
Altar breads, stoles for clergy, scarves for pastors and lay readers.

Office Book: ASB & the Service Book of the Province of the Anglican Church in S E Asia.

Bishop Visitor
Rt Revd Melter Jiki Tais, Bishop of Sabah

Benedictine Community of the Holy Cross, Costock

CHC

Founded 1857

Holy Cross Convent
Highfields
Nottingham Road
Costock
LE12 6XE
UK
Tel: 01509 852761
Email: sisters@ holycrosschc.org.uk

Website: www. holycrosschc.org.uk

[SOUTHWELL & NOTTINGHAM DIOCESE]

6.15 am Matins

7.30 am Lauds

9.15 am Terce

12.15am Sext
(Subject to change)

1.30 pm None

4.30 pm Vespers
(4 pm on Thu & Fri)

8.00 pm Compline

9.30 am Mass
(Subject to change)

Office Book:
CHC Office

The Community of the Holy Cross was founded in 1857 by Elizabeth Neale (sister of John Mason Neale, the hymnographer), at the invitation of Father Charles Fuge Lowder. The foundation was intended for Mission work in Father Lowder's parish of London Docks, but succeeding generations felt that the Community was being called to a life of greater withdrawal, and in the twentieth century the Benedictine Office, and later *The Rule of St Benedict*, were adopted. The Community aims to achieve the Benedictine balance of prayer, study and work. All the work, whether manual, artistic or intellectual, is done within the Enclosure. The daily celebrations of the Eucharist and the Divine Office are the centre and inspiration of all activity.

The Community also provides hospitality for retreats and quiet days, deals with a large postal apostolate and produces greeting cards and publications as described below.

The care of the grounds and conservation work in the woodland, old orchard and fields ensures a flourishing of the wildlife much enjoyed by visitors.

SISTER MARY LUKE WISE CHC
(Mother Superior, elected 8 November 1991)
SISTER MARY JULIAN GOUGH CHC *(Assistant Superior)*
Sister Mary Michael Titherington
Sister Mary Bernadette Priddin
Sister Mary Joseph Thorpe
Sister Mary Cuthbert Aldridge
Sister Mary Hannah Kwark
Sister Mary Catherine Smith

Oblates and Associates: The Community has women & men Oblates who are attached to it in a union of mutual prayer. Each has a rule of life adapted to his or her particular circumstances. Oblates are not Religious but they seek to live their life in the world according to the spirit of *The Rule of St Benedict.* There are also Associates who have a much simpler rule.

Community Wares: A great variety of prayer and greeting cards are available for sale. Many are produced by the sisters and others are from a number of different sources.

Community Publications: A yearly Newsletter published in Advent. Available free from the Publications Secretary.

Bishop Visitor: Most Revd David Hope

Registered Charity: No 223807

Community History

Alan Russell, *The Community of the Holy Cross Haywards Heath 1857 - 1957: A Short History of its Life and Work*, 1957.

A leaflet: A short history of the Community of the Holy Cross. Available from the Publications Secretary.

Guest and Retreat Facilities

There is limited accommodation for residential, private retreats. The Community also provides for Quiet Days for individuals or groups up to 20. The Guest House is closed after Christmas and Easter.

Community of the Holy Name

CHN

Founded 1888

Community House
40 Cavanagh Street
Cheltenham
Victoria 3192
AUSTRALIA

Tel: 03 9583 2087
Fax: 03 9585 2932
Email: chnmelb @bigpond.com
Website: www.chnmelb.org

Eucharist
7.30 am / 5.30 pm

Mattins 9.00 am

Midday Office
12.45 pm

Vespers 5.30 / 5.00 pm

Compline 7.30 pm

The Community of the Holy Name was founded in 1888 within the Diocese of Melbourne by Emma Caroline Silcock (Sister Esther). The work of the Community was initially amongst the poor and disadvantaged in the slum areas of inner-city Melbourne. Over the years, the Sisters have sought to maintain a balance between a ministry to those in need and a commitment to the Divine Office, personal prayer and a daily Eucharist.

For many years, CHN was involved in institutions, such as children's homes and a Mission house. There were many and varied types of outreach. The Holy Name Girls' High School was established in Papua New Guinea, and the indigenous Community of the Visitation of Our Lady *(see separate entry)* fostered there.

Today, Sisters are engaged in parish work in ordained and lay capacities, and in a variety of other ministries, including hospital chaplaincies, spiritual companionship and leading of Quiet Days and retreats. The offering of hospitality to people seeking spiritual refreshment or a place away from their normal strains and stresses has become an important part of the life and ministry. St. Julian's Retreat Centre is now closed as we are building new accommodation for the sisters on that site. Our original Convent will become the new Retreat and Spirituality Centre which will open in 2018.

Other Australian Addresses

68 Pickett Street, Footscray, VIC 3011

2/7 James Street, Brighton, VIC 3186

Office Book

CHN adaptation of the Anglican Office Book.

Community Wares: Cards, marmalade and handicrafts are sold at the Community House.

CAROL CHN
(Mother Superior, assumed office 12 April 2011, re-elected 2014 & 2017)
ANDREA CHN *(Assistant Superior)*
Council members: AVRILL, MARGOT & VALMAI

Avrill
Elizabeth Gwen
Felicity
Hilary
Jean *(in care)*
Josephine Margaret
Lyn
Maree *(in care)*
Margaret Anne *(priest)* *(in care)*
Margot *(priest)*
Pamela
Sheila *(priest)*
Sheila Anne
Shirley
Valmai

Novices: 1

Obituaries

26 May 2016	Philippa, aged 95, professed 69 years
19 Oct 2016	Ruth, aged 81, professed 55 years

Oblates and Associates

The **Order of Oblates** is for women and men who desire to lead lives of prayer and dedication in close association with the Community. The Oblates have a personal Rule of Life based on the Evangelical Counsels of Poverty, Chastity and Obedience and renew their dedication annually.

The **Associates and Priest Associates** support and pray for the Community. Each of these Groups meet regularly at the Community's House for fellowship and spiritual input. Priest Associates offer the Eucharist with special intention for the Community and seek to promote the Religious Life.

Guest and Retreat Facilities

Day groups of up to 25 people are welcome in the Prayer Group and Gathering Space. There is accommodation for six residential guests at the Community House and a Sister is available for help and guidance if requested. A self-contained hermitage in the grounds is available for private retreats. All guests are invited to join the sisters in worship.

Most convenient time for guests to telephone: 10am - 12.30 pm, 2pm - 5pm

Community Publication

An Associates Letter is published four times a year. Write to Sister Avrill, the Associates Sister, for a subscription, which is by donation.
Oblates Letter
Community newsletter and Prayer Pamphlets are available on the website or by email on request.

Community History

Sister Elizabeth CHN, *Esther, Mother Foundress*, Melbourne, 1948.
Lynn Strahan, *Out of the Silence*, OUP, Melbourne, 1988.
Sister Sheila Smith Dunlop CHN, *Some Suitable Women*, Morning Star Publishing, Northcote, VIC, 2014.

Bishop Visitor: Most Revd Dr Philip Freier, Archbishop of Melbourne
Warden: Rt Revd Garry Weatherill, Bishop of Ballarat

Community of the Holy Name (UK Province)

CHN

Founded 1865

Convent of the Holy Name
Morley Road
Oakwood
Derby
DE21 4TB
UK

Tel: 01332 671716
Fax: 01332 669712

Email:
bursarsoffice @tiscali.co.uk

Website:
www.comholyname.org

Bishop Visitor
Rt Revd John Inge, Bishop of Worcester

The Sisters combine the life of prayer with service to others in their evangelistic and pastoral outreach and by maintaining their houses as centres of prayer where they can be available to others. They run a small guest house in Derby. In our houses, and from the Convent in Derby, the Sisters are involved in parish work, hospital visiting, retreat-giving and work among the wider community, and with those who come for spiritual guidance.

The members of the Fellowship of the Holy Name are an extension of its life and witness in the world.

We encourage those who wish to live alongside for a period of time.

Sister Edith Margaret CHN
(Provincial Superior, assumed office 11 December 2015)
Sister Diana CHN *(Assistant Superior)*

Sister Marjorie Jean
Sister Barbara
Sister Brenda
Sister Verena
Sister Jean Mary
Sister Lilias
Sister Theresa Margaret
Sister Mary Patricia
Sister Lisbeth
Sister Vivienne Joy
Sister Pauline Margaret
Sister Carol
Sister Monica Jane
Sister Pippa
Sister Rosemary
Sister Irene
Sister Lynfa
Sister Julie Elizabeth
Sister Catherine

Novices: 1

Obituaries

19 Aug 2015 Sister Ruth, aged 96, professed 64 years
10 Oct 2015 Sister Charity, aged 93, professed 50 years
6 Dec 2015 Sister Elaine Mary, aged 83, prof. 29 years
22 Jan 2016 Sister Elizabeth Clare, aged 87, prof. 48 years

Fellowship of the Holy Name

The Fellowship is comprised of ecumenically-minded Christians who feel called to share with the Community in their life of prayer and service.

Members have a personal Rule of Life, which they have drawn up in consultation with a particular Sister. This will include daily private prayer, regular prayer and worship with the local Christian community, as well as time and space for their own well-being and creativity. Each rule varies with the individual. A six-month probation living the rule is required before formal admission to the Fellowship. This usually takes place at the Convent in the context of the

Prime
7.45 am

Eucharist
8.00 am
(12.20 pm Tue & Thu)

Mattins
9.15 am
(8.45 am Tue & Thu)

Midday Office
12.45 pm
(12.05 pm Tue & Thu)

Vespers
5.00 pm

Office Book
Daily Office CHN

Most convenient time to telephone:
10.00 am - 12 noon
2.00 pm - 5.00 pm
5.30 pm - 8.30 pm

Registered Charity:
No. 250256

Eucharist. There are regional meetings for members living in the same area, and the Community distributes newsletters throughout the year and encourages members to contribute articles for the Community magazine.

Other Addresses

St John's Rectory, St John's Road, Longsight, Manchester M13 0WU Tel: 01612 248596

64 Allexton Gardens, Welland Estate, Peterborough PE1 4UW Tel: 01733 352077

Community History

History of the Community of the Holy Name, 1865 to 1950, published by CHN, 1950.

Una C. Hannam, *Portrait of a Community*, printed by the Church Army Press, 1972. This was a heavily edited version of the original manuscript by the late Sister Constance CHN. A revised and updated version of the complete manuscript is now published as:
Sister Constance CHN, *What's in a Name?: Portrait of a Community*, CHN, 2015.

Community Publication

Community magazine - contact the editor.
Set of four leaflets: Community of the Holy Name; Fellowship of the Holy Name; Living Alongside; Facilities.

Community Wares

Various cards.

Booklet of Stations of the Cross, from original paintings by Sister Theresa Margaret CHN, with biblical texts. Can be ordered from the Convent: £5.00 each, or for orders of ten or more £4.50 each.

Sister Pauline Margaret CHN, *Jesus Prayer,* £3.50. Can be ordered from the Convent or SLG Press.
Sister Verena CHN, *A Simplified Life*, Canterbury Press, Norwich. Available from the Convent £10.

Examples of icons can be viewed by request at the Convent. Commissions can be taken. Contact Sister Theresa Margaret CHN at the Convent.

Guest and Retreat Facilities

There are opportunities for individuals to make a private retreat at the guest house, and Sisters may be prepared to give help and guidance if requested. Six single rooms, one double - see our website. Individuals and groups can contact the Convent for day bookings (usually between 10am – 4 pm).

Community of the Holy Name

(Lesotho Province)

CHN

Founded 1865 (in UK)
1962 (in Lesotho)

Convent of the Holy Name
PO Box 22
Ficksburg 9730
SOUTH AFRICA
Tel: 22400249

Website:
www.comholyname.org

Morning Prayer
6.30 am
(6.45 am Sun)

Terce
7.45 am (Sun only)

Eucharist
7.00 am (8.00 am Sun; 12 noon Wed)

Midday Office
12.15 pm (12.30 pm Sun, 11.45 am Wed)

Evening Prayer 5 pm

Compline 8.15 pm

Office Book
South African Prayer Book, supplemented by CHN Office Book

The Basotho Community of St Mary at the Cross was founded in Leribe, Lesotho, in 1923, under CSM&AA, Bloemfontein. In 1959, CHN Sisters were invited to take over this work and started at Leribe in 1962. They had invited the Sisters of S. Mary at the Cross to become members of CHN and the full amalgamation of the two communities was completed in 1964. As a multi-racial community, the witness against racism at a time when apartheid was in the ascendant in South Africa was an important strand of the Community's vocation. In succeeding years, the Sisters have continued the evangelistic and pastoral work which is also an important part of the CHN vocation. Sisters are involved in children's work, prison visiting, as well as other outreach in both Lesotho and South Africa. There is a church sewing room and wafer room. The Sisters in Leribe run a hostel for secondary school students. Some Sisters are 'Volunteers of Love' for families where there is HIV/AIDS. This work is enabled and strengthened by the daily round of prayer, both corporate and private, which is at the heart of the Community's Rule. A daily Eucharist at the centre of this life of prayer is the aim. There is a small guest house.

SISTER MALINEO CHN
(Provincial Superior, assumed office 18 January 2016)
SISTER MPOLOKENG CHN *(Assistant Superior)*

Sister Calista
Sister Alphonsina
Sister Hilda Tsepiso
Sister Julia
Sister Angelina
Sister Mary Selina
Sister Josetta
Sister Gertrude
Sister Ryneth
Sister Lineo
Sister Exinia Tsoakae
Sister Lebohang
Sister Malefu

Novices: 1

Obituaries

5 Feb 2016 Sister Lucia, aged 76, professed 51 years
Sister Provincial 1995-2001

Other houses: Please contact the main house.

Community Wares: Church sewing (including cassocks, albs, stoles); communion wafers; Mothers Union uniforms; mohair and woven goods from the Leribe Craft Centre and the disabled workshop, started by the Community.

Bishop Visitor: Rt Revd Adam Taaso

Community of the Holy Name

(Zulu Province)

CHN

Founded 1865 (in UK)
1969 (in Zululand)

Convent of the Holy Name
Pt. Bag 806
Melmoth 3835
Zululand
SOUTH AFRICA
Tel: 3545 02892
Fax: 3545 07564

Email:
chnsisters @telkomsa.net

Website:
www.comholyname.org

Terce 6.30 am

Eucharist
6.30 am (Wed & Fri)
6.45 am (Tue & Thu)
4.30 pm (Mon)

Mattins 8.30 am

Midday Office
12.30 pm

Evening Prayer
4.00 pm (Mon & Wed)
5.00 pm (Tue & Thu)
4.30 pm (Fri)

Compline 7.45 pm

The Community of the Holy Name in Zululand was founded by three Zulu Sisters who began their Religious life with the Community in Leribe. All three Provinces of CHN have the same Rule of life, but there are differences of customary and constitutions to fit in with cultural differences. The daily life of the Community centres around the daily Office, and the Eucharist whenever the presence of a priest makes this possible.

The Sisters are involved extensively in mission, pastoral and evangelistic work. The Zulu Sisters have evangelistic gifts, which are used in parishes throughout the diocese at the invitation of parish priests. Several Sisters have trained as teachers or nurses. They work in schools or hospitals, where possible within reach of one of the Community houses. Their salaries, and the large vestment-making department at the Convent at Kwa Magwaza, help to keep the Community solvent. The sisters also facilitate the care of many orphans in their extended families.

MOTHER ZAMANDIA CHN
(Provincial Superior, assumed office 2017)

Sister Claudia
Sister Olpha
Sister Nestar Gugu
Sister Nokuthula
Sister Sibongile
Sister Zodwa
Sister Mantombi
Sister Bonakele
Sister Nonhlahla
Sister Jabu
Sister Thulisiwe
Sister Thembelihle
Sister Sebenzile
Sister Benzile
Sister Samukelisiwe
Sister Thandazile
Sister Thandiwe
Sister Nondumiso
Sister Thokozile
Sister Duduzile
Sister Patricia
Sister Phindile
Sister Nqobile
Sister Sibekezelo
Sister Philisiwe
Sister Nokubongwa
Sister Nomathemba
Sister Thandukwazi
Sister Sindisiwe
Sister Bongile
Sister Maureen
Sister Neliswa
Sister Hlengiwe
Sister Nkosikhoma
Sister Thembekile
Sister Sizeka
Sister Thandeka

Novices: 0

Office Book: Offices are mainly in Zulu, based on the South African Prayer Book & the CHN Office Book.

Community Wares
Vestments, cassocks, albs and other forms of dressmaking to order.

Other Houses

PO Box 175, Nongoma 3950, SOUTH AFRICA
St Benedict House, PO Box 27, Rosettenville 2130, SOUTH AFRICA

Bishop Visitor: Rt Revd Monument Makhanya, Bishop of Zululand

---

Community of the Holy Spirit

CHS

Founded 1952

454 Convent Ave
New York
NY 10031-3618
USA
Tel: 212 666 8249

Email: chssisters @chssisters.org

Website
www.chssisters.org

The daily schedule varies with the seasons.
Please call ahead for current schedule.
Monday is a Sabbath in each house of the Community, during which there is no corporate worship.

Office Book
CHS Office book

Each person is given an invitation to follow Christ. The Sisters of our monastic community respond to that invitation by an intentional living out of the vows of poverty, chastity, and obedience within the structure of a modified Augustinian Rule. Through the vow of poverty, we profess our trusting dependence upon God by embracing voluntary simplicity and responsible stewardship of creation. Through chastity, we profess the sanctity of all creation as the primary revelation of God. Through obedience, we profess our desire to be dependent on God's direction and to live and minister in ways that respect all creation, both now and for generations to come. Compassionate, respectful love is God's gift to life. Prayer and the worship of God are the lifeblood and heart of our Community and the source of inspiration for all that we undertake. Through our prayer, worship, and creative talents we encourage others to seek God. Through our ministries of hospitality, retreat work, spiritual direction, and education through simple, sustainable, spiritual living, we seek to grow in love and communion with all whose lives touch us and are touched by us. We also provide spiritual support for women and men who wish to be linked with our Community as Associates. By adopting a personal rule of life, they extend the Community's ministry through prayer, worship and service.

Other Address:

The Melrose Convent - Bluestone Farm and Living Arts Center, 118 Federal Hill Road, Brewster, NY 10509-5307, USA
Tel: 845 363 1971 Fax: 845 746 2205

Email: inquiries@chssisters.org

Community Council *(assumed office June 2015)*
*members indicated on list below by **

Sister Élise
Sister Mary Elizabeth
*Sister Emmanuel
*Sister Heléna Marie
*Sister Faith Margaret
*Sister Catherine Grace
*Sister Leslie
*Sister Claire Joy
*Sister Carol Bernice

Obituaries

25 Sep 2015 Sister Mary Christabel, aged 93, professed 57 years
18 Mar 2017 Sister Maria Felicitas, aged 95, professed 39 years

Associates

From the Community's early days, Christian women and men have sought an active association with the Sisters, wishing to live out their baptismal commitments by means of a rule of life.

The Community provides four rules: Fellowship, St Augustine, Confraternity and Priest Associate. Each consists of prayer, reading, self-denial and stewardship. Each provides an opportunity for growth toward God and daily renewal of life in Christ. Each calls for a commitment to pray daily for the Sisters and all others in their life, worship and ministry, using the collect for Pentecost and the Lord's Prayer.

In consultation with the Sister for Associates, they may formulate their own rule if the ones provided cannot be fulfilled as they stand, or if they need to be expanded. As far as is possible Associates support the Community through gifts of time, talents and financial resources. There is an annual fee of $75, if possible.

Community Wares: [From Bluestone Farm]: Food items as available; crafts.

Community Publication: Periodic electronic newsletter. Please send email address to inquiries@chssisters.org.

Community History: The Revd Mother Ruth CHS, *"In Wisdom Thou Hast Made Them",* Adams, Bannister, Cox, New York, 1986.

Guest and Retreat Facilities

St Cuthbert's at Melrose; eight rooms, total capacity fifteen. Closed irregularly; email in advance to make reservations.
Visit www.chssisters.org for further information.
Email: vibhachokhani@mindkindinstitute.com

Most convenient time to telephone:

Generally, phones are staffed irregularly between 9.00 am and 5.00 pm EST Tuesday through Saturday, though you may leave a message at any time.

Bishop Visitor

Rt Revd Allen K. Shin, suffragan Bishop of New York

Community of the Holy Transfiguration

CHT

Founded 1982

St David's Bonda Mission
P Bag T 7904
Mutare
ZIMBABWE

The Community started in 1982 with 8 members who broke away from the Community of the Holy Name (Chita Che Zita Rinoyera). The Community is stationed at St David's Bonda Mission and it is an open community. We assist the Church in evangelistic work and other ministerial duties. Some members are employed by the diocese as priests and some as Evangelists. We run an orphanage with a maximum number of thirty young children. As of now, the age-group is going beyond this age range because of the HIV/AIDS pandemic. We are also a self-reliant community through land tilling and poultry. There is now another house at St Francis Mission, Shurugwi, in the diocese of Masvingo.

SISTER EMILDAH CHT
(Mother, assumed office 2006)
Postulants: 2

Sister Merina
Sister Dorothy
Sister Felicity
at Shurugwi:
Sister Gloria *(superior)*
Sister Winnie
Sister Lucy
Sister Gloria Mary
Rev Friar Fungayi Leonard
Sister Francesca

Obituaries: Sister Violet

Community of Jesus' Compassion

CJC

Founded 1993

PO Box 153
New Hanover
3230
SOUTH AFRICA

Tel: 072 027 0393 (Mother's mobile)
Email:cjcsisters@gmail.com

Founded in the Diocese of Natal by a sister from the Community of the Holy Name in Zululand, CJC have been based in Newcastle and Ixopo. However, the sisters have now settled at New Hanover, which is half an hour's drive from the cathedral at the city of Pietermaritzburg. The main work of the sisters is evangelising in the local parish, prison, Christian community radio station and children's ministry. The Sisters care for few children now due to some constraints.

On the 19th December 1998, the first professions within the community were received. The Community's formal recognition by the Church of the Province of South Africa followed in 2000 with the first life professions. In 2006, Sister Thandi became the first nun in the diocese to be ordained to the stipendiary ministry. However, she has now stepped down due to unforeseen circumstance and is currently furthering her studies in theology.

Other address: Unit 1, 2 & 3 Kruisfontein, Old Main Road, New Hanover 2330, SOUTH AFRICA

Community Wares
Girdles, Prayer Book and Bible covers, vegetables.

Morning Prayer, followed by Terce
5.30 am

Midday Prayer
12.30 pm

Evening Prayer
4.30 pm

Compline
8.15 pm

MOTHER LONDIWE CJC
(Mother Superior, assumed office 8 January 2000)
SISTER THANDI CJC *(Assistant Superior)*

Sister Yekisiwe	Sister Mbali
Sister Ntombi	Sister Thelma
Sister Zandile	Sister Ayanda
Sister Nontokozo	Sister Makhosazana
Sister Thokozile	Sister Sibongile
Sister Nqobile	*Novices:* 2

Office Book: Anglican Prayer Book 1989 of the CPSA Midday Office book & Celebrating Night Prayer

Bishop Visitor: Rt Revd Dino Gabriel, Bishop of Natal

Community of Nazareth CN

Founded 1936

4-22-30 Mure
Mitaka
Tokyo 181-0002
JAPAN
Tel: 0422 48 4560
Fax: 0422 48 4601

Morning Prayer
6.25 am

Eucharist 7.00 am

Terce 8.15 am

Sext 12 noon

None after lunch

Evening Prayer
5.00 pm

Night Prayer 8.00 pm

Under the guidance of the Sisters of the Community of the Epiphany (England), the Community of Nazareth was born and has grown. The Community is dedicated to the Incarnate Lord Jesus Christ, especially in devotion to the hidden life which he lived in Nazareth.

In addition to the Holy Eucharist, which is the centre and focus of our community life, the Sisters recite a sixfold Divine Office. We run a Retreat house and make wafers.

We welcome enquirers and aspirants.

SISTER NOBU CN
(Reverend Mother, assumed office 2008)
SISTER MIYOSHI CN *(Assistant Mother)*

Sister Yachiyo	Sister Asako	*Novices:* 1
Sister Kayoko	Sister Setsuko	
Sister Chizuko	Sister Mana	

Associates: Clergy and laity may be associates.

Other Address
81 Shima Bukuro, Naka Gusuku Son, Naka Gami Gun, Okinawa Ken 901-2301, JAPAN

Community Wares: Wafers, vestments.

Guest and Retreat Facilities: There are some rooms for meditation and retreat, but not tourists. Please contact us to ask further details about staying.

Office Book: BCP of Nippon Seiko Kai Office Book

Bishop Visitor: Rt Revd Yoshimichi Ohata, Bp of Tokyo

Benedictine Community of Our Lady & Saint John

Alton Abbey

OSB

Founded 1884

Alton Abbey
Abbey Road
Beech, Alton
Hampshire
GU34 4AP
UK
Tel: 01420 562145
& 01460 563575

Morning Prayer
7.00 am

Conventual Mass
9.00 am (10 am Sun)

Midday Office
12.30 pm

Evening Prayer
4.45 pm

Night Prayer
8.30 pm (7.30 pm Sun)

The monks follow the Rule with its balance of prayer, work and study, supported by the vows of stability, conversion of life and obedience. A wide ministry of hospitality is offered, and visitors are welcome at the daily Mass and Divine Office. The purpose built monastery is built around two cloister garths; the Abbey Church dates from the beginning of the twentieth century. Set in extensive grounds, with contrast between areas that are cultivated and others that are a haven for wildlife, the Abbey is situated about four miles from Alton.

RT REVD DOM GILES HILL OSB
(Abbot, assumed office September 2013)
VERY REVD DOM ANDREW JOHNSON OSB *(Prior)*

Dom Anselm Shobrook OSB
Rt Revd Dom Timothy Bavin OSB
Brother John Towson OSB (*Guest Master)*
Brother Anthony Witherspoon OSB

Obituaries
9 Jul 2016 Revd Dom Nicholas Seymour OSB, aged 76, professed 29 years

Oblates
For details of the Oblates of St Benedict, please contact the Oblate Master.
For details of the Companions of Our Lady and Saint John, please contact the Master of the Companions.

Community Wares
Incense: contact Alton Abbey Supplies Ltd.
Tel: 01420 565977

Guest and Retreat Facilities
Guest house facilities for up to eighteen persons, for both group and individual retreats. There is a programme of retreats each year, available from the Guestmaster.
No smoking in the house.

Most convenient time to telephone: 4.00 pm - 4.30 pm.

Office Book: Alton Abbey Office Book

Website: www.altonabbey.com

Bishop Visitor: awaiting appointment

Registered Charity: No. 229216

Community of the Resurrection

CR

Founded 1892

House of the Resurrection
Mirfield
West Yorkshire
WF14 0BN
UK
Tel: 01924 494318
Fax: 01924 490489
Email: community @mirfield.org.uk

Website: www.mirfieldcommunity.org.uk

Mattins
6.45 am (7.30 am Sun)

Midday Office
12.00 noon

Mass 12.15 pm
On festivals on week days, the time of Mass may change.

Evensong 6.00 pm

Compline 9.15 pm

Office Book
CR Office

Registered Charity
No. 232670

The Community consists of priests and laymen living a life of worship, work and study within the monastic life. They undertake a wide range of pastoral ministry including retreats, teaching and counselling.

GEORGE GUIVER CR
(assumed office 29 December 2002)
OSWIN GARTSIDE CR *(Prior)*

Roy France
Eric Simmons
Aidan Mayoss
Robert Mercer
Simon Holden
Crispin Harrison
Antony Grant
Nicolas Stebbing
John Gribben
Peter Allan
Philip Nichols
Thomas Seville
Steven Haws
Dennis Berk
Jacob Pallett

Novices: 2

Oblates, Companions & Associates

OBLATES, clergy and lay, are those who desire to make a special and permanent offering of themselves to God in association with the Community of the Resurrection.

COMPANIONS seek to live the baptismal vocation of all Christians through a commitment to each community to which they belong and also to the Community of the Resurrection; a commitment to Eucharistic worship, corporate and private prayer and the use of the sacrament of reconciliation; a commitment of time, talents and money. Those who wish to be Companions keep their commitments for at least a year before being admitted, and thereafter, with all Companions, renew their commitment each year. All Companions have a spiritual director or soul friend with whom their commitments are discussed and who undertakes to support them on their journey.

ASSOCIATES have a less demanding relationship with the Community for whatever reason, but do have an obligation of prayer and worship. For more information contact the Chaplain to the Companions at Mirfield.

SOCIETY OF THE RESURRECTION: This is a new group initiated in 2015, and after a probationary period, launched at Corpus Christi 2017, its members then making their first promises. It is akin to being an oblate, but open to men and women, ordained or lay, married or single. It has a fairly demanding rule and a strong sense of community sustained partly through social media.

Bishop Visitor: Rt Revd Graham James, Bp of Norwich

Community History: Alan Wilkinson, *The Community of the Resurrection: A centenary history,* SCM Press, London, 1992.

CR: a brief history, Mirfield Pubs, 2014; £3.50 from Mirfield.

Community Publication: *CR Quarterly*. Many subscribe to this who are not Oblates, Companions or Associates. Minimum annual subscription is £15.00.

Community Wares: Postcards, theological and spiritual books, leaflets on prayer, CDs of Community's music, clothes with logo: apply to Mirfield Publications at the House of the Resurrection. Purchases available online through the website.

Guest and Retreat Facilities: Retreats are listed on the website.

House of the Resurrection

Twenty-four single rooms, two double rooms, nine en-suite rooms, one small flat.

Most convenient time to telephone: 9.00 am - 12 noon, 2.00 pm - 6.00 pm

Mirfield Centre

The Centre offers a meeting place at the College for about fifty people. Small residential conferences are possible in the summer vacation. Day and evening events are arranged throughout the year to stimulate Christian life and witness.

The Mirfield Centre (College of the Resurrection), Mirfield, West Yorks WF14 0BW, UK Tel: 01924 481920 Fax: 01924 418921
Email: centre@mirfield.org.uk

College of the Resurrection

The College, founded in 1902 and run by its own independent Council, trains men and women and also provides opportunities for others to study for degrees.

Principal: Fr Peter Allan CR

College of the Resurrection, Mirfield, West Yorkshire WF14 0BW, UK
Tel: 01924 481900 Email: registrar@mirfield.org.uk

Community of the Resurrection of Our Lord CR

Founded 1884

St Peter's, PO Box Grahamstown 6140 SOUTH AFRICA Tel & Fax: 046 622 4210

This Community was founded in 1884 by Bishop Allan Becher Webb and Cecile Isherwood to undertake pastoral and educational work in Grahamstown. These two types of work, and later Social Welfare work, have predominated throughout the Community's history. The regular life of monastic Offices and personal prayer and intercession has always been maintained in all houses, wherever situated. Grahamstown is now the only centre where the Community life continues. The Sisters are involved in various ministries: at the Cathedral and other churches as needed; in the Raphael Centre for people suffering from HIV/Aids etc; in visiting at Old Age Homes and the hospital; soup kitchens; and needlework/banners. In April 2012, the Community opened an orphanage, named Ikhay Lethu, in our old convent, with two sisters and a brother, aged 1-6. Since then we have received two more, the youngest two being 9 months and one year old. So the total of children is five: three girls and two boys.

Email:
motherzelma
@geenet.co.za

Morning Office
7.00 am

Eucharist
7.30 am

Midday Office
12.30 pm

Evening Office
5.30 pm

Compline 7.30 pm

Greater Silence: 9 pm

Office Book
Anglican Prayer Book 1989, CPSA; Traditional Midday Office & Compline

Community Wares
Cards, banners, girdles, stoles and altar linens etc, corporals and purificators.

Bishop Visitor
Rt Revd Patrick Glover

MOTHER ZELMA CR *(priest)*
(Mother Superior, assumed office 24 November 2005)
SISTER KEKELETSO CR *(Assistant Superior)*
Sister Carol *(priest)*
Sister Neheng

Obituaries

20 May 2015 Sister Dorianne, aged 100, professed 71 years

Oblates and Associates

OBLATES OF THE RISEN CHRIST live under a Rule drawn up for each individual according to circumstances, on their observance of which they must report monthly to the Oblate Sister.

ASSOCIATES undertake a simple Rule, including regular prayer for the Community. Priest Associates undertake to give an address or preach on Religious Vocation at least once a year.

FRIENDS are interested in the Community and pray for it, and keep in touch with it.

There is a Fellowship Meeting twice a year, after Easter and near the Foundress's birthday on 14 November.

Also there is a Festival gathering of UK Associates at St Peter's Bourne, Whetstone, north London, on the Saturday nearest to St Peter's Day, 29 June, each year, at which two Sisters from South Africa are always present to preserve our links with the UK.

Community Publication: A Newsletter is sent out three times a year to all bishops and Religious communities of CPSA, and also to all the Oblates and Associates of the Community.

Guest and Retreat Facilities: Ten or more guests can be accommodated; though prior consultation is needed. The charge is negotiable. There is also a guest flatlet for two.

Community History and Books

A pictorial record of the Community's history, with commentary, was published in its centenary year, 1984. It was a collaborative work.

A Sister of the Community (compiler), *Mother Cecile in South Africa 1883-1906: Foundress of the Community of the Resurrection of Our Lord,* SPCK, London, 1930.

A Sister of the Community, *The Story of a Vocation: A Brief Memoir of Mother Florence, Second Superior of the Community of the Resurrection of Our Lord,* The Church Book Shop, Grahamstown, no date.

Guy Butler, *The Prophetic Nun*, Random House, 2000. (Life and art works, with colour illustrations, of Sisters Margaret and Pauline CR, and Sister Dorothy Raphael CSMV.) This is a coffee-table type book available in South Africa and the UK.

Community of the Sacred Name

CSN

Founded 1893

**300 Tuam Street
Christchurch 8011
NEW ZEALAND
Tel: 03 366 8245
Email: comsacnm
@xtra.co.nz**

Morning Prayer
7.15 am

Mass 8.00 am
(Thu & Fri)

Midday Office
12 noon

Vespers 5.15 pm

Compline 7.00 pm

Office Book
A New Zealand Prayer Book
He Karakia Mihinare o Aotearoa

Community Wares
Cards, vestments.

Bishops Visitor
Rt Revd
Victoria Matthews
&
Rt Revd
Winston Halapua

The Community of the Sacred Name was founded in Christchurch in 1893 by Sister Edith (Deaconess). She was released from the Community of St Andrew in London to establish an indigenous community to respond to the needs of the colonial Church. A wide variety of teaching, childcare and parish work has been undertaken over the years. Since 1966, the Sisters have run a large children's home in Fiji but since 2016 a new Community, established by the Archbishop of Polynesia, are now running the Orphanage. Our Sisters, still in the same Compound, are looking after our retreat house. We no longer look after St. Mary's hostel for girls. Mother Alena and Sister Keleni are in Christchurch, looking after the Retreat House. We have moved to our new House at 181 Barbadoes Street again and that has given more space for the retreat house; and we are still using the 300 Tuam Street address. Four Sisters are based in Ashburton, where we do ecclesiastical embroidery. Underpinning all the work is a life of worship.

MOTHER ALENA CSN
(Mother Superior, assumed office 9 November 2016)
SISTER KELENI CSN *(Assistant)*

Sister Annette	Sister Mele	Sister Fehoko
Sister Brigid	Sister Litia	Sister Sandra
Sister Lu'isa	Sister Judith	Sister Veronika
Sister Anne	Sister Miria	

Oblates and Associates

The Community has Oblates, men and women called by God to live the contemplative life in the world.

We also have Companions, Associates, Friends of St Christopher's. For women or men, priests or lay people.

Community History

Ruth Fry, *The Community of the Sacred Name - a Centennial History,* 1993; copies available from Revd Mother.

Guest and Retreat Facilities

13 bedrooms with one 2-bedded room. Retreat House closed at Christmas and New Year. Contact (03) 366 8245

Most convenient time to telephone: 9.15 am - 5.15 pm

Community Publication: Community *Newsletter*, three times a year. Write to the Reverend Mother.

Other addresses

53 Morris Road, RD2, Ashburton 7772, NEW ZEALAND Tel: (03) 307 1121

P.O Box 8869, Nakasi Suva, FIJI Tel: 3411441

PO Box 1824, Nuku'alofa, TONGA Tel: 27998

Community of the Sacred Passion

CSP

Founded 1911

Convent of the Sacred Passion
22 Buckingham Road
Shoreham-by-Sea
West Sussex
BN43 5UB
UK
Tel: 01273 453807
Email: communitysp@yahoo.co.uk

Morning Prayer
7.10 am

Prayer before noon
8.05 am

Mass 9.30 am
(Mon, Thu, Fri)

Midday Office
12.10 pm

Evening Prayer
6.00 pm

Compline 7.30 pm

The Community was founded to serve Africa by a life of prayer and missionary work, bringing to Africans a knowledge of God's love. After the Church in Tanzania gained independence, and the Community of St Mary of Nazareth and Calvary (CMM), which they nurtured, became self-governing, CSP withdrew from Tanzania and now offers support from England. Much of the help is channelled through CMM to whom they offer encouragement, advice and financial support. The Sisters also collect money for some of the work that they founded, including the Polio Hostel at Kwa Mkono, caring for disabled children.

At Shoreham, the Sisters offer hospitality for small day events and meetings. They are involved in guidance of individuals and have various contacts in the local community. The Sister who lives in Clapham has contacts with people of various faiths.

Prayer remains the foundation of the life of the Community.

MOTHER PHILIPPA CSP
(Revd Mother, assumed office 30 August 1999)
SISTER JACQUELINE CSP *(Deputy Superior)*

Sister Dorothy
Sister Gillian Mary
Sister Rhoda
Sister Angela
Sister Lucia

Oblates: Men and women who feel called to associate themselves with the aims of the community, by prayer and service, and by a life under a Rule. Their own Rule of Life will vary according to their particular circumstances. Oblates are helped and advised by the Oblates' Sister.

Associates: Men and women who share in the work of the community by prayer, almsgiving and service of some kind. They pray regularly for the community.

Priest Associates: Pray regularly for the community and offer Mass for it three times a year, of which one is Passion Sunday (the Sunday before Palm Sunday).

Friends: Pray regularly for the community and help it in any way they can. Although those who are enrolled as 'Associates' will continue in that category no more Associates will be enrolled but interested people will be welcomed as 'Friends'. Oblates and Priest Associates will continue to be accepted.

All those who are connected with the community are prayed for daily by the Sisters and remembered by name on their birthdays. They receive the four-monthly intercession paper and newsletter.

Other Address:
725 Wandsworth Road
London SW8 3JF
UK

Bishop Visitor
Rt Revd Ian Brackley

Registered charity No:
800080

Community Wares
Commissions for icons are accepted.

Guest and Retreat Facilities
One room. Donations. Women only for overnight stay.

Most convenient time to telephone: 4 pm - 7.30 pm.

Community History
Sister Mary Stella CSP, *She Won't Say 'No': The History of the Community of the Sacred Passion*, 1984
Margaret Gooch, *Zanzibar to Shoreham in 100 years,* Paul Davies, Great Yarmouth, 2011 - obtainable from the Convent, £10 plus £1.30 p & p, cheques payable to Community of the Sacred Passion.

Community of St Andrew

CSA

Founded 1861

Correspondence address:
Revd Mother Lillian, CSA
St Mary's Convent & Nursing Home,
Burlington Lane,
Chiswick,
London W4 2QE

Tel: 020 8742 8434

Email: teresajoan@ btinternet.com

Office Book
Common Worship - Daily Prayer

Registered Charity:
No 244321

In the mid 19th century Elizabeth Ferard felt called to restore the diaconate of women. She was authorized by the Bishop of London, A. C. Tait, to begin an Institute to train women as Deaconesses which started on St Andrew's Day, 1861. The Bishop commissioned Elizabeth as the first Deaconess of the Church of England on 18 July 1862. The Bishop laid hands on the head of each person to be made Deaconess, give her his blessing and she would be admitted to the Community of the London Diocesan Deaconess Institution. From about 1887 the Community evolved into a Religious Community known as the Deaconess Community of St Andrew; thus the dual vocation of life commitment in community and ordained ministry in the Church. The fundamental ministry is the offering of prayer and worship, evangelism, pastoral work and hospitality, now mainly through retirement ministries.

Associates: Our Associates are part of our extended Community family. They may be men, women, clergy or lay, and follow a simple Rule of Life, which includes praying for the Sisters and their work. The Sisters pray for the Associates every day.

Bishop Visitor: *vacancy*

REVD MOTHER LILLIAN CSA *(deacon)* Tel: 020 8742 0001
(Mother Superior, 1982-94, 2000-)
Revd Sister Donella *(deacon)* Tel: 020 8742 3172
Revd Sister Patricia *(deacon)* Tel: 020 8742 8434
all resident at: St Mary's Convent & Nursing Home, Burlington Lane,
Chiswick, London W4 2QE

Sister Pamela *(deaconess)*
resident at: Tower House, Reading Road, Shiplake,
Henley on Thames, Oxon RG9 3JN

Revd Dr Sister Teresa *(priest)*
resident at: 12 Ramsay Hall, 9-13 Byron Road, Worthing, West Sussex, BN11 3HN
Tel: 01903 238017 Email: teresajoan@btinternet.com

Community History

Sister Joanna [Baldwin], Dss. CSA, "The Deaconess Community of St Andrew", *Journal of Ecclesiastical History*, Vol. XII, No.2, October 1961, 16pp.

Henrietta Blackmore, editor, *The Beginnings of Women's Ministry: The Revival of the Deaconess in the 19th-Century Church of England*, Boydell & Brewer, Woodbridge, 2007, ISBN 978-843-308-6.

Sister Teresa [Joan White], CSA, *The (Deaconess) Community of St Andrew, 1861-2011,* St Andrew's House, 2012, reprinted 2013, 225 pp. plus photos.

Sister Edna Mary [Skinner], Dss.CSA, *The Religious Life*, Penguin, Harmondsworth, 1968.

Community of St Clare

OSC

Founded 1950

St Mary's Convent
178 Wroslyn Road
Freeland, Witney
OX29 8AJ
UK
Tel: 01993 881225
Email: community @oscfreeland.co.uk

We follow a contemplative tradition that is eight hundred years old with a fresh and informal spirit. In the pattern of St Clare, hierarchy is tempered by mutuality and warm relations within the community. As the Second Order of the international Society of St Francis, we have brothers and sisters in the First and Third Orders, and we enjoy close, though informal, ties with the Roman Catholic Poor Clares.

Our worship and prayer throughout the day are interspersed with domestic tasks in the convent and guest house, and environmentally friendly work in the large garden and grounds where we raise fruit and vegetables to eat, and keep hens who give us eggs. We also engage in our industries (altar breads, printing, cards) which with the guest house help us to earn our living, and where possible to share with others. Responding to God's call in our daily lives within the enclosure, we also enjoy visitors, holidays and the use of books, newspapers and the internet for a wider view of daily life.

Women seriously interested in the contemplative life (with or without the intention of joining the community) are welcome to take part for up to a year in our life of Franciscan simplicity and joy.

Sister Paula Fordham OSC
(Abbess, elected May 2016)

Sister Alison Francis Hamilton
Sister Carolin Clare Clapperton
Sister Damien Davies
Sister Kathleen Marie Staggs
Sister Mary Kathleen Kearns
Sister Mary Margaret Broomfield
Sister Susan Elisabeth Leslie

Community Wares: Printing, cards, crafts, altar breads.

Guest and Retreat Facilities
Men, women and children are welcome at the guest house. It is not a 'silent house' but people can make private retreats if they wish. 10 rooms (some double or twin-bedded). Donations, no fixed charge. Closed annually 16 Dec - 7 Jan.

Most convenient time to telephone:
For those wishing to stay at the Guest House – 6 pm - 7 pm Mon to Fri. For altar breads, printing, etc. 9.30 am - midday.

Community History: Petà Dunstan, *This Poor Sort,* DLT, London 1997, pp157-167

Bishop Protector
Rt Revd Stephen Cottrell, Bishop of Chelmsford

Website
www.oscfreeland.co.uk

Guest House
(for guests arriving)
The Old Parsonage
168 Wroslyn Road
Freeland, Witney
OX29 8AQ, UK
Tel: 01993 881227

Morning Prayer
7.30 am

Eucharist 8.30 am

Midday Prayer
12.30 pm

Evening Prayer
5.00 pm

Night Prayer 8.00 pm

Office Book
The Daily Office SSF

Community of St Francis

CSF

Founded 1905

As Franciscan sisters, an autonomous part of the Society of St Francis, our primary vocation is to live the gospel in the places to which we are called. The context is our life in community, under vows. Our wide range of backgrounds, abilities and gifts contributes to many ways of expressing the three elements of prayer, study and work. Prayer together and alone, with the Eucharist being central, is the heart of each house and each sister's life. Six sisters are priests. Two live the solitary life. One sister is in residential care. Study nurtures our spiritual life and enables and enriches our ministries. Work encompasses practical domestic tasks and a wide range of ministries: currently these include hospitality, spiritual direction, theological college and hospice chaplaincy, administration, teaching computer skills, local church and diocesan ministry roles, supporting people with various disabilities, preaching,

Minister General
Tel: 01325 462954
Email: minister generalcsf@franciscans.org.uk

UK Houses:

St Matthew's House
2 Yukon Way
Leicester LE1 2AF
Tel: 0116 253 9158
Email: leicestercsf@franciscans.org.uk

San Damiano
38 Drury Street
Metheringham
Lincs LN4 3EZ
Tel: 01526 321115
Email: metheringhamcsf@franciscans.org.uk

11 St Mary's Road
Plaistow
London E13 9AE
Tel: 020 8552 4019
Email: plaistowcsf@franciscans.org.uk

St Alphege Clergy House
Pocock Street
Southwark
London SE1 0BJ
Tel: 020 7928 8912
Email:southwarkcsf@franciscans.org.uk

Website
www.franciscans.org.uk

Office Book
Daily Office SSF

Registered Charity:
No. 286615

leading quiet days and retreats, writing, being a presence in poor urban areas, and work with deaf blind people. Some of this work is salaried, much is voluntary. Each new sister brings her unique gifts, thus enriching our shared life. Now in our second century, we are excited by the challenge of living the Franciscan life in today's world.

HELEN JULIAN CSF
(Minister General, assumed office February 2012)

EUROPEAN PROVINCE

SUE CSF
(Minister Provincial, assumed office February 2012, re-elected 2017)

Beverley	Hilary	Nan
Chris	Jannafer	Patricia Clare
Christine James	Joyce	*Resident in Korea:*
Elizabeth	Judith Ann	Frances
Gina	Liz	Jemma
Gwenfryd Mary	Maureen	Juliana

Obituaries
26 Sep 2015 Angela Helen, aged 82, professed 28 years

Companions & Third Order
Companions are individual Christians who wish to associate themselves with the Society through prayer, friendship and in seeking to live the spirit of the Gospel in the way of St Francis. For more information about becoming a Companion contact the Secretary for Companions, Hilfield Friary, Dorchester, Dorset DT2 7BE, UK.
For the Third Order SSF, *see separate entry.*

Community Publication
franciscan, three times a year. Subscription (Feb 2017): UK £9.00 per year, EU £16, Rest of World £16 surface mail or £19 airmail. Write to the Subscriptions Secretary, The Friary of St Francis, Hilfield, Dorset DT2 7BE, UK.
UK: Email to franciscansubscriptions@franciscans.org.uk.
Australia: Email to treasurer@tssforg.uk
Canada & USA: Email to djmoore@samnet.net
New Zealand: Email to a.moody@vodafone.net.nz

Community History
Elizabeth CSF, *Corn of Wheat,* Becket Pubs, Oxford, 1981.
Helen Stanton, *For Peace and for Good,* Canterbury Press, Norwich, 2017.

Bishop Protector
Rt Revd Stephen Cottrell, Bishop of Chelmsford

Minister Provincial:
Tel: 020 7928 7121
Email: ministercsf @franciscans.org.uk

Guest and Retreat Facilities

METHERINGHAM

In rural Lincolnshire on the edge of a peaceful village, the sisters welcome day visitors, either in the house or the comfortable hermitage in the garden. The house also has one room for a residential guest for retreat or quiet break. Two meeting rooms are available for groups of up to 8 and 24. The house is normally open to guests from Wednesday to Sunday. The sisters sometimes also welcome Working Guests who stay for a period sharing in the life and work.

SOUTHWARK

In central London the house welcomes day guests, and also has two rooms available for residential guests. Two meeting rooms accommodate groups of up to 8 and 20.

For more information please see the website, or contact the relevant house.

44-23, Suryu-gil,
Haepyeong-myeon,
Gumi-si
Gyeongsangbuk-do
730-872
REPUBLIC OF KOREA
Tel: (054) 451 2317
Email: csfkorea @gmail.com

AMERICAN PROVINCE

The Sisters came to the United States in 1974, and for over forty years we have engaged in many types of ministry, but with special concern for the poor, the marginalized, and the sick. We can be found in hospitals and nursing homes; among the homeless, immigrants, and people with AIDS; teaching student deacons and serving on diocesan commissions; providing spiritual direction and directing retreats in parishes. In all things we strive to be instruments of God's love.

PAMELA CLARE CSF
(Minister Provincial, assumed office June 2010)

Cecilia	Maggie
Jean	Ruth

St Francis House
3743 Cesar Chavez Street
San Francisco
CA 94110
USA
Tel: 415 824 0288

Email: csfsfo@aol.com

Website: www. communitystfrancis.org

Associates

Contact: Sister Jean SSF, Secretary for Associates.
Email: jeancsf@aol.com

Community Wares:

We sell the *CSF Office Book,* home retreat booklets, Franciscan prayer cards.

Community Publication

The Canticle. Contact St Francis House to subscribe to this electronic newsletter.

Community History
Elizabeth CSF, *Corn of Wheat,* Becket Pubs, Oxford, 1981.
Pamela Clare CSF, 'The Early History of the First Order Brothers and Sisters of the Society of St Francis', *The Historiographer,* Vol L, No 4, (Fall 2012), The National Episcopal Historians and Archivists and The Historical Society of the Episcopal Church, Phoenx, AZ, USA.

Guest and Retreat Facilities: At the San Francisco house, there is a guest apartment, which has one bedroom (two beds) and a small kitchen. It has its own entrance. The suggested cost is $50 per night.

Most convenient time to telephone: 9.00 am - 5.00 pm, 7.45 pm - 9.00 pm.

Office Book: CSF Office Book

Bishop Protector: Rt Revd Nedi Rivera (retired)

Community of St John Baptist (UK)

CSJB

Founded 1852

Harriet Monsell House
Ripon College
Cuddesdon
Oxfordshire
OX44 9EX
Tel: 01865 877100
(office)
01865 877102
(Community Room)

Email:
carol.wotherspoon @csjb.co.uk

Website
www.rcc.ac.uk/sisters

Registered Charity:
No 236939

Founded by Harriet Monsell and Thomas Thelluson Carter to help women rejected by the rest of society, we are now a Community of women who seek to offer our gifts to God in various ways. These include parish and retreat work, spiritual direction, and ministry to the elderly. Two sisters are ordained to the priesthood and preside regularly at the Community and College Eucharists. One is part of the College Chaplaincy team and the other assists in local benefices. Sisters are also available to facilitate quiet days.

We have close links with the sisters of our affiliated community at Mendham, New Jersey, USA *(see separate entry);* and we also have links with the Justice and Peace Movement.

Daily life centres on the Eucharist and the Divine Office, and we live under the three vows of poverty, chastity and obedience. Following the *Rule of St Augustine*, we are encouraged to grow into 'an ever-deepening commitment of love for God and for each other as we strive to show forth the attractiveness of Christ to the world'.

In 2012, we moved to Ripon College, Cuddesdon, where we hope to contribute to the life of the community and the spiritual development of the students.

[There is no named leader of the Community]
Sister Jane Olive Stencil
Sister Monica Amy *(in residential care)*
Sister Elizabeth Jane Barrett *(in residential care)*
Sister Mary Stephen Britt
Sister Anne Proudley

Bishop Visitor: Bishop of Oxford

Morning Prayer
7.30 am

Eucharist
8.00 am (during term)
9.30 am
(Sat and vacations)

Mid-day Office
12.30 pm

Evening Prayer
5.00 pm

Compline
8.30 pm

(all subject to variation in term time)

Office Book
Common Worship Daily Prayer, with our own plainsong hymns and antiphons

Oblates & Associates
CSJB has women oblates. Men and women may become Associates or members of the Friends of Clewer - these answer to a call to prayer and service while remaining at home and work. This call includes a commitment to their own spiritual life development and to active church membership. Oblates, Associates and Friends support the Sisters by prayer and in other ways, and are likewise supported by the Community, and are part of the extended family of CSJB.

Community Publication
Associates' Letter, published twice a year. Contact the editor at carol.wotherspoon@csjb.co.uk

Community History
Books by Valerie Bonham, all published by CSJB:
A Joyous Service: The Clewer Sisters and their Work (1989) - revised edition 2012
A Place in Life: The House of Mercy 1849-1883 (1992)
The Sisters of the Raj: The Clewer Sisters in India (1997)

Guest and Retreat Facilities
Facilities vary according to the time of year and the needs of the student body. These should be booked through Ripon College Cuddesdon.

Most convenient time to telephone:
10 am-12.15 pm; 2.30 pm-4.30 pm, Mon to Sat.

Community of St John Baptist (USA)

CSJB

Founded 1852 (in UK)
1874 (in USA)

PO Box 240 -
82 W. Main Street
Mendham, NJ
07945
USA
Tel: 973 543 4641
Fax: 973 543 0327
Email:
csjb@csjb.org

Lauds
7.30 am

Eucharist
8.00 am

Terce
9.30 am

Noonday Office
12 noon

Vespers
5.45 pm

Compline
8.30 pm

Website
www.csjb.org

The Community of St John Baptist was founded in England in 1852. The spirit of the Community is to "prepare the way of the Lord and make straight in the desert a highway for our God." We follow the call of our patron through a life of worship, community, and service.

Our Community is made up of monastic women, who share life together under the traditional vows of poverty, chastity and obedience. Our life includes daily participation in the Eucharist and the Divine Office, prayer, and ministry to those in need. We also have married or single Oblates, who commit themselves to a Rule of life and service in the Church, and Associates, who make up the wider family of CSJB.

We live by an Augustinian Rule, which emphasizes community spirit. Those who live with us include Oblates and friends, as well as our pony, dog, and cat. Our Retreat House and guest wing are often full of persons seeking spiritual direction and sacred space. Our buildings are set in a beautiful wooded area. Our work includes spiritual direction, retreats, hospitality, youth ministry and ordained ministry (two sisters are priests). The Community participates in a mission in Africa, helps the homeless, and works in parishes.

SISTER ELEANOR FRANCIS CSJB
(Sister Superior, assumed office 14 December 2009)
SISTER BARBARA JEAN CSJB *(Novice Director)*

Sister Suzanne Elizabeth
Sister Laura Katharine
Sister Pamela
Sister Mary Lynne
Sister Margo Elizabeth
Sister Deborah Francis
Sister Linda Clare
Sister Victoria Michelle
Sister Monica Clare

Oblates & Associates

Oblates make promises which are renewed annually. The Rule of Life includes prayer, study, service, spiritual direction, retreats. Associates keep a simple Rule. Membership is ecumenical.

Address of other house

St Mary's Mission House, 145 W. 46th Street, New York, NY 10036, USA. Tel: 212 869 5830

Office Book
Our own book based upon the Book of Common Prayer of the Episcopal Church of the USA

Community Publication
Community Notes, Michaelmas, Christmas, Easter Newsletters.

Most convenient time for guests to telephone:
between 10 am and 4.45 pm

Bishop Visitor
Rt Revd Allen K. Shin suffragan Bishop of New York

Community History & Books
J. Simpson & E. Story, *Stars in His Crown*, Ploughshare Press, Sea Bright, NJ, 1976.

Books by Valerie Bonham, all published by CSJB:
A Joyous Service: The Clewer Sisters & their Work (2nd ed 2012)
A Place in Life: The House of Mercy 1849-1883 (1992)
The Sisters of the Raj: The Clewer Sisters in India (1997)
Living Stones: The CSJB in America (2016)

P. Allan, M. Berry, D. Hiley, Pamela CSJB & E. Warrell, *An English Kyriale.*

Guest and Retreat Facilities
ST MARGUERITE'S RETREAT HOUSE
This has twenty-seven rooms. The address is the same as for the Convent but the telephone number is: 973 543 4582 There is one new room for a disabled person with disabled-access bathroom.

CONVENT GUEST WING
This has six rooms (for women only). The cost is $75.00 for an overnight stay with three meals. Closed Mon and Tue.

Community Wares
Tote bags, mugs, cards, jewelery, candles, ornaments, tapes, prayer beads.

Community of St John the Divine

CSJD

Founded 1848

Registered Charity
No. 210 254

These last two years have been a transition for the Community, letting go of securities and responding to new challenging circumstances. As a small Community, we believed our stewardship of a large house had come to an end and it was time to take a major step in faith of selling the house to others who would continue to have a Christian ministry in Birmingham. The five Sisters who comprise the Community have now bought a smaller house in Marston Green on the outskirts of the city where we hope to continue a ministry of welcoming people to the house for quiet days and for spiritual direction albeit on a smaller scale than previously. We are already involved in the local churches and have received a very warm welcome in the parish of St Leonard's, Marston Green.

Many smaller Communities are facing a similar situation and under the guidance of the Holy Spirit, we are all exploring how Religious life might be lived in a new way today.

SISTER CHRISTINE CSJD
& SISTER MARGARET ANGELA CSJD
(Leaders of the Community, assumed office April 2007)

Sister Elaine
Sister Ivy
Sister Shirley

St John's House
113 Coleshill Road
Marston Green
Birmingham
B37 7HT
UK

Tel: 0121 788 0391

Email: csjdivine@btconnect.com

Website
http://csjdivine.wordpress.com

Office Book
The Daily Office SSF
(Revised edition 2010)

Bishop Visitor
Rt Revd
David Urquhart,
Bishop of Birmingham

Associates
Associates are men and women from all walks of life who desire to have a close link with the life and work of the Community. They make a simple Commitment to God, to the Community and to one another. Together with the Sisters, they form a network of love, prayer and service. (Guidelines available.)

Community History
The brochure written for the 150th anniversary contains a short history.

Community Wares
Various hand-crafted cards for different occasions.

Community Publication
Annual report called *Making Connections*

Guest and Retreat Facilities
Quiet Days for individuals and groups. Facilities for residential individual private retreats. Openness to be used as a resource.

Most convenient time to telephone:
9.00 am, 2.30 pm, 6.00 pm

The new CSJD house in Marston Green

Community of St John the Evangelist

CSJE

Founded 1912

St Mary's Home
Pembroke Park
Ballsbridge
Dublin 4
IRISH REPUBLIC
Tel: 668 3550

Founded in Dublin in 1912, CSJE was an attempt to establish Religious Life in the Church of Ireland, although it did not receive official recognition. The founder believed that a group of sisters living hidden lives of prayer and service would exercise a powerful influence. When he died in 1939, there were twenty-four professed sisters and six novices. From the 1930s, the Community had a branch house in Wales, which became the Mother House in 1967. In 1996, however, the Sisters returned to Dublin to the house originally taken over in 1959 from another small community. This present house was formerly a school and then a home for elderly ladies of the Church of Ireland. It is now a Registered Nursing and Residential Home under the care of the Community but run by lay people. The remaining Sister of CSJE continues to live the Religious Life to the best of her ability and leaves the future in the hands of God.

Sister Verity Anne CSJE

Obituaries

16 Jan 2016 Sister Kathleen Brigid, aged 98, professed 55 years

Associates and Companions: Associates have a simple Rule, Companions a fuller and stricter Rule. Both groups are now much reduced in number.

Community History

A private booklet was produced for Associates in 1962.

Office Book: Hours of Prayer with the Revised Psalter.

Community of St Laurence

CSL

Founded 1874

Registered Charity: No. 220282

The Community was founded in 1874. The Sisters cared for the 'Treasures' of the Church - those in need of love and care, including elderly ladies. In 2001 the Community moved to a new purpose-built convent in Southwell, adjacent to Sacrista Prebend Retreat House and the Cathedral. The Convent closed in 2012.

Sister Dorothea CSL
Sister Margareta Mary CSL

Associates

Associates pray regularly for the community, and include priests and lay people. We have over one hundred associates.

Community of St Mary (Eastern Province)

CSM

An Anglican/ Episcopalian Order founded in 1865

St Mary's Convent
242 Cloister Way
Greenwich
NY 12834-7922
USA

Convent Phone:
518 692 3028
Farm Phone:
518 791 4142
Website: www.
stmaryseast.org

Home of:
St Mary's Institute for Christian Studies
St Mary's on-the-Hill Cashmere
St Mary's Scriptorium

Matins 6.30 am
(7.30 am Sat & Sun)

Mass 7.00 am
(8.00 am Sat & Sun)

Terce 9.30 am

Sext 12 noon

Vespers 5.30 pm

Compline 7.30 pm

The Sisters of St Mary live a vowed life in community, centered on the daily Eucharist and a modified five-fold Divine Office. Each sister has time daily for private prayer and study. Our way of life is a modern expression of traditional monastic practice including silent meals in common, plainchant in English for much of our corporate worship, a distinctive habit, and a measure of enclosure.

Our ministry is an outward expression of our vowed life of poverty, chastity and obedience. The specific nature of our work has changed over the years since Mother Harriet and our first sisters were asked to take charge of the House of Mercy in New York City in 1865. Being "mindful of the needs of others," as our table blessing says, we have been led in many ways to care for the lost, forgotten and underprivileged. Today our work is primarily prayer, Benedictine hospitality, retreats, and Christian education, a micro-farm in Greenwich, NY, and care of orphans in Malawi. Sisters also go out from time to time to speak in parishes, lead quiet days and provide a praying community within the Diocese of Albany's Spiritual Life Center and the Diocese of Northern Malawi.

MOTHER MIRIAM CSM
(Mother Superior, assumed office 31 August 1996)
SISTER MARY JEAN CSM *(Assistant Superior)*

Sister Mary Angela
Sister Catherine Clare
Sister Mary Elizabeth
Sister Martha
Sister Monica
Sister Jane
Sister Silvia
Sister Esther *(Junior)*

Novices: 2

Address of other house

Sisters of St Mary, St Mary's Convent, PO Box 20280, Luwinga, Mzuzu 2, MALAWI, South Central Africa

Community Publication: *St Mary's Messenger*, (print). Contact Subscription Editor, St Mary's Convent, Greenwich, NY 12834-7922. Cost to subscribers in the USA is $15, to those outside the USA $25.
ENews available at no cost via subscription to MotherMiriam@stmaryeast.org.

Guest and Retreat Facilities

Accommodations for seven in the Convent Guest wing and a further 50 accommodations on first-come, first-serve basis at adjacent Spiritual Life Center, in Greenwich, NY.

Most convenient time to telephone: 10 am - 7 pm ET.

Office Book
The Monastic Diurnal Revised, (CSM, New York, 1989): a modern English version of the *Monastic Diurnal* by Canon Winfred Douglas with supplemental texts based upon the American 1979 BCP. Copies are for sale.

Community Wares
Assorted illuminated greeting cards, cashmere yarn from the Sisters's micro-farm.

Bishop Visitor
Rt Revd William Love, Bishop of Albany

Associates
Associates of the Community of St Mary are Christian men and women, lay and clerical, who undertake a Rule of life and share in the support and fellowship of the Sisters, and of one another, whilst living dedicated and disciplined lives in the world. Any baptized, practicing Christian who feels called to share in the life and prayer of the Community of St Mary as part of our extended family is welcome to inquire about becoming an Associate. Each prospective Associate plans his or her own Rule with the advice of a Sister. An outline is provided covering one's routine participation in the Eucharist and the Divine Office, private prayer; abstinence and fasting, and charity and witness. Individual vocations and circumstances vary so widely in today's world that a 'one size fits all' Rule is no longer appropriate. The fellowship of Associates is the extended family of the Sisters and an active part of bringing the world to Christ. Contact the Mother Superior for more information.

Community History: Sister Mary Hilary CSM, *Ten Decades of Praise,* DeKoven, Racine, WI, 1965. (*out of print*).
Morgan Dix, *Harriet Starr Cannon,* Longman, NY, 1896.
Video: *The Hidden Life,* heritage videos, 2002 (58 minutes)

Community of St Mary (Western Province)

CSM

Founded 1865

St John's -on-the-Lake
1840 N Prospect Avenue #504, Milwaukee WI 53202 USA
Tel: 414 239 7908

Email: srletitia504 @gmail.com

The Western Province of the Community of St Mary as set apart as a separate branch of the community in 1904. We share a common Rule, but have separate administration. Our basic orientation is toward a life of prayer, corporate and personal, reaching out to the Church and the world according to the leading of the Holy Spirit. We live singly or in small groups, each sister using her gifts for ministry as she feels led with the support of the whole group.

SISTER LETITIA PRENTICE CSM
(*President, assumed office January 1992*)
Sister Mary Grace Rom CSM

Associates
Associates (both men and women) are part of the community family. They follow a Rule of Life and assist the sisters as they are able.

Bishop Visitor
Rt Revd Steven A. Miller, Bishop of Milwaukee

Community of St Mary (Southern Province)

CSM

Founded 1865

1100 St Mary's Lane
Sewanee
TN 37375
USA
Tel: 931 598 0046
Fax: 931 598 9519
Email:
stmsis@att.net

Morning Prayer & Holy Eucharist
7.00 am
(8.00 am Holy Eucharist Sat & Sun)

Noonday Prayer
12 noon
(12.30 pm Sun)

Evening Prayer
5.00 pm

Compline 7.00 pm
(not Sat & Sun)

Office Book
BCP of ECUSA plus Plainsong Psalter, Book of Canticles

Bishop Visitor
Rt Revd John Bauerschmidt, Diocese of Tennesee

The Community of St Mary began in New York in 1865. It was the first women's monastic community founded in the United States, and now has three provinces. The Southern Province has its mother house in Sewanee, Tennessee, and a branch house in the Mountain Province, Philippines. The primary focus of our life together is prayer and worship. The sisters gather four times a day for corporate prayer. We nourish ourselves spiritually through meditation, spiritual reading, Bible study and retreats. The sisters take the three-fold vows of simplicity, chastity and obedience. We live in community and hold all things in common. We choose to live a simple life and endeavour to treat God's creation with care. Hospitality and mission are important components of our community's life.

SISTER MADELEINE MARY CSM
(Leader, assumed office 2013)

Sister Elizabeth Grace	Sister Margaret
Sister Mary Martha	Sister Mary Hope
Sister Mary Zita	Sister Ines *(Philippines)*

Associates and Oblates

Associates are a fellowship of men and women who help CSM through friendship, prayer, support and by their dedicated lives in the world. Each associate writes his/her own rule of life, according to guidelines. We offer associates hospitality, retreats and spiritual companionship.

Oblates are a fellowship of men and women who pattern their lives on the monastic tradition of prayer and service. Oblates work closely with the sisters.

Other Address

St Mary the Virgin Church, St Mary's Convent, 2619 Sagada, Mountain Province, PHILIPPINES

Website: stmary-conventsewanee.org

Community wares: Photo cards, hand-painted note cards, rosaries (Anglican & Dominican).

Community publication: *The Messenger*

Community history: James Waring, *Saint Mary's, the Sewanee Sisters and their School,* Sewanee Trust, 2010

Guest and Retreat Facilities: St Dorothy's guest house. A one-bedroom unit with small kitchen and bath and a two-bedroom unit with kitchen and bath. All welcome. Contact CSM for the current fees.

Most convenient time to telephone
Mon-Sat, 9.30 am - 11.30 am, 2 pm - 5 pm

Community of St Mary the Virgin

CSMV

Founded 1848

St Mary's Convent
Wantage
Oxfordshire
OX12 9DJ
UK

OX12 9AU

Tel: 01235 763141

Email: guestwing @csmv.co.uk

Website:
www.csmvonline.org.uk

Lauds 7.00 am

Terce 8.15 am

Eucharist 10.00 am (9.30 am Sun & main feasts)

Sext 12.30 pm

Vespers 5.00 pm

Compline 8.15 pm

Office Book
CSMV publication

Registered Charity:
No 240513

As Sisters of CSMV, we are called to respond to our life in Community in the spirit of Mary, Mother of Jesus: "Here I am, the servant of the Lord; let it be with me according to your word." Our common life is centred in the worship of God through the Eucharist, the Daily Office, in personal prayer and reflection on the Scriptures. From this all else flows. For some, it will be expressed with those staying on our Guest Wing, in spiritual direction and retreat work; for others there will be creative ministry in icon writing, in the making and embroidery of vestments. There are regular contacts with the parish church and with children and staff in our local C of E primary school.

In early 2016, after exploring the possibility of moving from Wantage, we agreed corporately to rediscover our roots and vision in the Convent, together with our many links in this expanding market town. Parts of our building are being made available for Conference work in close connection with the Oxford Diocesan Schools Trust. In our grounds our Arts and Crafts period house, White Lodge, now provides additional quiet accommodation for individuals and small groups.

Sister Stella CSMV
(Sister-in-charge, assumed office 15 August 2016)

Sister Barbara Noreen	Sister Jean Frances
Sister Catherine Naomi	Sister Christine Ann
Sister Honor Margaret	Sister Eileen
Sister Helen Philippa	Sister Lorna
Sister Valeria	Sister Trudy
Sister Phoebe Margaret	Sister Elizabeth Jane

Obituaries

13 Apr 2016 Sister Mary Jennifer, aged 84, prof. 51 years

Oblates & Associates

Oblates

The Oblates of the Community respond to their vocation in the same spirit as Mary: "Here I am, the servant of the Lord. Let it be with me according to your word." Oblates may be married or single, women or men, ordained or lay. Most are Anglicans, but members of other denominations are also welcome. There is a common Rule of Life, based on Scripture and the Rule of St Augustine, and each Oblate is encouraged to draw up a personal Rule. There is a two-year period of mutual discernment by the Novice Oblate and the Oblate Council; the Promise made at Oblation with life intention is renewed annually. In addition to a close personal link with the Community, Oblates meet where possible in regional groups and gather annually for a day's summer meeting. A monthly letter and information is sent out as part of prayer and support for the Oblate Fellowship, and there are annual retreat and quiet days.

ASSOCIATES

Associates are those who wish to be received as 'friends' of the Community. Along with the Sisters, they too seek to live in the spirit of Mary's 'Fiat'. They live by a simple Rule of Life and undertake to pray regularly for the Community and for one another. The Associates' Link Sister acts as a bridge between the Associates and the Community, but she delegates the running of the Associates' fellowship to a Steering Group which keeps in touch with Associates by means of a quarterly newsletter, regular retreats and an annual Associates' Day held at the Convent.

Guest and Retreat Facilities

ST MARY'S CONVENT GUEST WING

The guest wing is a quiet place, enabling space and refreshment for all who come. Everyone is welcome at the Eucharist and Daily Office in St Mary Magdalene's Chapel. St Mary's Chapel is also available for private prayer and reflection. Facilities include sitting rooms, one with a library, a separate fiction library, dining room, informal quiet room, computer access and art room. There are attractive, secluded gardens and a water garden. For group retreats and group quiet days we offer a variety of rooms to accommodate most requirements. Conference facilities are also available. Those coming for individual quiet days are allocated a room, where they may rest. All other facilities are available to day guests and they are able to share in a meal in the guests' dining room if they so wish. The Community library may be available for reading on request. The Guest Wing is closed from after lunch on Sunday until Monday morning each week.

Rooms: Twenty bedrooms, including two twin rooms, one bedroom with sitting room, one small flat with en suite facilities, one ground-floor room with en suite shower for the less able.

WHITE LODGE

Arts & Crafts period six-bedroomed house in Convent grounds; can be booked for up to six people a night. Further details: www.white-lodge.org

Most convenient time to telephone

Contact the Guest Wing (01235 763141) 9.00 am - 7.00 pm, Mon to Sat.
Answerphone outside these hours. Email: guestwing@csmv.co.uk

Community History

A Hundred Years of Blessing, SPCK, London, 1946.

Sister A. F. Norton, *A History of CSMV*, Parts I & II (1974 MA thesis) & Parts III & IV (1978 MPhil thesis), available for reading in the Convent library.

Community Publication

CSMV Annual Newsletter Wantage Annual Overseas Review

Community Wares: Books, cards, crosses and other church items.

Acting Bishop Visitor: Rt Revd Steven Croft, Bishop of Oxford

Community of St Paul

CSP

Founded 1980

Maciene
MOZAMBIQUE

The Community was founded in 1980 in Maputo (Lebombo Province). The present house in Maciene was originally the branch house of the community and is where the sisters live today. They have been supported by CHN sisters from Zululand. The four sisters in life vows are all Portuguese-speaking.

Their present work includes a local ministry centred on the Cathedral, with hospitality offered through Bishop's House, support for the Sunday School and pastoral visiting.

Sister Cassilda
Sister Julieta
Sister Francina
Sister Persina

Community of St Peter, Horbury

CSPH

Founded 1858

St Peter's Convent
14 Spring End Road
Horbury
Wakefield
West Yorkshire
WF4 6DB
UK
Tel: 01924 272181

Email: stpetersconvent @virginmedia.com

Bishop Visitor
Rt Revd Tony Robinson,
Bishop of Wakefield

The Community seeks to glorify God by a life of loving dedication to him, by worship and by serving him in others. A variety of pastoral work is undertaken including Quiet Days, spiritual direction and ministry to individuals in need. The spirit of the community is Benedictine and the recitation of the Divine Office central to the life.

TEAM LEADERSHIP *(assumed office 4 August 2014)*
Sister Gwynneth Mary
Sister Mary Clare *(priest)*
Sister Phyllis
Sister Jean Clare
Sister Robina
Sister Elizabeth

Sister Margaret Ann
2 Main Street, Bossall, York YO2 7NT, UK
Tel: 01904 468253

Oblates and Associates
The Community has both oblates and associates.

Guest and Retreat Facilities
There are no overnight facilities for guests.

Community Publication: Annual newsletter at Petertide

Lauds 7.30 am

Mass 8.00 am

Midday Office 12.00 noon

Vespers 6.00 pm

Compline 7.15 pm

Community of St Peter

CSP

Founded 1861

St Peter's Convent
c/o St Columba's House
Maybury Hill
Woking, Surrey
GU22 8AB
UK
Tel: 01483 750739
(9.30am-5pm Mo-Th)
Fax: 01483 766208

Email: reverendmother@stpetersconvent.co.uk

Office Book: CCP

Community Publication:
Associates' newsletter at Petertide and Xmas.

Community History
Elizabeth Cuthbert, *In St Peter's Shadow,* CSP, Woking, 1994

Bishop Visitor
Rt Revd David Walker, Bishop of Manchester

Registered Charity:
No. 240675

The Community was founded by Benjamin Lancaster, a Governor of St George's Hospital, Hyde Park, London. He wished his poorer patients to have convalescent care before returning to their homes. The Sisters also nursed cholera and TB patients, and opened orphanages and homes for children and the elderly. They were asked to go to Korea in 1892. They have close links with the Society of the Holy Cross in Korea, which was founded by the Community *(see separate entry).* Since the closure of their Nursing/Care Home, new work is undertaken outside the Community in the way of continued care, using Sisters' abilities, talents and qualifications. The Sisters live in houses located where they can carry out their various works and ministry. They recite their fourfold daily Office either together in their houses or individually.

REVD MOTHER ANGELA CSP
(Mother Superior, assumed office June 2015)
41 Sandy Lane, Woking, Surrey, GU22 8BA

Sister Margaret Paul:
St Mary's Convent & Nursing Home, Burlington Lane, Chiswick, London W4 2QE

Sister Lucy Clare: Fosbrooke House, Apartment 33, 8 Clifton Drive, Lytham, Lancashire, FY8 5RQ

Obituaries

1 Jul 2016 Sister Georgina Ruth, aged 82, prof. 30 years
5 May 2017 Sister Rosamund, aged 94, prof. 32 years, Mother Superior 2001-2006

Associates and Companions

The associates support the community in prayer and with practical help, as they are able. They have a simple rule and attend the Eucharist in their own Church. Companions have a stricter rule and say the Daily Office.

Guest and Retreat Facilities

Chaplain & Programme Developer: Rachel Moore
St Columba's House (Retreat & Conference Centre)
Maybury Hill, Woking, Surrey GU22 8AE, UK
Tel: 01483 713006 or 07069 067116 Fax: 01483 740441
Website: www.stcolumbashouse.org.uk

22 en-suite single bedrooms (2 with disabled facilities), 5 twin bedrooms (4 ensuite). Programme of individual and group retreats. Conference centre for residential and day use, completely refurbished in 2009 for retreatants, parish groups etc. Outstanding liturgical space with a pastoral, and liturgical programme.

Most convenient time to telephone: 9.30 am - 5.00 pm.

Community of the Servants of the Will of God

CSWG

Founded 1953

The Monastery of the Holy Trinity
Crawley Down
Crawley
West Sussex
RH10 4LH
UK

Tel: 01342 712074

Email:
(for guest bookings & enquiries)
brother.andrew@ cswg.org.uk

Vigils 5.00 am

Lauds 7.00 am

Terce 9.30 am

Sext 12.00 noon

Vespers 6.30 pm

Mass
7.00 pm Mon – Fri
11.00 am Sat & Sun

This monastery is set in woodland. The Community lives a contemplative life, uniting silence, work and prayer in a simple life style based on the *Rule of St Benedict.* The Community is especially concerned with uniting the traditions of East and West, and has developed the Liturgy, Divine Office and use of the Jesus Prayer accordingly.

FATHER COLIN CSWG
(Father Superior, assumed office 3 April 2008)
FATHER PETER CSWG *(Prior)*
Brother Martin
Brother Christopher Mark
Brother Andrew

Obituaries
12 Nov 2015 Brother John of the Cross, aged 71, professed 21 years
23 May 2016 Father Alex Brighouse, aged 70, postulant

Associates
The associates keep a rule of life in the spirit of the monastery.

Community Publication
CSWG Journal: *Come to the Father*, issued Pentecost and All Saints. Write to the Monastery of the Holy Trinity.

Community History
Father Colin CSWG, *A History of the Community of the Servants of the Will of God,* 2002. Available from the Monastery of the Holy Trinity.

Guest and Retreat Facilities
Six individual guest rooms; meals in community refectory; Divine Office and Eucharist, all with modal chant; donations c.£20 per day.

Most convenient time to telephone: 9.30 am - 6.00 pm.

Community Wares
Mounted icon prints, Jesus Prayer ropes, candles and vigil lights, booklets on monastic and spiritual life.

Office Book
CSWG Divine Office and Liturgy

Bishop Visitor
Rt Revd John Hind

Community of the Sisters of the Church

CSC

Founded 1870

for the whole people of God

Worldwide Community Website: www. sistersofthechurch .org

ENGLAND
Registered Charity No. for CEA: 200240

CANADA
Registered Charity No. 130673262RR0001

AUSTRALIA
Tax Exempt - NPO

Founded by Emily Ayckbowm in 1870, the Community of the Sisters of the Church is an international body of lay and ordained women within the Anglican Communion. We are seeking to be faithful to the gospel values of Poverty, Chastity and Obedience, and to the traditions of Religious Life while exploring new ways of expressing them and of living community life and ministry today. By our worship, ministry and life in community, we desire to be channels of the reconciling love and acceptance of Christ, to acknowledge the dignity of every person, and to enable others to encounter the living God whom we seek.

The Community's patrons, St Michael and the Angels, point us to a life both of worship and active ministry, of mingled adoration and action. Our name, Sisters of the Church, reminds us that our particular dedication is to the mystery of the Church as the Body of Christ in the world.

Each house has its own timetable of corporate worship. The Eucharist and Divine Office (usually fourfold) are the heart of our Community life.

Community houses provide different expressions of our life and ministry in inner city, suburban, coastal town and village setting.

LINDA MARY SHUTTLE CSC
(Mother Superior, assumed office July 2009)
Email: lindacsc@bigpond.com
29 Lika Drive, Kempsey, NSW 2440, AUSTRALIA

ENGLAND
SUSAN HIRD CSC
(*UK Provincial, assumed office September 2008*)
Email: provincial@sistersofthechurch.org.uk
CATHERINE HEYBOURN CSC *(Assistant Provincial)*

Aileen Taylor
Anita Cook
Annaliese Brogden
Dorothea Roden
Hilda Mary Baumberg
Jennifer Cook
Judith Gray
Mary Josephine Thomas
Rosina Taylor
Ruth White
Sheila Julian Merryweather
Sue McCarten
Teresa Mary Wright
Vivien Atkinson

Addresses in the UK

St Michael's Convent, Vicarage Way, Gerrards Cross, Bucks SL9 8AT
Email for general enquiries: info@sistersofthechurch.org.uk

82 Ashley Road, Bristol BS6 5NT Tel: 01179 413268
Email: bristol@sistersofthe church.org.uk

St Gabriel's, 27A Dial Hill Road, Clevedon, N. Somerset BS21 7HL
Tel: 01275 544471 Email: clevedon@sistersofthe church.org.uk

10 Furness Road, West Harrow, Middlesex HA2 0RL
Tel: 020 8423 3780 Email: westharrow@sistersofthe church.org.uk

CANADA

Arrived in Canada 1890. Established as a separate Province 1965.

MARGARET HAYWARD CSC
(Provincial, assumed office 26 September 2009)
Email: margaretcsc@sympatico.ca

Heather Broadwell
Marguerite Mae Eamon
Michael Trott

Obituaries

27 Apr 2017 Rita Dugger, aged 89, *(CWC 1983-95, CSC 1995-2017)*

Addresses in Canada

Sr Margaret Hayward CSC
(& the Community of the Sisters of the Church, c/o Sr Margaret)
Apt 1003 - 6 John St, Oakville, ON, L6K 3T1
Tel: 905 849 0225
General email: sistersofthechurch@sympatico.ca

Sr Michael Trott CSC, Apt 604 - 6 John St, Oakville, ON, L6K 3T1
Tel: 905 845 7186

Sr Marguerite Mae Eamon CSC, Unit 1110 - 1240 Marlborough Court, Oakville, ON, L6H 3K7 Tel: 905 842 5696

Sr Heather Broadwell CSC,
Unit 303 - 28 Duke St, Hamilton, ON, L8P 1X1 Tel: 289 396 6103

AUSTRALIA

Arrived in Australia 1892. Established as a separate Province 1965.

LINDA MARY SHUTTLE CSC
(*Provincial, assumed office November 1999*)
Email: lindacsc@bigpond.com

Elisa Helen Waterhouse
Fiona Cooper
Frances Murphy
Helen Jamieson
Rosamund Duncan

Obituaries

18 Apr 2017 Audrey Floate, aged 92, professed 54 years, Provincial 1972-1981

Addresses in Australia

Sisters of the Church, PO Box 1105, Glebe, NSW 2037
Email: cscaust@hotmail.com

Sisters of the Church, 29 Lika Drive, Kempsey, NSW 2440
Tel: 2 6562 2313

Unit 15/75, St John's Road, Glebe, NSW 2037

PO Box 713, Melton, Victoria 3337 **Tel: 3 8716 1403**
Email: elisahelen.waterhouse@gmail.com

SOLOMON ISLANDS-PACIFIC

Arrived in Solomon Islands 1970. Established as a separate Province 2001.

VERONICA VASETHE CSC
(Provincial, assumed office March 2017)
Email: veronica@sistersofthechurch.org
EMILY MARY IKAI CSC (*Assistant Provincial)*
Email: emily@sistersofthechurch.org

Agnes Maeusia
Anneth Kagoa
Annie Meke
Beglyn Tiri
Betsy Samo
Beverlyn Aosi
Caroline Havideni
Catherine Tawai
Daisy Gaoka
Dexter Wilkins
Doreen Awaisi
Eleanor Ataki
Ellen Marou
Evelyn Yaiyo
Grace Papahu
Jennifer Clare
Jennifer Imua
Jessica Maru
Kathleen Kapei
Kristy Arofa
Lillian Mary Manedika
Lucia Sadias
Margaret Mauvo
Margosa Funu
Marina Tuga
Mary Gharegha
Mary Gladys Nunga
Mary Kami
May Peleba
Neslyn Elonoda
Patricia Kalali
Phyllis Sau
Priscilla Iolani
Rachel Teku
Rita Zimae
Rose Glenda Kimanitoro
Ruth Hope Sosoke
Shirley Hugo
Sophie Leguvako

Novices: 6
Postulants: 6

Addresses in the Solomon Islands

Tetete ni Kolivuti, Box 510, Honiara

Patteson House, Box 510, Honiara **Tel: 677 22413 & 677 27582**

PO Box 7, Auki, Malaita **Tel: 677 40423**

St Gabriel's, c/o Hanuato'o Diocese, Kira Kira, Makira/Ulawa Province **Fax: 677 50128** **Mobile: 7553947**

St Mary's, Luesalo, Diocese of Temotu, Santa Cruz
Mobile phone: 7440081

St Scholastica's House, PO Box 510, Honiara

Sisters of the Church, Henderson, PO Box 510, Honiara

Associates

Associates are men and women who seek to live the Gospel values of Simplicity, Chastity and Obedience within their own circumstances. Each creates his/her own Rule of Life and has a Link Sister or Link House. They are united in spirit with CSC in its life of worship and service, fostering a mutually enriching bond.

Community History

A Valiant Victorian: The Life and Times of Mother Emily Ayckbowm 1836-1900 of the Community of the Sisters of the Church, Mowbray, London, 1964.

Ann M Baldwin CSC, *Now is the Time: a brief survey of the life and times of the Community of the Sisters of the Church,* CSC, 2005.

Community Publication: *Newsletter*, twice a year.

Information can be obtained from any house in the community and by email.

Community Wares

Books by Sister Sheila Julian Merryweather: *Colourful Prayer; Colourful Advent; Colourful Lent.* All published by Kevin Mayhew, Buxhall, Stowmarket.

Some houses sell crafts and cards. Vestments are made in the Solomon Islands.

Guest and Retreat Facilities: Hospitality is offered in most houses. Gerrards Cross and Tetete ni Kolivuti have more accommodation for residential guests as well as day facilities. Please contact individual houses for other information.

Office Book: The Office varies in the different Provinces. Various combinations of the Community's own Office book, the New Zealand psalter, the UK *Common Worship* and the most recent prayer books of Australia, Canada and Melanesia are used.

The new CSC house at Gerrards Cross, UK

Bishops Visitor

UK Province: Rt Revd Christopher Chessun, Bishop of Southwark
Australia Province: Rt Revd Sarah Macneil, Bishop of Grafton
Canada Province: Rt Revd Michael Bird, Bishop of Niagara
Solomon Islands Pacific Province: Rt Revd Nathan Tome, Bishop of Guadalcanal

Address of Affiliated Community

Community of the Love of God (*Orthodox Syrian*)
Nazareth, Kadampanad South 691553, Pathanamthitta District, Kerala, INDIA
Tel: 473 4822146

Community of the Sisters of the Love of God

SLG

Founded 1906

Convent of the Incarnation
Fairacres
Parker Street
Oxford OX4 1TB
UK
Tel: 01865 721301
Fax: 01865 250798
Emails:
sisters@slg.org.uk
guests@slg.org.uk

Website:
www.slg.org.uk

Matins
6.00 am (6.15 am Sun & Solemnities)
Terce & Mass
9.05 am (no Mass Sat, ecept on major feasts)
Sext 12.15 pm
None
2.05 pm (3.05 pm Sun)
Vespers 5.30 pm
Compline 8.05 pm (7.35 pm in Winter)
Sat: unless a major feast, Office said privately until Vespers at 5.30 pm

A contemplative community with a strong monastic tradition founded in 1906, which seeks to witness to the priority of God and to respond to the love of God - God's love for us and our love for God. We believe that we are called to live a substantial degree of withdrawal, in order to give ourselves to the work of prayer which, beginning and ending in the praise and worship of God, is essential for the peace and well-being of the world. Through offering our lives to God within the Community, and through prayer and daily life together, we seek to deepen our relationship with Jesus Christ and one another. The Community has always drawn upon the spirituality of Carmel; life and prayer in silence and solitude is an important dimension in our vocation. The Community also draws from other traditions and the Divine Office and Eucharist are central to our life.

Sister Clare-Louise SLG
(Revd Mother, elected 27 May 2015)
Sister Avis Mary SLG *(Prioress)*

Sister Benedicta
Sister Adrian
Sister Anne
Sister Barbara June
Sister Susan
Sister Edmée
Sister Christine
Sister Rosemary
Sister Catherine
Sister Julie
Sister Shirley Clare
Sister Alison
Sister Tessa
Sister Margaret Theresa
Sister Raphael
Sister Stephanie Thérèse
Sister Freda
Sister Judith
Sister Eve
Sister Elizabeth
Sister Helen

Obituaries

31 Jul 2015	Sr Jane Frances, aged 84, prof. 49 years
31 May 2016	Sr Mary Kathleen, aged 92, prof. 49 years
14 June 2016	Sr Isabel, aged 82, professed 56 years
20 Aug 2016	Sr Helen Columba, aged 88, prof. 39 years
10 Sep 2016	Sr Mary Margaret, aged 90, prof. 56 years

Oblates and associates

The Community includes Oblate Sisters, who are called to the contemplative life in the world rather than within the monastic enclosure. There are three other groups of associates: Priest Associates, Companions, and the Fellowship of the Love of God. Information about all these may be obtained from the Revd Mother at Fairacres.

Community Publication: *Fairacres Chronicle.* Published twice a year by SLG Press (see under Community Wares).

Community Wares

SLG Press publishes the *Fairacres Chronicle* and a range of books and pamphlets on prayer and spirituality. Contact details:

The Editor, SLG Press, Convent of the Incarnation, Fairacres, Parker Street, Oxford OX4 1TB, UK

Tel: 01865 241874 Fax: 01865 241889

Best to telephone: Mon-Fri 10.00 am - 2.45 pm. A message can be left if there is no-one currently in the office.

Email: General matters: editor@slgpress.co.uk
Orders only: orders@slgpress.co.uk Website: www.slgpress.co.uk

Guest and Retreat Facilities

There is limited accommodation for private retreats, for both men and women, at Fairacres. Please write to or email the Guest Sister to make a booking.

Email: guests@slg.org.uk Tel (for guest sister): 01865 258152 (with voicemail)

Most convenient time to telephone:

10.30 am - 12 noon; 3.30 pm - 4.30 pm; 6.00 pm - 7.00 pm

Sunday and Friday afternoons, and Saturdays, are ordinarily covered by an answer phone, but messages are cleared after Vespers.

Office Book: SLG Office

Bishop Visitor: Rt Revd Michael Lewis, Bishop of Cyprus & the Gulf

Registered Charity: No. 261722
SLG Charitable Trust Ltd: registered in England 990049

Community of the Sisters of Melanesia

CSM

Founded 1980

KNT/Headquarter
Verana'aso
PO Box 19
Honiara
SOLOMON ISLANDS

First Office, Mattins & Mass 5.45 am

Morning Office 7.45 am

Mid-day Office & Intercession 11.55 am

Afternoon Office 1.30 pm

Evensong & Meditation 5.30 pm

Compline 8.45 pm

Office Book
CSM Office Book (adapted from MBH Office book)

The community of the Sisters of Melanesia is a sisterhood of women in Melanesia. It was founded by Nester Tiboe and three young women of Melanesia on 17 November 1980. Nester believed that a Religious community of women in Melanesia was needed for the work of evangelism and mission, similar to the work of the Melanesian Brotherhood, founded by Brother Ini Kopuria.

On 17 November 1980, the four young women made their promises of Poverty, Celibacy, and Obedience to serve in the community. The ceremony took place at St Hilda's Day at Bunana Island and officiated by the Most Reverend Norman Kitchener Palmer, the second Archbishop of the Province of Melanesia.

The community aims to offer young women in Melanesia an opportunity of training for ministry and mission, so that they may serve Christ in the church and society where they live. To provide pastoral care for women and teenage children and uphold the Christian principles of family life. To be in partnership with the Melanesian Brotherhood and other Religious communities by proclaiming the Gospel of Jesus Christ in urban and rural areas in the islands. To give God the honour and glory, and to extend His Kingdom in the world.

Professed. c. 50, Noviciate c. 40

Addresses of other houses in the Solomon Islands
Joe Wate Household, Longa Bay, Waihi Parish, Southern Region, Malaita
Marau Missionary Household, Guadalcanal
NAT Household, Mbokoniseu, Vutu, Ghaobata Parish, East Honiara, Guadalcanal
Sir Ellison L. Pogo Household, Honiara

Community Wares
Vestments, altar linen, weaving and crafts.

Associates: The supporters of the Community of the Sisters of Melanesia are called Associates, a group established in 1990. It is an organization for men and women, young and old, and has over one thousand members, including many young boys and girls. All promise to uphold the Sisters in prayer, and they are a great support in many ways. The Associates of the Community of the Sisters of Melanesia are in the Solomon Islands, Australia and Canada.

Bishop Visitor
Most Revd George Takeli, Archbishop of Melanesia

Community of the Transfiguration

CT

Founded 1898

495 Albion Avenue
Cincinnati
Ohio 45246
USA
Tel: 513 771 5291
Fax: 513 771 0839
Email:
ctsisters@aol.com

Website www.ctsisters.org

Lauds
7.00 am (Sun 6.45am)

Morning Prayer
7.30am (Sun 7.05am)

Holy Eucharist
7.40 am

Noon Office 12.35 pm
(Sat Intercessions 12.25pm)

Evensong 5.00 pm

Compline
8.00 pm (Sun 7.30pm)

Office Book
CT Office Book
& the BCP

Community Publication
The Quarterly

Bishop Visitor
Most Revd Michael B Curry

The Community of the Transfiguration, founded in 1898 by Eva Lee Matthews, is a Religious community of women dedicated to the mystery of the Transfiguration. Our life is one of prayer and service, reflecting the spirit of Mary and Martha, shown forth in spiritual, educational and social ministries. The Mother House of the community is located in Cincinnati, Ohio, where our ministries include a retreat and spirituality center, a school and a recreation center.

The Sisters live their life under the vows of poverty, chastity and obedience. The motto of the community is Benignitas, Simplicitas and Hilaritas - Kindness, Simplicity and Joy.

SISTER TERESA MARIE CT
(Mother Superior, assumed office 24 June 2008)

Sister Joan Michael
Sister Monica Mary
Sister Priscilla Jean
Sister Ann Margaret
Sister Jacqueline Marie
Sister Johanna Laura
Sister Jean Gabriel
Sister Rachel Margaret
Sister Nadine Elizabeth
Sister Eleanor Grace
Sister Hope Mary
Sister Diana Dorothea
Sister Lynn Julian
Sister Marian Therese
Sister Carina Elsa

Obituaries

17 Aug 2014 Sister Mary Elizabeth, aged 67, professed 37 years
12 Jun 2015 Sister Marcia Francis, aged 71, professed 21 years
13 Jan 2017 Sister Hilary Mary, aged 86, professed 54 years

Other addresses

Transfiguration Spirituality Center, 469 Albion Avenue, Cincinnati, Ohio 45246, USA Website: tscretreats.org

Bethany School, 555 Albion Ave, Cincinnati, Ohio 45246, USA
Website: www.bethanyschool.org

Sisters of the Transfiguration, 4527 Harris Road, Butler, Ohio, USA

St Monica's Recreation Center, 10022 Chester Road, Lincoln Heights, Ohio 45215, USA

Associates & Oblates: The Community has Associates and Oblates.

Guest and Retreat Facilities
Transfiguration Spirituality Center: 40 beds
Various guest houses and rooms: 16 beds.

Community Wares: Cards, crafts

Community history and books
Mrs Harlan Cleveland, *Mother Eva Mary CT: The story of a foundation,* Morehouse, Milwaukee, WI, 1929.
Sibyl Harton, *Windfall of Light: a study of the Vocation of Mother Eva Mary CT*, Roessler, Cincinnati, OH, 1968.
Sister Monica Mary Heyes CT, *Women of Devotion*, Orange Frazer Press, Cincinnati, OH, 2014.

Community of the Sisters of the Visitation of Our Lady

CVL

Founded 1964

Convent of the Visitation
Hetune, Box 18
Popondetta
Oro Province
PAPUA NEW GUINEA

Mattins 5.30 am (6.15 am Sat)

Mass 7.30 am

Mid-day prayer 12 noon

Spiritual reading 4.30 pm

Evening Prayer 5.00 pm

Compline 8.00 pm

In 1964, Sister Margaret CHN walked to the site of the convent with Cora Aiga, Edith Genolla and Roseline. They set up a tent to sleep in and from that day they started the community and settled down. When the years passed, the community grew and it is now known as Hetune Convent. Not all the sisters were able to continue and some went back to their homes, but the late Sister Cora stayed until she became ill and died.

It has been a struggle through the years and numbers have gone up and come down. In 2016 the chapel had to be pulled down and now we worship in the classroom. We would like to open a new house and we know God will find a way for us to do that.

SISTER BEVERLEY TUNBARI CVL
(Guardian, assumed office 10 June 2016)
SISTER PEGGIE CVL *(Assistant)*
Sister Bridget Maku *(Novice Formator)*
Sister Ann Kovari
Sister Angela
Sister Winnie *(Secretary)*
Sister Edna Benuni

Novices: 6
(Iossie John, Mavice, Ela, Brenda, Jean, Genuine)

Community Wares: Sewing vestments, crafts

Office Book: PNG Anglican Prayer Book

Bishop Visitor: Most Revd Clyde Igara, Archbishop of Papua New Guinea

Congrégation des Compagnons de Saint Benoît

(Congregation of the Companions of St Benedict)

CCSB

Founded 2007

Prieuré Sainte Scholastique
BP 20629, Yaoundé, CAMEROON

Email: sanctibenedicti fratres @rocketmail.com

5.30 am Vigils (5.50 Sat, 7.00 Sun)

7.00 am Lauds (7.20 Sat, 8.30 Sun)

7.20 am Mass (5.30 Sat, 10.00 Sun)

12.15 pm Sext

5.30 pm Vespers

7.30 pm Compline

The Congregation of the Companions of St Benedict is an Anglican Religious order comprising priests, lay brothers and sisters faithful to Anglican doctrine and morals. Its main branch is situated at St Scholastica's Priory, Yaoundé, Cameroon. A women's branch could be joined to it to form a spiritual family according to the norms of the Anglican Church.

The Congregation, Benedictine in its spirituality, has a double purpose: divine praise according to the Book of Common Prayer (ECUSA); and the second to care for abandoned children with a view to ensure their academic professional and familial integration. Its members lead a semi-contemplative life based on the three vows of poverty, chastity and obedience.

Concerning its commitment to social justice, the Congregation intends to found in the near future a reception centre to house at least fifty children.

BROTHER EMMANUEL OBA'A CCSB
(Prior-General, assumed office 11 July 2007)
REVD BROTHER FRANÇOIS MBOZO'O CCSB *(Sub-prior)*

Brother Benoît Essaga Ndjana
Brother Calvin Bayiga
Brother Jean Flore Zeh
Brother Jean Zoa
Brother Magloire Bessala
Brother Max Ngamao
Brother Robert Meva'a
Brother Odilon Attey Epopa
Brother Joseph Owono
Brother Gabriel Mva'a Zombo
Brother Laurent Charles
Brother Ortaire Marie Zeh Oba'a

Novices: 5 *Postulants:* 5

Other Address

Saints Comas and Damian Priory, P.O. Box 443, Ebolowa, CAMEROON

Bishop Visitor:

Rt Revd Dibo Thomas Babynton Elango,
Bishop of the Anglican Diocese of Cameroon

Fikambanan'ny Mpanompovavin I Jesoa Kristy

(Society of the Servants of Jesus Christ)

FMJK

Founded 1985

Convent Hasina, BP 28
Ambohidratrimo 105
Antananarivo 101
MADAGASCAR

6.00 am
Morning meditation

6.30 am
Morning Prayer

9.00 am
Silent prayer for the Nation

12.10 pm
Midday Prayer
& midday meditation

3.00 pm
Silent prayer for the Nation

4.30 pm
Silent prayer

5.00 pm
Evening Prayer

8.00 pm
Compline

The FMJK sisters were founded by Canon Hall Speers in 1985. They live in the village of Tsinjohasina, on the high plateau above the rice fields, situated some fifteen kilometres from Antananarivo, the capital of Madagascar. The sisters work in the village dispensary and are active in visiting, Christian teaching and pastoral work in the villages around. They are an independent community but have been nurtured by a connection with CSMV, Wantage, in the UK.

SISTER ISABELLE FMJK
(Masera Tonia, assumed office 12 April 2016)
SISTER CHAPITRE FMJK *(Prioress)*

Sister Ernestine
Sister Georgette
Sister Jacqueline
Sister Odette
Sister Voahangy
Sister Vololona
Sister Fanja

Novices: 2

Community Wares: Crafts and embroidery.

Office Book: FMJK Office and Prayer Book

Other house:
Antaralava, Soamanandray, BP 28, Ambohidratrimo 105, Antananarivo 101, MADAGASCAR

Bishop Visitor
Most Revd Ranarivello Samoelajaona, Archbishop of the Indian Ocean

Little Brothers of Francis

LBF

Founded 1987

Franciscan Hermitage
"Eremophilia"
PO Box 162
Tabulam
NSW 2469
AUSTRALIA

Website: www.franciscanhermitage.org

Brothers have times of Solitude in their hermitage, which vary from a day to weeks or months, where they have their own personal rhythm of prayer and manual work.

Office Book
LBF Office book, developed to provide for our needs as a Franciscan Hermitage

Bishop Protector
Rt Revd
Godfrey Fryar

We are a community of Brothers who desire to deepen our relationship with God through prayer, manual work, community, and times of being alone in our hermitages. We follow the Rule written by Saint Francis for Hermitages in which three or four brothers live in each fraternity. As others join us we envisage a federation of fraternities with three or four brothers in each. There are several sources of inspiration for the Little Brothers of Francis. They are:

The Gospels

The four Gospels (Matthew, Mark, Luke and John) are central to our spirituality, and the main source material for our meditation and prayer life.

St Francis

Francis would recall Christ's words and life through persistent meditation on the Gospels, for his deep desire was to love Christ and live a Christ-centred life. He was a man of prayer and mystic who sought places of solitude, and hermitages played a central role in his life. Significant events, like the initiation of the Christmas Crib tradition, happened at the hermitage at Greccio, and, of course, he received the stigmata while he was at the hermitage at Mount La Verna.

Though the early brothers embraced a mixed life of prayer and ministry, Francis wanted places of seclusion - hermitages, for the primacy of prayer, in which three or four brothers lived, and for which he wrote a rule.

St Francis's Rule for Hermitages

In his brief rule for life within the hermitage, Francis avoided a detailed document and set out the principles that are important. Liturgy of the Hours is the focus, and sets the rhythm of the daily prayer. Each hermitage was to have at the most four Brothers, which meant they would be both 'little' and 'fraternal'. Within this framework, Brothers could withdraw for periods of solitude. The hermitages were not to be places or centres of ministry.

Desert Fathers

The stories and sayings of the Desert Fathers contain a profound wisdom for any who are serious about the inner spiritual journey. This is why they have held such prominence in monastic circles in both East and West down through the centuries, and why they are a priority source for us.

The Land

A strong connectedness to a spiritual and physical

Vigil Office
followed by
Lectio Divina
(private)
2.00 am or 4.00 am

Meditation
6.00 am

Angelus and Mattins
7.00 am

Terce
9.00 am

Angelus and Sext
12 noon

None (private)
3.00 pm

Vespers
6.00 pm

Compline
8.00 pm

home has always been a part of our charism, not unlike St Francis' love for his 'Portiuncula' or Little Portion. In shaping and building our hermitage over the years our environment has shaped and formed us. Droughts, bushfires, floods and bountiful years have brought us into a real and living relationship with the land in this place.

Brother Howard LBF
Brother Wayne LBF
Brother Geoffrey Adam LBF

Friends

Friends are individuals, or self-organized groups, who value the contemplative life as lived by the Brothers and support them in various ways.

Contact person for Australia:
Father Dennis Claughton Email: parish@ang.org.au
Contact person for New Zealand:
Ian Lothian Email: ianlothian@xtra.com.nz

Community Publication: The *Bush Telegraph.*
Contact the Brothers for a subscription, which is by donation.

Community Wares: Hand-carved holding crosses, jam, marmalade, cards and honey.

Guest and Retreat Facilities: There is a guest hermitage for one person. A fee of $60 per night is negotiable.

The Melanesian Brotherhood

MBH

Founded 1925

Email: mbhches @solomon.com.sb

SOLOMON ISLANDS REGION
The Motherhouse of the Melanesian Brotherhood
Tabalia
PO Box 1479
Honiara
SOLOMON ISLANDS
TEL: +677 26355
FAX: +677 23079

PAPUA NEW GUINEA REGION
Dobuduru Regional Headquarters
Haruro
PO Box 29
Popondetta
Oro Province
PAPUA NEW GUINEA

SOUTHERN REGION
Tumsisiro Regional Headquarters
PO Box 05
Lolowai, Ambae
VANUATU

The Melanesian Brotherhood was founded by Ini Kopuria, a native Solomon Islander from Guadalcanal, in 1925. Its main purpose was evangelistic, to take and live the Gospel in the most remote islands and villages throughout the Solomon Islands, among people who had not heard the message of Christ. The Brotherhood's method is to live as brothers to the people, respecting their traditions and customs: planting, harvesting, fishing, house building, eating and sharing with the people in all these things. Kopuria believed that Solomon Islanders should be converted in a Melanesian way.

Today, the work of the Brotherhood has broadened to include work and mission among both Christians and non-Christians. The Melanesian Brotherhood now has three Regions in the Pacific: Solomon Islands (includes Brothers in the Philippines and Vancouver); Papua New Guinea; and Southern (Vanuatu, New Caledonia & the Diocese of Polynesia). There is a Region for Companions and any Brothers in Europe.

Following an ethnic conflict in the Solomon Islands 1998-2003, the Melanesian Brotherhood have been increasingly called upon as peace makers and reconcilers, work for which they were awarded the United Nations Pacific Peace Prize in 2004. The Brotherhood has also led missions in New Zealand, Australia, Philippines and UK; their missionary approach includes music, dance and a powerful use of drama.

The Brotherhood aims to live the Gospel in a direct and simple way following Christ's example of prayer, mission and service. The Brothers take the vows of poverty, chastity and obedience, but these are not life vows but for a period of three years, which can be renewed. They train for four years as novices and normally make their vows as Brothers at the Feast of St Simon and St Jude. Most of the Brothers are laymen but a few are ordained.

THE MOST REVD GEORGE TAKELI,
ARCHBISHOP OF MELANESIA *(Father of the Brotherhood)*

NELSON BAKO MBH
(Head Brother, elected 15 March 2017)
JESSIE ARAIASI *(Assistant Head Brother)*

Mr Alphonse Garimae *(Brotherhood Secretary)*
Email: agarimae@yahoo.com

Timetable of the Main House

First Office and Mattins
5.50 am
(6.20 am Sun & holidays)

Holy Communion
6.15 am
(7.15 am Sun & holidays)

Morning Office
8.00 am

Midday Office
12 noon
(Angelus on Sun & holidays)

Afternoon Office
1.30 pm
(not Sun & holidays)

Evensong 5.30 pm
(6.00 pm Sun & holidays)

Last Office 9.00 pm

Office Book
Offices and Prayers of the Melanesian Brotherhood 1996 (not for public sale)

Website:
www.orders.anglican.org/mbh

SOLOMON ISLANDS REGION
THE MOST REVD GEORGE TAKELI,
ARCHBISHOP OF MELANESIA *(Regional Father)*

SOUTHERN REGION
THE RT REVD JAMES LIGO,
BISHOP OF VANUATU & NEW CALEDONIA
(Regional Father)

PAPUA NEW GUINEA REGION
THE MOST REVD CLYDE MERVIN IGARA,
ARCHBISHOP OF PNG
(Regional Father)

EUROPE REGION *(for Companions)*
THE RT REVD DR ROWAN WILLIAMS, LORD WILLIAMS OF OYSTERMOUTH, *former Archbishop of Canterbury*
(Regional Father)

Professed Brothers: 282
(Solomon Islands: 148; PNG: 80: Southern Region: 49: Palawan: 4; Canada: 1)
Novices: 171
(Solomon Islands: 102; PNG: 12: Southern Region: 53; Palawan: 4)

SOLOMON ISLANDS REGION
The Solomon Islands Region is divided into Sections according to each Diocese. Each Section has its own Section Father.

CENTRAL MELANESIA DIOCESAN SECTION
Address for all SI houses in this Section:
PO Box 1479, Honiara, Guadacanal, SOLOMON ISLANDS

Central Headquarters, Tabalia

St Barnabas Cathedral Working Household, Honiara
Tel: 24609 Fax: 23079
Bishopsdale Working Household, Honiara
Tel: 27695 Fax: 23079
Chester Rest House
Tel: 26355 Fax: 23079
Email: mbhches@solomon.sb.com
Working Household, Bellona Island

PALAWAN MISSION DISTRICT, PHILIPPINES
Iglesia Philipina Independiente (I.F.I.), De los Reyos Road 2, 5300
Puerto Princesa City, 5300 Palawan, PHILIPPINES

CENTRAL SOLOMONS DIOCESAN SECTION
Thomas Peo Section Headquarters,
c/o Central Solomons Diocesan Office, PO Box 52, Tulagi, Central Province
Nathaniel Sado Working Household, Savo Island
Lango Working Household, Small Ngella Island

GUADALCANAL DIOCESE SECTION
Address for other houses in this section:
c/o Central Headquarters, Tabalia, PO Box 1479, Honiara
Ini Kopuria Household, Kolina, Guadalcanal
Olimauri Household, Mbambanakira, Guadalcanal
Calvary Household, Surapau, Guadalcanal
Selwyn Rapu Working Household, Guadalcanal

MALAITA DIOCESAN SECTION
Address for houses in this Section:
c/o Malaita Diocesan Office, PO Box 7, Auki, Malaita Province
Airahu Section Headquarters
Kokom Working Household, Auki
Apalolo Household, South Malaita

YSABEL DIOCESAN SECTION
Address for houses in this section:
c/o Ysabel Diocesan Office, PO Box 6, Buala, Isabel Province
Welchman Section Headquarters, Sosoilo
Poropeta Household, Kia
Alfred Hill Working Household, Jejevo
John Pihavaka Household, Gizo
Noro Working Household, New Georgia Island

HANUATO'O DIOCESAN SECTION
Address for houses in this section:
c/o Hanuato'o Diocesan Office, Kirakira, Makira Province
Fox Section Headquarters, Poronaohe, Makira
Simon Sigai Household, Makira
Mumunioa Working Household, Makira
John Hubert Waene Working Household, Makira

TEMOTU DIOCESAN SECTION
Address for houses in this section:
c/o Temotu Diocesan Office, Lata, Temotu Province

Makio Section Headquarters, Santa Cruz Island
Utupua Working Household, Utupua
Lata Working Household, Santa Cruz Island

SOUTHERN REGION

VANUATU SECTION

Tumsisiro Regional Headquarters, Ambae
Saratabulu Household, West Ambae
Hinge Household, Lorevilko, East Santo
Suriau Household, Big Bay, Santo Bush
Caulton Weris Working Household
Patterson Household, Port Vila

BANKS & TORRES SECTION

Lency Section Headquarters, Vanua Lava Island
Towia Working Household

PAPUA NEW GUINEA REGION

POPONDOTA SECTION

Dobuduru Regional Headquarters, Popondetta
Gorari Household; Nedewari Household; Domara Household

PORT MORESBY SECTION

ATS Section Headquarters, Oro Village
Pivo Household; Moro Guina

DOGURA SECTION

Sirisiri Section Headquarters
Pumani Household; Podagha Project Household; Tabai Isu Working Household

AIPO RONGO SECTION

Aiome Section Headquarters
Kumburub Household; Kuiyama Household; Saniap Working Household

NEW GUINEA ISLANDS SECTION

Hosea Sakira Section Headquarters
Aseke Household; Saksak Household

Companions

The Melanesian Brotherhood is supported both in prayer, in their work and materially by the Companions of the Melanesian Brotherhood (C.O.M.B.). They have their own Handbook with both Pacific and Europe versions.

For more information about becoming a Companion, please contact:
Mrs Barbara Molyneux, 11 Milton Crescent, Heswall, Merseyside, CH60 5SS, UK
Tel: (0)151 342 6327 Email: bjmolyneux@hotmail.com

or Companions Chief Secretary, PO Box 1479, Honiara, Solomon Islands
or at the same address: Mr Alphonse Garimae, Secretary to the Brotherhood,
Tel: +677 26377 (8 am - 4 pm) Email: agarimae@yahoo.com

Alongside Companions, the Brotherhood also has associates whose ministry is more closely associated with the community, except that they do not take the threefold vow. They work voluntarily without wages just like the brothers.

Community Publications

Companions' Newsletter for the Europe Region (once a year)
- contact Mrs Barbara Molyneux, address under 'Companions' below.

Community History and other books

Brian Macdonald-Milne, *The True Way of Service: The Pacific Story of the Melanesian Brotherhood, 1925-2000,* Christians Aware, Leicester, 2003.

Richard Carter, *In Search of the Lost: the death and life of seven peacemakers of the Melanesian Brotherhood*, Canterbury Press, Norwich, 2006.

Charles Montgomery, *The Shark God: Encounters with myth and magic in the South Pacific,* Fourth Estate/Harper Collins, London, 2006.

Guest and Retreat Facilities

The Community offers hospitality ministry through Chester Rest House in Honiara, Solomon Islands. Two Brothers are mandated to welcome guests and offer a Christian welcome to any person who may want accommodation in their Rest House. This Rest House was funded by Chester Diocese in UK. It is an alcohol-free environment and every guest is ensured to be safe and enjoy the environment. It has 8 twin-bedded rooms, self-catering at £30 per room per night, and 8 self-contained single rooms, self-catering at £75 per room per night. A conference room to accommodate 10-15 people is also available at £10 per day, self-catering. Contacts for advance bookings can be made through email: mbhches@solomon.com.sb or telephone +677 26355.

All the Brotherhood's Headquarters and Section Headquarters can provide simple accommodation for visitors. Retreats can be made by prior arrangement with the relevant Chaplain at Central, Regional or Section headquarters. Tabalia Headquarters has a guest house with eight twin-bedded rooms, self-catering, no cost but a contribution is much appreciated. Meetings, workshops and Retreats can be made by prior arrangement with the Section Elder Brother/Elder Brother at Tabalia.

Women are not allowed to enter the Brotherhood square (St Simon & Jude), which usually is outside the chapel of every Brotherhood station (not in Honiara). Women are not allowed to enter Brothers' dormitories.

Order of the Holy Cross

OHC

Founded 1884

Holy Cross Monastery
PO Box 99
(1615 Rt. 9W)
West Park
NY 12493
USA
Tel: 845 384 6660
Fax: 845 384 6031

Email:
ohcsuperior@gmail.com

Website: www.holycrossmonastery.com

Mattins 7.00 am

Holy Eucharist
9.00 am

Midday Prayer
12 noon

Vespers 5.00 pm

Compline 8.00 pm

Mondays are observed as a sabbath day on which there are no scheduled liturgies.

The Order of the Holy Cross is a Benedictine monastic community open to both lay and ordained. The principles governing the Order's life are those of *The Rule of St Benedict* and *The Rule of the Order of the Holy Cross*, written by its founder James Otis Sargent Huntington.

The liturgical life of each house centers around the corporate praying of the Divine Office and the celebration of the Holy Eucharist. Members are also expected to spend time in private prayer and meditation.

The work of the Order is varied, depending on the nature of the household and the gifts and talents of its members. Houses range from traditional monastic centers with active retreat ministries to an urban house from which brothers go forth to minister. Four brothers live independently as Monks Not In Residence.

Members are engaged in preaching, teaching, counselling, retreat conducting, spiritual direction, parish and diocesan support work, evangelism, hospice care, and ministry with the homeless. The South African community administers educational and scholarship programs for local children and operates a primary school.

Other Addresses

Mount Calvary Monastery and Retreat House, PO Box 1296, Santa Barbara, CA 93102, USA
Tel: 805 682 4117
Website: www.mount-calvary.org

Holy Cross Priory, 204 High Park Avenue, Toronto, Ontario M6P 2S6, CANADA
Tel: 416 767 9081
Website: www.ohc-canada.org

Mariya uMama weThemba Monastery, PO Box 6013, Grahamstown 6141, SOUTH AFRICA
Tel: 46 622 8111 **Fax: 46 622 6424**
Website: www.umaria.co.za

Community Publications
Mundi Medicina (West Park, NY) - thrice a year
Uxolo (Grahamstown, South Africa) - twice a year
Mount Calvary Monastery (Santa Barbara, CA) - thrice a year
Holy Cross Priory (Toronto, Ontario) - twice a year
Cost: by donation

Office Book
A Monastic Breviary (OHC) or *Lauds and Vespers* (Camaldolese Monks OSB).

Robert James Magliula OHC
(*Superior, assumed office 10 June 2017*)
Scott Wesley Borden OHC (*Assistant Superior*)

Thomas Schultz
Christian George Swayne
Laurence Harms
Rafael Campbell-Dixon
Bede Thomas Mudge
Brian Youngward
Roy Parker
Adrian Gill
David Bryan Hoopes
Adam McCoy
Carl Sword
William Brown
Timothy Jolley
James Robert Hagler
Robert Michael Pierson
Leonard Abbah
Reginald-Martin Crenshaw
Richard Paul Vaggione
Lary Pearce
Robert Leo Sevensky
John Forbis
Bernard Jean Delcourt
James Randall Greve
Daniel Ludik
James Michael Dowd
Roger Stewart
Josép Martinez-Cubero
Aidan Owen
Joseph Wallace-Williams

Novices: 3
Postulants: 2

Obituaries
13 Apr 2016 Ronald Grant Haynes, age 76, professed 43 years
26 Aug 2016 Samuel Beard DeMerell, aged 85, professed 47 years

Associates: The Associates of Holy Cross are men and women of many different Christian traditions affiliated to the Order through a Rule of Life and annual retreats and reports.

Guest and Retreat Facilities
West Park: 39 rooms at US$80 per night ($95 weekends). Accommodations for couples and individuals. Closed Mondays.
Santa Barbara: 24 beds at US$90 per night ($100 weekends). Closed Mondays.
Grahamstown: 19 rooms (doubles and singles).
Apply to Guestmaster for rates.
Closed Mondays.
Toronto: 2 single rooms.
Apply to Guestmaster for rates.

Community History
Adam Dunbar McCoy OHC,
Holy Cross: A Century of Anglican Monasticism,
Morehouse-Barlow, Wilton, CT, 1987.

Community Wares
Incense and Publications (West Park).

Bishop Visitor
Rt Revd Andrew M. L. Dietsche

Order of the Holy Paraclete

OHP

Founded 1915

St Hilda's Priory
Sneaton Castle,
Whitby
North Yorkshire
YO21 3QN
UK
Tel: 01947 602079
Fax: 01947 820854
Email:
ohppriorywhitby@btinternet.com

Website:
www.ohpwhitby.org.uk

Morning Prayer
7.30 am

Eucharist
8.00 am (Wed, Fri & Sat)
9.30 am (Sun)
12.30 pm (Thu)

Midday Office
12.40 pm
12.15 pm (Thu)
12 noon (Sat)

Vespers 6.00 pm
(4.30 pm Sun)

Compline 7.45 pm

No services in chapel on Tuesdays

Founded as an educational order, the sisters have diversified their work in UK to include hospitality, retreats and spiritual direction, inner city involvement, preaching and mission, and development work overseas.

The Mother House is at St. Hilda's Priory, Whitby. Other UK houses are in York, Dormanstown (near Redcar), Bishopsthorpe and Sleights (near Whitby).

The Order has had a long-standing commitment to Africa since 1926. Most of the work begun by the sisters has been handed over to local people who continue to run the projects. The Order has two houses in Ghana. In Jachie, Sister Aba runs an eye clinic. In Sunyani, Sister Mavis and Sister Benedicta Anne make communion hosts, have a shop and run a vocational school teaching computer and crafts to girls who were unable to complete their education. Both houses still foster vocations to the Religious life.

Central to the Order's life in all its houses are the Divine Office and Eucharist, and a strong emphasis on corporate activity.

Houses in the UK

St Oswald's Pastoral Centre, Woodlands Drive, Sleights, Whitby, N Yorks YO21 1RY
Tel: 01947 810496
Email: ohpstos@globalnet.co.uk

1A Minster Court, York YO7 2JJ
Tel: 01904 557276
Email: sistersohp@googlemail.com

3 Acaster Lane, Bishopthorpe, York, N Yorks YO23 2SA
Tel: 01904 777294
Email: ohpbishopthorpe@archbishopofyork.org

All Saints House, South Avenue, Dormanstown, TS10 5LL **Tel: 01642 486424**
Email: sisteranita@btinternet.com

Houses in Africa

Resurrection House, PO Box 596, Sunyani, Brone Ahafo, GHANA
Tel: +233 243 770 6840
Email: ohpjac@yahoo.com

Jachie, Convent of the Holy Spirit, PO Box AH 9375, Ahinsan, Kumasi Ashanti, GHANA
Tel: +233 26 861 4521
Email: Adedzewa2@gmail.com

SISTER CAROLE OHP
(Prioress, assumed office November 2015)
SISTER JOCELYN OHP *(Sub-Prioress)*

Sister Barbara Maude	Sister Dorothy Stella	Sister Linda
Sister Olive	Sister Benedicta	Sister Aba
Sister Janet	Sister Caroline	Sister Helen
Sister Alison	Sister Margaret Elizabeth	Sister Karan
Sister Anita	Sister Marion Eva	Sister Helena
Sister Hilary Joy	Sister Heather Francis	Sister Louisa Ann
Sister Grace	Sister Erika	
Sister Janette	Sister Maureen Ruth	*Novices:* 2
Sister Janet Elizabeth	Sister Margaret Anne	
Sister Betty	Sister Mavis	

Obituaries

11 Sep 2016	Sister Pam, aged 75, professed 20 years
28 Sep 2016	Sister Muriel, aged 84, professed 55 years
5 Jan 2017	Sister Ursula, aged 93, professed 68 years
25 Mar 2017	Sister Michelle, aged 83, professed 59 years

Tertiaries and Associates

THE OHP TERTIARY ORDER is a fellowship of women and men, united under a common discipline, based on the OHP Rule, and supporting one another in their discipleship. Tertiaries are ordinary Christians seeking to offer their lives in the service of Christ, helping the Church and showing love in action. They value their links with each other and with the Sisters of the Order, at Whitby and elsewhere, and when possible they meet together for mutual support in prayer, discussion and ministry. The Tertiary Order is open to communicant members of any Trinitarian Church.

THE OHP ASSOCIATES are friends of the Order who desire to keep in touch with its life and work while serving God in their various spheres. Many have made initial contact with the Sisters through a visit or parish mission, or via another Associate. All are welcome, married or single, clergy or lay, regardless of religious affiliation.

THE FRIENDS OF OHP is a group open to men and women, of any religious affiliation or none, with an interest in OHP. The annual subscription of £10 includes a copy of the OHP newsletter and an invitation to an annual meeting.

Community Publication: *OHP Newsletter.* Write to The Publications Secretary at St Hilda's Priory. Annual subscription: £5.00 for the UK, £6.50 for the rest of Europe and £8.00 for the rest of the world.

Community Wares

Cards and craft items. St Hilda's Priory has a shop selling books, cards, church supplies and religious artefacts.
Email: sneatonshop@btinternet.com

Community History
A Foundation Member, *Fulfilled in Joy,* Hodder & Stoughton, London, 1964.
Rosalin Barker, *The Whitby Sisters,* OHP, Whitby, 2001.

Guest and Retreat Facilities
ST HILDA'S PRIORY: six rooms (four single; one double; one twin) available in the Priory or nearby houses. Individuals or small groups are welcome for personal quiet or retreat, day or residential. If requested in advance, some guidance can be provided. There is no programme of retreats at the Priory. Contact the Guest Sister with enquiries and bookings.
SNEATON CASTLE CENTRE: seventy-one rooms (one hundred and twenty beds). The Centre has conference, lecture and seminar rooms with full audio-visual equipment, and recreational facilities. There are two spacious dining rooms and an excellent range of menus. Guests are welcome to join the community for worship or to arrange their own services in the Chapel.
Contact the Bookings Secretary, Sneaton Castle Centre, Whitby YO21 3QN.
Tel: 01947 600051 See also the website: www.sneatoncastle.co.uk
ST OSWALD'S PASTORAL CENTRE: 13 rooms (16 beds). 3 self-catering units.
Most convenient time to telephone:: 9 am - 5 pm, Mon-Fri; 10 am - 12 noon Sat

Office Book: OHP Office

Registered Charity: No. 271117

Bishop Visitor: Most Revd John Sentamu, Archbishop of York

Order of Julian of Norwich OJN

Founded 1985

W704 Alft Rd
White Lake
WI 54491-9715
USA

Tel: 715-882-2377

Email: ojn@ orderofjulian.org

The Order of Julian of Norwich is a contemplative order of the Episcopal Church. The monks and nuns of the Order live the monastic life together under the vows of poverty, chastity, obedience, and prayer 'in the spirit of our Mother St Julian'. Our life in community is grounded in the Eucharist and 4-fold Daily Office, and includes study, work, and times of solitude and recreation. The practice of enclosure allows us the solitude and liberty to live as deeply as we can into the life of prayer and friendship with God. Serving God in each other, in our guests, and before God's altar, we are committed to prayer, intercession, and conversion of heart, centred on our relationship with Jesus Christ and our transformation in Him, growing up into Christ through our life in common. As the three windows of Julian's anchorhold opened, one to the altar, one to the room of her lay sisters, and one to the public lane, so the life of the Order looks to the worship of God, to the support and fellowship of the wider community of the Order—our Oblates and Associates—and to the service of the Church and the world.

REVD MOTHER HILARY CRUPI OJN
(*Guardian, assumed office 30 April 2010*)
SISTER THERESE POLI OJN *(Prior)*
Revd Father John-Julian Swanson
Sister Cornelia Barry
Brother Barnabas Leben
Postulants: 1

Website:
www.orderofjulian.org

Silent Prayer/ Morning Prayer
3.45 am

Mass
7.30 am

Midday Office
11.30 am

Silent Prayer/ Evensong
4.00 pm

Compline
7.00 pm

Office Book
The BCP of ECUSA with enrichments

Community Publication
Julian's Window quarterly. Subscription free. Contact Sister Cornelia OJN

Bishop Visitor
Rt Revd Wendell N. Gibbs, Jr., Bishop of Michigan

Associates and Oblates

ASSOCIATES AND OBLATES of the Order are those who respond to the Holy Spirit's invitation to draw nearer to Jesus under the patronage of St Julian of Norwich, called to the contemplative life in the world. Their rules of life, adaptations of the monastic Rule, unite their lives of prayer to that of the monastery and commit them to a regular practice of silent prayer, worship and study, in the context of their own particular vocations. In varying degree, they bring this contemplative practice into their parishes and communities by their transformation of their lives through the deepening of their relationship with Christ.

ASSOCIATES are committed to a simple form of the rule adaptable to many different walks of life.

OBLATES, after a period of discernment and formation, profess vows requiring regular discipline and reflection in the Christian commitment, with a rule of life closely modelled on that of the Order's monastics. A vow of celibacy is possible for Oblates within the Order.

Guest and Retreat Facilities

Two guest rooms for individual silent retreat. There is no charge.

Community History and other books

Teunisje Velthuizen, ObJN, *One-ed into God: The first decade of the Order of St Julian of Norwich,* The Julian Press, 1996.

Gregory Fruehwirth OJN, *Words for Silence,* Paraclete Press, Orleans, MA, 2008.

John Julian Swanson OJN, *The Complete Julian,* Paraclete Press, Orleans, MA, 2009.

Community Wares

Original icons, mounted icon prints and icon cards; prayer benches; and soap are all made by the community for their support. The Shop specializes in books about Julian of Norwich and contemplative and monastic spirituality.
Email: jshop@orderofjulian.org

Order of St Anne at Bethany

OSA

Founded 1910

25 Hillside Avenue
Arlington
MA 02476-5818
USA

Tel: 781 643 0921
Fax: 781 648 4547

Email: bethany convent@aol.com

Morning Prayer
7.00 am

Eucharist
8.00 am (Tue-Fri)
7.30 am (Sun)

Midday prayers
12 noon

Evensong 5.00 pm

Compline 7.30 pm

Office Book
SSJE Office Book

We are a small multi-cultural community of women committed to witnessing to the truth that, as Christians, it is here and now that we demonstrate to the Church and the world that the Religious Life lived in community is relevant, interesting, fulfilling and needed in our world and our times. We strive to recognize and value the diversity of persons and gifts. We believe that God has a vision for each one of us and that opportunities to serve the Church and the world are abundant. For this to become real, we know that our spirits and hearts must be enlarged to fit the dimensions of our Church in today's world and the great vision that God has prepared for our Order. We are especially grateful for our continuing ministry within the Diocese of Massachusetts.

The Rule of the Order of St Anne says our houses may be small, but our hearts are larger than houses. Our community has always been 'people-oriented' and we derive a sense of joy and satisfaction in offering hospitality at our Convent, at the Bethany House of Prayer and in our beautiful chapel. Always constant in our lives are our personal prayer and our corporate worship, our vows of Poverty, Celibacy and Obedience, our commitment to spiritual growth and development of mind and talents, and our fellowship with one another and other Religious communities, as friends and sisters.

SISTER ANA CLARA OSA
(Superior, assumed office 1992)

Sister Olga
Sister Felicitas
Sister Maria Agnes
Sister Maria Teresa

Associates
We have an associate program and continue to receive men and women into this part of our life.

Community Wares: Communion altar bread.

Community History
Sister Johanna OSA (editor), *A Theme for Four Voices,* privately printed, Arlington, Mass., 1985

Revd Charles C Hefling & Sister Ana Clara OSA, *Catch the Vision: celebrating a century of the Order of St Anne,* Order of St Anne-Bethany, Arlington, Mass., 2010

Bishop Visitor: Rt Revd Alan M. Gates, Bishop of Massachusetts

Guest and Retreat Facilities

The Bethany House of Prayer, 181 Appleton Street, on the grounds of the Convent and Chapel, sponsors, coordinates and offers a variety of programs and events including Quiet Days, Special Liturgies, contemplative prayer, spiritual direction, day-retreats, hospitality and workshops. For more information call 781 648 2433.

Order of St Anne

Chicago

OSA

Founded 1910

1125 North LaSalle Blvd
Chicago
Illinois 60610
USA

Tel: 312 642 3638

Email: stannechicago@hotmail.com

Website: www.sistersofstannechicago.org

Matins 6.40 am

Eucharist 7.00 am
(Church of the Ascension)

Terce 8.30 am

Sext 12 noon

Vespers 5.00 pm

Compline 7.00 pm

Office Book: Monastic Diurnal revised

The Order of St. Anne was founded in 1910 by Father Frederick Cecil Powell of the Society of St. John the Evangelist in Arlington Heights, Mass. The Sisters live a modified Benedictine Rule, dedicated to a life of prayer and good works beneficial to all people including children. The Sisters of St. Anne came to Chicago in 1921 invited by then rector of the Church of the Ascension, the Revd Stoskopf, to do parish work and other needed services in the Diocese of Chicago. The Chicago convent is autonomous, although Sisters live as part of the church of the Ascension.

According to our Rule "the Order of St. Anne cannot be designated as professing exclusively the contemplative, the mixed or active spirit" since all three may be found within the Order. The principal of the Order is the life of God within it and whatsoever He may say to us – whether to sit at His feet only or feed His lambs - which we must do. While our works are important, it must be kept in mind that God calls us to a life of prayer. The Sisters are involved in parish work, especially at the Church of the Ascension doing whatever is needed. The sisters also work with the homeless, alcoholics, addicts and other emotionally and mentally disturbed people. The sisters work as teachers, counsellors and hospital chaplains. A future plan is for a recovery home for addicts, alcoholics and emotionally disturbed women.

SISTER JUDITH MARIE OSA
(Superior, assumed office 2007)
Sister Barbara Louise OSA
Resident Companion: Ms Dorothy Murray

Associates

We have an associate program for men and women.

Community Publication: PROEIS

Guest and Retreat Facilities

Two guest rooms in Convent (women only). No charge, donations accepted. Individual retreats; spiritual direction and counselling available.

Bishop Visitor: Rt Revd Jeffrey Lee, Bishop of Chicago

Order of St Benedict

St Mark's Abbey, Camperdown

OSB

Founded 1975

Benedictine Abbey
PO Box 111
Camperdown
Victoria 3260
AUSTRALIA

Tel: 3 5593 2348

Email: benabbey@dodo.com.au

Website: www.anglicanbenedictine.org.au

Vigils 5.00 am

Lauds 6.30 am

Terce & Conventual Mass 8.15 am

Sext 11.45 am

None 2.10 pm

Vespers 5.00 pm

Compline 7.30 pm

Office Book
Camperdown breviary

Abbot Visitor: Rt Revd Dom Guillermo Arboleda Tamayo OSB

The community was founded in the parish of St Mark, Fitzroy, in the archdiocese of Melbourne on 8 November 1975. In 1980, after working in this inner city parish for five years, and after adopting the Rule of Saint Benedict, the community moved to the country town of Camperdown in the Western District of Victoria. Here the community lives a contemplative monastic life with the emphasis on the balanced life of prayer and work that forms the Benedictine ethos. In 1993, the Chapter decided to admit women and so establish a mixed community of monks and nuns. The community supports itself through the operation of a printery, mounting of icons, manufacture of incense, crafts and a small guest house. In 2005, the Chapter petitioned the Subiaco-Cassinese Congregation of the Benedictine Confederation for aggregation to the Congregation. After a period of probation, this was granted on the Feast of SS Peter and Paul 2007. Our founder, Abbot Michael King, died in 2014. The community continues its life and work of prayer and looks forward to growth in the future. Sister Raphael Stone was appointed Superior in 2016 for a period of three years. The community is supported by Oblates and friends and has recently begun an 'Alongsider' program.

SISTER RAPHAEL STONE OSB
(Superior, assumed office 30 July 2016)

Dom Placid Lawson
Father Aidan Melder

Alongsiders: 1

Oblates
Our confraternity includes Oblates of St Benedict, who promise to lead a Christian life according to the Gospel as reflected in the *Rule of St Benedict*. After a time of preparation, the candidates offer themselves to God through a promise which affiliates them with St Mark's Abbey and commits them to an individual rule of life.

Guest and Retreat Facilities: Small guest house: 4 rooms (2 twin), open to men and women, for private retreats. Guests eat main meal (midday) with the community, prepare own breakfast and evening meal in the guesthouse with provisions provided. Minimum donation of $70 per person per night requested.

Community Publication: Yearly newsletter in December - free download from website or $6 per hard copy.

Community Wares
Printing, icons, cards, incense, devotional items.

Diocesan Bishop: Rt Revd Garry Weatherill

Order of St Benedict

Community of St Mary at the Cross, Edgware

OSB

Founded 1866

Edgware Abbey
94A Priory Field Drive, Edgware
Middlesex
HA8 9PU
UK

Tel: 020 8958 7868

Email: info@edgwareabbey.org.uk *or* **nuns.osb.edgware@btconnect.com**

Website: www.edgwareabbey.org.uk

Vigils (private)

Lauds 8.00 am

Midday Office 11.55 am (not Sun)

Vespers 5.30 pm

Compline 8.00 pm

Mass weekdays: 7.45 am or 11.00 am
11 am (Sun/feast days)

Living under *The Rule of Benedict* and dedicated to St Mary at the Cross, the vocation of this community is to stand with Christ's Mother beside those who suffer; its heart in prayer, the Divine Office & the Eucharist are central to its life. Beginning in Shoreditch, Mother Monnica Skinner and Revd Henry Nihill worked together, drawn to the desperate poverty and sickness around them. Awareness of the needs, especially of 'incurable children', led to the building of a hospital, marking the beginning of the community's life work. Developing to meet the needs of each generation, this ministry continues today in the provision of Henry Nihill House, a care home with nursing for thirty residents, in the beautiful grounds of Edgware Abbey.

Edgware Abbey is a haven of peace which enfolds many visitors. All are offered Benedictine hospitality with space for rest and renewal. The small comfortable Guest Wing provides short stay retreat accommodation and space for parish Away Days and meetings. All guests are welcome to participate in the Community's offering of the Divine Office and Eucharist. Edgware Abbey is easily accessible from the M1, A1, tube and rail.

RT REVD DAME MARY THÉRÈSE ZELENT OSB
(Abbess, elected 30 March 1993)
Dame (Mary Eanfleda) Barbara Johnson

Oblates: Our Oblates are part of our extended Community family: living outside the cloister; following the spirit of the *Holy Rule of St Benedict*; bonded with the Community in prayer and commitment to service.

Community Publication: *Abbey Newsletter*, published yearly. There is no charge but donations are welcome. Obtainable from the Convent.

Guest and Retreat Facilities
The Guest Wing: Three comfortable bedrooms for B & B retreat accommodation; guest reception area with kitchenette; space for small day groups & clergy groups, parish quiet day groups etc.; use of chapel and garden; small parking area.

Bishop Visitor: Rt Revd Peter Wheatley

Office Book: Divine Office with own form of Compline.

Registered Charity: No. 209261

Order of St Benedict

Malling Abbey

OSB

Founded 1891

St Mary's Abbey
52 Swan Street
West Malling, Kent
ME19 6JX
UK
Tel: 01732 843309
Email: abbess@ mallingabbey.org

Website: www. mallingabbey.org

Vigils 4.30 am (5.00 am Sun)

Lauds 6.50 am (8.10 am Sun)

Eucharist 7.30 am (9.00 am Sun)

Terce 8.45 am

Sext 12.00 noon

None 3.00 pm

Vespers 4.45 pm (5.00 pm Sun)

Compline 7.30 pm

Office Book
Malling Abbey Office

In 2017 we began the second centenary of our Benedictine life at Malling Abbey. The rhythm of our day is shaped by the Eucharist and seven-fold Office and our times for personal prayer and lectio divina.

Silence and simplicity, prayer and hospitality, express our core values. We welcome opportunities to share our monastic heritage, to encourage ecumenical and interfaith understanding and to practise the responsible stewardship of God's creation.

In a venture of faith we have worked with the Diocese of Rochester to establish the St. Benedict's Centre at the Abbey. This Centre welcomes individuals and groups to meet, to retreat, to study and to pray. The Community has also welcomed the St. Augustine's College of Theology to share our Abbey grounds. We undergird their work of welcome and education with our monastic rhythm of prayer, and continue our own tradition of Benedictine hospitality in our separate guest facilities.

For more details of our daily life and work, or to arrange a visit, please see our website.

Mother Mary David Best OSB
(Abbess, elected 16 September 2008)
Sister Mary Stephen Packwood OSB *(Prioress)*
Sister Macrina Banner
Sister Mary Mark Brooksbank
Sister Mary John Marshall
Sister Ruth Blackmore
Sister Mary Cuthbert Archer
Sister Bartimaeus Ives
Sister Mary Michael Wilson
Sister Miriam Noke
Sister Mary Owen DeSimone
Sister Margaret Joy Harris
Sister Anne Clarke

Obituaries
4 Mar 2017 Sister Mary Gundulf Wood, aged 74 years, professed 43 years

Bishop Visitor: Rt Revd Laurie Green

Community Wares
Cards and booklets, created and painted by the sisters, are on sale at the Abbey.

Oblates & Alongsiders

Oblates

Oblates are men and women who have been regular Abbey guests and who feel called by God to follow the Benedictine way in their lives outside the cloister. They have a 2½ year period of training before making a promise of conversion of life. Their commitment is expressed in a personal Benedictine rule of life, which balances their personal prayer, worship and lectio divina with their responsibility to family and work.

Alongsiders

Alongsiders are women who, after visiting the Abbey Garth several times, wish to share in the life of the Community within the enclosure for a period of 3 months or more. This will enable them to experience a daily rhythm of prayer supported by an uncluttered, focussed and disciplined life. After living with the Community for a year, some alongsiders may wish to consider a longer stay involving a commitment of 2 or 3 years. Please see our website for details.

Community History

Sisters Mary David & Miriam (editors), *Living Stones: The Story of Malling Abbey*, privately published, Malling Abbey, 2005.

Guest and Retreat Facilities

In the Abbey Garth guest wing we can welcome four guests in single occupancy en-suite rooms. In addition we can accommodate one guest in the Gate House and two in St. Michael's Cottage. All guests are self-catering. Our guests come to share in the worship and God-centred quiet, and to have the space and time for spiritual reflection and refreshment. There is no charge, though donations are welcome. Please see our website for further details.

Day guests are now accommodated at the St. Benedict's Centre:
bookings@stbenedictscentre.org

Most convenient time to telephone: 9.30 am - 11.00 am

Order of St Benedict Mucknell Abbey

OSB

Founded 1941

Mucknell Abbey
Mucknell Farm Lane
Stoulton
Worcestershire
WR7 4RB
Tel: 01905 345900
Email: abbot@mucknellabbey.org.uk

Website
www.mucknellabbey.org.uk

Office of Readings 6.00 am

Lauds 7.00 am

Terce 8.45 am

Eucharist Noon (11 am Sun & solemnities)

None 2.15 pm

Vespers 5.30 pm (5.00 pm in winter)

Compline 8.30 pm (8.00 pm in winter)

The contemplative community of monks and nuns sold their former monastery in Burford in 2008 and bought a farm near Worcester and transformed it into a monastery incorporating as many 'sustainable' features as possible. Having moved into their new home in November 2010, the Community is seeking to maintain an atmosphere of stillness and silence in which the Community and its guests are enabled to be open and receptive to the presence of God. The recitation of the Divine Office and the celebration of the Eucharist constitute the principal work of the Community. The ministry of hospitality, the development of the surrounding 40 acres of land (which comprises a large kitchen garden, orchard, newly-planted woodland and hay meadows), the production of incense for a world-wide market, and various income-generating crafts provide a variety of manual work for members of the Community and those guests who wish to share in it. The monastery seeks to celebrate the wonder and richness of Creation and to model a responsible stewardship. The Community's concern has always been to pray for Christian Unity, and it now rejoices in having a Methodist presbyter in its number. Dialogue with people of other faiths and those seeking a spiritual way, either within or outside an established religious tradition, is a priority.

RT REVD BROTHER STUART BURNS OSB
(Abbot, elected 14 October 1996 - election pending September 2017)
BROTHER PHILIP DULSON OSB *(Prior)*

Brother Thomas Quin
Brother Anthony Hare
Brother Ian Mead
Sister Sally Paley
Brother Luke Fox
Sister Alison Fry
Brother Patrick Souter
Brother Michaël Brossard
Brother Aidan Mallam-Clark

Novices: 1
Alongsiders: 2

Obituaries

4 Jan 2016 Sister Mary Bernard Taylor, aged 91, professed 52 years, Prioress 1984-1996

Friends: There is a Friends' Association.
Contact: *friends@mucknellabbey.org.uk*

Community Wares: Incense: *incense@mucknellabbey.org.uk*
Hand-written icons, using traditional materials, and block mounted icon prints: *icons@mucknellabbey.org.uk*
Chinese brush painted cards: *cards@mucknellabbey.org.uk*
Rosaries and hand-carved Holding Crosses: *craftsales@mucknell.org.uk*

Bishop Visitor: Rt Revd John Inge, Bishop of Worcester

Community publications
There are up-dates on the Community's website.
The Rule of St Benedict – inclusive translation by Abbot Stuart.

Guest and Retreat Facilities
Six guest rooms and one room for an individual having a quiet day. No groups.

Most convenient time to telephone: 9.30 am-11.30 am; 2.30 pm-3.45 pm.
Email enquiries are preferred: *bookings@mucknellabbey.org.uk*

Office Book: Mucknell Abbey Office

Registered Charity: No. 221617

Order of St Benedict

Servants of Christ Priory

OSB

Founded 1968

A community united in love for God and one another following the Benedictine balance of prayer, study and work reflects the life of the monks. The remaining member of the community is now in care accommodation.

The Revd Lewis H. Long OSB

Obituaries
24 Sep 2016 The Very Revd Cornelis J. de Rijk OSB, aged 80

Oblates
Oblates follow a rule of life consistent with the *Rule of St Benedict* adapted to their lifestyle.

Bishop Visitor
Rt Revd Kirk Stevan Smith, Bishop of Arizona

Order of St Benedict

Salisbury

OSB

Founded 1914

St Benedict's Priory
19A The Close
Salisbury SP1 2EB
UK
Tel: 01722 335868
Email:
salisbury.priory@gmail.com

Vigils 6.00 am

Morning Worship & Eucharist
at Cathedral 7.30 am
(Cathedral Choral Eucharist
10.30 am Sun)

Lauds (at Priory)
8.00 am Sun

Terce 10.00 am

Midday Prayer
12.45 pm
(at Sarum College)
12.15pm Sat & Sun
(at Priory)

Evensong
at Cathedral
(times vary)

Compline 8.30 pm

The monastery aims to provide an environment within which the traditional monastic balance between worship, study and work may be maintained with a characteristic Benedictine stress upon corporate worship and community life. To this end, outside commitments are kept to a minimum.

VERY REVD DOM SIMON JARRATT OSB
(Conventual Prior, elected 13 December 2005)
DOM FRANCIS HUTCHINSON OSB *(Sub-Prior)*
Rt Revd Dom Kenneth Newing
Dom Bruce De Walt

Oblates
An extended confraternity of oblates, numbering over 250 men and women, married and single, seek to live according to a rule of life inspired by Benedictine principles. From the start, the community has believed in the importance of prayer for Christian unity and the fostering of ecumenism.

Community History
Petà Dunstan, *The Labour of Obedience: A history of Pershore, Nashdom, Elmore,* Canterbury Press, Norwich, 2009.

Community Publications
Books:
Augustine Morris, *Oblates: Life with Saint Benedict* £4.25.
Simon Bailey, *A Tactful God: Gregory Dix,* £12.99.

Guest and Retreat Facilities
The Community receives day visitors. There are no facilities for residential guests, although Sarum College next door is open for bed & breakfast.

Most convenient time to telephone
9.00 am - 9.50 am; 10.30 am - 12.15 pm; 3.30 pm - 4.45 pm
Tel: 01722 335868

Office Book: Own Office books at the Priory.

Bishop Visitor
Rt Revd Dominic Walker OGS

Registered Charity
Pershore Nashdom & Elmore Trust - No. 220012

St Gregory's Abbey Three Rivers OSB

Founded 1939

St Gregory's Abbey
56500 Abbey Road
Three Rivers
Michigan
49093-9595
USA
Tel: 269 244 5893
Fax: 269 244 8712
Email: abbot@saintgregorysthreerivers.org

Website
www.saintgregorysthreerivers.org

Matins 4.00 am
(5.30 am Sun & solemnities, with Lauds)

Lauds 6.00 am

Terce & Mass
8.15 am (8.30 am Sun & solemnities)

Sext 11.30 am
(12 noon Sun & solemnities, with None)

None 2.00 pm

Vespers 5.00 pm

Compline 7.45 pm

Office Book
Home-made books based on the Roman Thesaurus for the Benedictine Office.

St Gregory's Abbey is the home of a community of men living under the *Rule of St Benedict* within the Episcopal Church. The center of the monastery's life is the Abbey Church, where God is worshipped in the daily round of Eucharist, Divine Office, and private prayer. Also offered to God are the monks' daily manual work, study and correspondence, ministry to guests, and occasional outside engagements.

RIGHT REVD ANDREW MARR OSB
(*Abbot, elected 2 March 1989*)
VERY REVD AELRED GLIDDEN OSB (*Prior*)

Father Benedict Reid*	Brother Martin Dally
Father Jude Bell	Brother Abraham Newsom
Father William Forest	*Novices:* 1

**resident elsewhere*

Associates

We have a Confraternity which offers an official connection to the Abbey and is open to anyone who wishes to join for the purpose of incorporating Benedictine principles into their lives. For further information and an application form, please write the Father Abbot.

Community Publications and History

Abbey Newsletter, published four times a year. Free.

Singing God's Praises, published 1998. It includes articles from community newsletters over the past sixty years and also includes a history of St Gregory's. Copies can be bought from the Abbey, price $20 a copy, postpaid.

Come Let Us Adore: St Gregory's 1999-2011, a successor to the above. Published by iUniverse and available from online bookstores such as Amazon.

Andrew Marr OSB, *Tools for Peace: the spiritual craft of St Benedict and René Girard*, available from online bookstores.

Andrew Marr OSB, *Moving and Resting in God's Desire: A Spirituality of Peace,* 2016. Published by St. Gregory's Abbey Press and available from online bookstores.

Community Wares: The Abbey calendar.

Guest and Retreat Facilities

Both men and women are welcome as guests. There is no charge, but $40 per day is 'fair value for services rendered' that is not tax-deductible. For further information and arrangements, contact the guest master by mail, telephone or e-mail at *guestmaster@saintgregorysthreerivers.org*

Bishop Visitor: Rt Revd Arthur Williams (retired)

Order of St Helena

OSH

Founded 1945

Convent of St Helena
414 Savannah Barony Drive
North Augusta
SC 29841
USA
Tel: 803 426 1616
Email: sisters@osh.org

Website
www.osh.org

Matins 7.30 am
Eucharist 8.00 am
Diurnum and intercessions 12 noon
Vespers 5.00 pm
Compline 7.00 pm

Bishop Visitor
Rt Revd Neil Alexander, Dean of the School of Theology, University of the South at Sewanee, TN

Registered Charity No: US Government 501 (c)(3)

The mission of the Order of Saint Helena is to show forth Christ through a life of monastic prayer, hospitality and service. Our core values are: **Prayer:** We celebrate the Holy Eucharist and pray the Divine Office daily. We practice individual prayer, intercession and meditation. **Hospitality:** We offer an oasis of welcome for guests, both individuals and groups. **Service:** We minister and serve where our gifts meet the world's needs. **Tradition and Innovation:** We are women living communally under a vow of monastic poverty, celibate chastity and obedience to God. From Benedictine roots, we discern new ways to interpret traditional monasticism, striving to grow in diversity and inclusivity. As an Order, we are not restricted to any single area of work but witness and respond to the Gospel, with individual sisters engaging in different ministries as they feel called by God and affirmed by the community. Our ministries are thus wonderfully varied: for example, parish ministry, leading retreats, spiritual direction, teaching, chaplaincy, interfaith dialogue, and community service. Four sisters are ordained priests. The Order is led by a three-member Leadership Council.

SISTER MARY LOIS MILLER OSH *(Administration)*
REVD SISTER CAROL ANDREW OSH *(Vocations/Formation)*
REVD DR ELLEN FRANCIS POISSON OSH *(Administration/Pastoral)*

Sister Ruth Juchter
Sister Ellen Stephen
Sister Barbara Lee
Sister Benedicta
Revd Sister Rosina Ampah
Sister June Thomas
Sister Ann Prentice
Sister Linda Elston
Sister Faith Anthony
Sister Miriam Elizabeth

Associates
ASSOCIATES - open to all women and men.

Guest and Retreat Facilities: Guest house, 8 single rooms.

Community Publication
OSH newsletter and article blog: subscribe on OSH website (www.osh.org) for subscription (paper or electronic); no charge.

Community Wares and Books
Hand-made rosaries: write to Sister Mary Lois for Dominican rosaries and to Sr Linda for Anglican rosaries.
Icon reproductions: www.ellenfrancisicons.org
Greeting cards by Sister Faith Anthony, see OSH website.
Sister Cintra Pemberton OSH, *Soulfaring: Celtic pilgrimage then and now,* SPCK & Morehouse, 1999.

Doug Shadel and Sister Ellen Stephen OSH, *Vessel of Peace: The voyage toward spiritual freedom*, Three Tree Press, 1999.
Sister Ellen Stephen, OSH, *The Poet's Eye: collected poetry,* Academica Press, 2012.
Sister Ellen Stephen, OSH, *Some Antics,* Order of Saint Helena, 2012.
Sister Rosina Ampah, *The Beautiful Cloth: stories and proverbs of Ghana,* Yellow Moon Press, 2010.
Sister Ellen Stephen OSH, *Together and Apart: a memoir of the Religious Life*, Morehouse, Harrisburg, PA, 2008.

Office Book
The Saint Helena Breviary, Monastic Edition is our office book. It is also available on CD (in PDF) for a minimum donation of $25.

Sisterhood of the Holy Nativity SHN

Founded 1882

W14164 Plante Dr.
Ripon
WI 54971
USA

Tel: 920 748 1479

Email: abizac50@hotmail.com

Matins 7.30 am

Eucharist 8.00 am

Noonday Prayer 12 noon

Vespers 5.30 pm (6.30 pm Sun)

Compline 8.00 pm

Ours is a mixed life, which means that we combine an apostolic ministry with a contemplative lifestyle. The Rule of the Sisterhood of the Holy Nativity follows the model of the Rule of St Augustine of Hippo. As such, we strive to make the love of God the motive of all our actions. The 'charisms', which undergird our life, are Charity, Humility, Prayer, and Missionary Zeal. Our work involves us with children's ministries such as Sunday School, Summer Camp and Vacation Bible School, as well as ministry to those we meet in everyday life.

SISTER ABIGAIL SHN
(Revd Mother, assumed office 2012)

Sister Charis SHN

Obituaries
11 Sep 2015 Sister Margaretta, aged 87, professed 59 years
24 Sep 2016 Sister Kathleen Marie, aged 92, prof. 35 years
30 Oct 2016 Sister Columba, aged 82, professed 54 years

Associates
These are men and women who connect themselves to the prayer life and ministry of the community, and keep a Rule of Life.

Community Publication
We put out a newsletter occasionally. There is no charge. Anyone interested may contact us at the address above or by email.

Office Book: *The Monastic Breviary*, published by the Order of the Holy Cross.

Bishop Visitor
Rt Revd Mathew Gunter, Bishop of Fond du Lac

Sisterhood of St John the Divine

SSJD

Founded 1884

St John's Convent
233 Cummer Ave
Toronto
Ontario M2M 2E8
CANADA
Tel: 416 226 2201
ext. 301
Fax: 416 222 2131
Emails:
convent@ssjd.ca
guesthouse@ssjd.ca

Website www.ssjd.ca

Morning Prayer
8.30 am

Holy Eucharist
12 noon (8.00 am Sun)

Mid-day Office
12.15 pm (when Eucharist not at noon)

Evening Prayer
5.00 pm

Compline 8.10 pm
(Tue, Wed, Thu & Fri)

Office Book
Book of Alternative Services 1985;
SSJD Daily Office Binder with inclusive language psalter.

The Sisterhood of St John the Divine is a monastic community of women within the Anglican Church of Canada. Founded in Toronto, we are a prayer- and gospel-centred monastic community, bound together by the call to live out our baptismal covenant through the vows of poverty, chastity and obedience. These vows anchor us in Jesus' life and the transforming experience of the Gospel. Nurtured by our founding vision of prayer, community and service, we are open and responsive to the needs of the Church and the world, continually seeking the guidance of the Holy Spirit in our life and ministries.

St John's Convent nurtures and supports the life of the whole Sisterhood. Our guest house welcomes individuals and groups who share in the community's prayer and liturgy; offers regularly scheduled retreats and quiet days, spiritual direction, and discernment programs for those seeking guidance in their life and work; and provides Sisters to preach, teach, speak, lead retreats and quiet days. Our programs help people build bridges between secular culture, the Church, and the monastic tradition. The Sisterhood witnesses to the power of Christ's reconciling and forgiving love through the gospel imperatives of prayer, spiritual guidance, justice, peace, care for creation, hospitality, ministering to those in need, and promoting unity, healing, and wholeness.

The Sisters advocate for a vision of health care at the St. John's Rehab site of Sunnybrook Hospital which expresses SSJD's values in a multi-faith, multi-cultural setting. The Sisters provide spiritual and pastoral support for patients, staff and volunteers.

Other address

ST JOHN'S HOUSE, 3937 St Peters Rd, Victoria, British Columbia V8P 2J9
Tel: 250 920 7787 Fax: 250 920 7709
E-mail: bchouse@ssjd.ca

A community of Sisters committed to being a praying presence in the Diocese of British Columbia. Prayer, intentional community, hospitality, and mission are at the heart of our life in the Diocese and beyond.

Community Wares

A variety of cards made by Sisters or Associates. Good selection of books on spiritual growth for sale at the Convent (not by mail) and a few CDs. Anglican rosaries made by the Sisters, some knitted items and prayer shawls.

Bishop Visitor: Rt Revd. Linda Nicholls, Bishop of Huron

SISTER ELIZABETH ROLFE-THOMAS SSJD
(Reverend Mother, assumed office 6 May 2015)
SISTER DOREEN MCGUFF SSJD *(Prioress)*

Sister Wilma Grazier
Sister Beryl Stone
Sister Patricia Forler
Sister Jocelyn Mortimore
Sister Margaret Ruth Steele
Sister Sarah Jean Thompson
Sister Anitra Hansen
Sister Jessica Kennedy
Sister Constance Joanna Gefvert *(priest)*
Sr Elizabeth Ann Eckert *(Novice Director)*
Sister Brenda Jenner
Sister Anne Norman
Sister Helen Claire Gunter
Sister Sue Elwyn
Sister Louise Manson
Sister Dorothy Handrigan
Sister Susanne Prue

Novices: 3

Associates, Oblates and Alongsiders

Our approximately seven hundred **Associates** are women and men who follow a Rule of Life and share in the ministry of the Sisterhood. The Sisterhood of St John the Divine owes its founding to the vision and dedication of the clergy and lay people who became the first Associates of SSJD. A year of discernment is required before being admitted as an Associate to see if the Associate Rule helps the person in what she/he is seeking; and to provide the opportunity to develop a relationship with the Sisters and to deepen his or her understanding and practice of prayer. The Associate Rule provides a framework for the journey of faith. There are three basic commitments: belonging to a parish; the practice of prayer, retreat, study of scripture, and spiritual reading; and the relationship with SSJD. Write to the Associate Director nearest you for further information.

The 23 **Oblates** of the Community are women who wish to make a promise of prayer and service in partnership with the Sisterhood. Each Oblate develops her own Rule of Life in partnership with the Oblate Director, her spiritual director, and a support group. A year of discernment is also required, as well as an annual residency program. Write to The Reverend Mother at the Convent in Toronto for more information.

An **Alongsider** is a woman who lives "alongside" the community of the Sisterhood of St. John the Divine, moving back and forth between the monastery and the world outside. She lives in the cloister with the Sisters and participates in many of the community activities (including worship, conference and recreation) and shares in household tasks. Alongside the Sisters, she is committed to a daily practice of personal prayer, spiritual reading and reflection on sacred Scripture and assists the Sisters in their ministries.

Companions are young women (ages 21 – 39) who have a desire to deepen their relationship with God, a willingness to follow Jesus in his radical obedience, and an openness to the leading of the Holy Spirit in the path of life. They live on the edge of the enclosure, join in the community worship, conference and recreation, form community among themselves, assist the Sisters in their work and ministry and have the opportunity to take courses at Wycliffe College, part of the Toronto School of Theology.

Community History and Books

Sister Eleonora SSJD, *A Memoir of the Life and Work of Hannah Grier Coome, Mother-Foundress of SSJD, Toronto, Canada,* OUP, London, 1933 (out of print).

The Sisterhood of St John the Divine 1884-1984, published 1931 as *A Brief History;* 4th revision 1984, (out of print).

Sister Constance Joanna SSJD, *From Creation to Resurrection: A Spiritual Journey,* Anglican Book Centre, Toronto, 1990.

Sister Constance SSJD, *Other Little Ships: The memoirs of Sister Constance SSJD,* Patmos Press, Toronto, 1997.

Sister Thelma-Anne McLeod SSJD, *In Age Reborn, By Grace Sustained*, Path Books, Toronto, 2007.

Dr Gerald D Hart, *St John's Rehab Hospital, 1885-2010, the Road to Recovery,*York Region Printing, Autora, ON, 2010

Jane Christmas & Sister Constance Joanna SSJD (editors), *A Journey Just Begun: The Story of an Anglican Sisterhood*, Dundurn, 2015.

Community Publication: *The Eagle* (newsletter). Contact the Convent Secretary. Published three times a year. $10.00 suggested annual donation.

Guest and Retreat Facilities: Guest House has 37 rooms (42 people) used for rest, quiet time and retreats. Contact the Guest Sister at the Convent for details about private accommodation, scheduled retreats, quiet days and other programs.

The Sisters in Victoria also lead quiet days and retreats and have room for one guest. Please contact St John's House, BC, for detailed information.

Sisterhood of St Mary

SSM

Founded 1929

St Andrew's Mission
PO Haluaghat
Mymensingh
BANGLADESH

Prayer 6.30 am

Meditation 8.00 am

Prayers
9.00 am, 11.30 am,
3.00 pm, 6.00 pm

Compline 8.00 pm

The community is located on the northern border of Bangladesh at the foot of the Garo hills in India. The community was formed in Barisal at the Sisterhood of the Epiphany, and was sent here to work among the indigenous tribal people, side by side with St Andrew's Mission. Membership of the Sisterhood has always been entirely indigenous. The first sisters were Bengalis. The present sisters are the fruit of their work - Garo and Bengali. They take the vows of Poverty, Purity and Obedience and live a very simple life. They lead a life of prayer and formation of girls. They also look after the Church and do pastoral work among women and children in the Parish.

SISTER MIRA MANKHIN SSM
(Sister Superior, assumed office 2002)

Sister Anita Raksam
Sister Bregita Doffo
Sister Mala Chicham

Novices: 2

Community Wares: Some handicrafts and vestments for church use and sale.

Office Book: Church of Bangladesh BCP & own book for lesser Offices.

Bishop Visitor: Most Revd Paul Sarker, Bp of Dhaka

Sisters of Charity

SC

Founded 1869

83 Fore Street
Plympton
Plymouth
PL7 1NB
UK
Tel: 01752 336112
Email:
plymptonsisters@gmail.com

Morning Prayer
9.00 am

Vespers 5.00 pm

Compline 7.00 pm

Office Book
Common Worship

Registered Charity:
No. X33170

A Community following the Rule of St Vincent de Paul and so committed to the service of those in need. The Sisters are involved in parish work and the Community also has a nursing home in Plympton.

MOTHER ELIZABETH MARY SC
(Revd Mother, assumed office 21 April 2003)
SISTER CLARE SC *(priest)* *(Assistant)*

Sister Angela Mary
Sister Mary Patrick
Sister Mary Joseph

Obituaries

5 Aug 2016 Sr Gabriel Margaret, aged 85, prof. 53 years
15 Mar 2017 Sr Theresa, aged 101, professed 70 years

Oblates and Associate Members

The Community has a group of Oblates and Associate Members, formed as a mutual supportive link. We ask them to add to their existing rule the daily use of the Vincentian Prayer. Oblates are also asked to use the Holy Paraclete hymn and one of the Daily Offices, thereby joining in spirit in the Divine Office of the Community. Oblates are encouraged to make an annual retreat. Associate Members support us by their prayers and annual subscription.

Other address

Saint Vincent's Nursing Home, Fore St, Plympton, Plymouth , PL7 1NE Tel: 01752 336205

Guest and Retreat Facilities

We welcome individuals for Quiet Days.

Most convenient time to telephone: 6.00 pm - 8.00 pm

Bishop Visitor: Rt Revd Martin Shaw

Sisters of the Incarnation

SI

Founded 1981

The sisters live under vows of poverty, chastity and obedience in a simple life style, and seek to maintain a balance between prayer, community life and work for each member and to worship and serve within the church. They combine the monastic and apostolic aspects of the Religious Life. The monastic aspects include prayer, domestic work at home, community life and hospitality. The sisters are engaged in parish ministry.

The community was founded in the diocese of Adelaide in 1981 as a contemporary expression of the Religious Life for women in the Anglican Church. In 1988, the two original sisters made their Profession of Life Intention win the Sisters of the Incarnation, before the Archbishop of

The House of the Incarnation
6 Sherbourne Terrace
Dover Gardens
SA 5048
AUSTRALIA
Tel: 08 8296 2166
Email: sisincar @bigpond.com

Office Book
A Prayer Book for Australia (1995 edition): MP, EP and Compline Midday Prayer is from another source.

Adelaide, the Visitor of the community. One member was ordained to the diaconate in 1990 and the priesthood in 1992. The governing body of the community is its chapter of professed sisters, which elects the Guardian, and appoints an Episcopal Visitor and a Community Advisor.

REVD SISTER JULIANA SI
(*Guardian, assumed office 2013*)
Sister Patricia

Friends
The community has a group of Friends who share special celebrations and significant events, many of whom have supported the community from the beginning, while others become Friends as we touch their lives. There is no formal structure.

Bishop Visitor: Rt Revd Dr K Rayner

Sisters of Jesus Way

Founded 1979

Website:
www.redacre.org.uk

Redacre
24 Abbey Road
West Kirby
Wirral
CH48 7EP
UK

Tel: 0151 6258775

Email:
sistersofjesusway @redacre.org.uk

Two Wesley deaconesses founded the Sisters of Jesus Way. There have been many strands that have been instrumental in the formation of the community but primarily these have been the Gospels, the Charismatic Renewal, the teaching and example of the Pietists of the 17th and early 18th centuries as practised in some German communities and the lives of saints from many denominations.

Our calling is to love the Lord Jesus with a first love, to trust the heavenly Father as his dear children for all our needs both spiritual and material and to allow the Holy Spirit to guide and lead us. Prayer, either using the framework of a simple liturgy or informal, is central to all that we do. We make life promises of simplicity, fidelity and chastity. Our work for the Lord varies as the Holy Spirit opens or closes doors. We welcome guests, trusting that as the Lord Jesus lives with us, they will meet with him and experience his grace. Music, some of which has been composed by the sisters, is very much part of our life. We work together, learning from the Lord to live together as a family in love, forgiveness and harmony.

Office Book: The Community uses its own liturgy.

Bishop Guardian
Rt Revd Dr Peter Forster, Bishop of Chester

Morning Prayer
8.00 am

Intercessory prayer
(community only)
12.30 pm

Evening Prayer
7.00 pm

Registered Charity
No 509284

SISTER MARIE
(Little Sister, assumed office 1991)
SISTER SYLVIA *(Companion Sister)*

Sister Hazel
Sister Florence
Sister Beatrice
Sister Susan
Sister Louise
Sister Pamela

Brother of the Way: Brother Elliot

Novices: 1

Associates
The Followers of the Lamb are a small group of women and men following a simple Rule of Life in their own homes and committed to assisting the Community.

Guest and Retreat Facilities
7 single rooms, 3 twin rooms. Several rooms for day visitors and small groups.

Most convenient time to telephone:
9.45 am-12.30 pm; 2.00 pm-5.45 pm; 7.30 pm-8.45 pm

Community Publication: Twice-yearly teaching and newsletter (no charge). Contact Sr Louise.

Community History
Written by the Sisters of Jesus Way and available from the Community:
To Love You Only: The Story of Lynda & a Community, Church in the Market Place Publications, 2013.
Precious in His Sight: The Love of the Father for His Children, Church in the Market Place Publications, 2017.

Community Wares
CDs: *Come Lord Jesus* and *Faithful Father* (both with music composed, sung & played by the Community).

Society of the Holy Cross

SHC

Founded 1925

15 Road 21
Seijong Daero
Jung-ku
Seoul 04519
KOREA
Tel: 2 735 7832
or 2 735 3478
Fax: 2 736 5028
Email:
holycross1925
@daum.net

Website
www.sister.or.kr

Morning Prayer
6.15 am

Holy Eucharist
6.45 am

Midday Prayer
12.30 pm
(12 noon Sun & great feast days)

Evening Prayer
5.00 pm

Compline 8.00 pm

Office Book
Revised Common Prayer for MP & EP and Compline; & SHC material for Midday Office

The community was founded on the feast day of the Exaltation of the Holy Cross in 1925 by the Rt Revd Mark Trollope, the third English bishop of the Anglican Church in Korea, admitting Postulant Phoebe Lee and blessing a small traditional Korean-style house in the present site of Seoul. The Community of St Peter, a Nursing Order in Woking, Surrey, England, sent eighteen Sisters as missionaries to Korea between 1892 and 1950, who nourished this young community for a few decades. Sister Mary Clare CSP, who was the first Mother Superior of this community, was persecuted by the North Korean communists and died during the 'Death March' in the Korean War in 1950. This martyrdom especially has been a strong influence and encouragement for the growth of the community. Our spirituality is based on a modified form of the Augustinian Rule harmonized with the Benedictine one. Bishop Mark Trollope, the first Visitor, and Sister Mary Clare CSP compiled the Divine Office Book and the Constitution and Rule of the Community. The activities that are being continuously practised even now include pastoral care in parishes, running homes for the elderly and those with learning difficulties, conducting Quiet Days, and offering people spiritual direction.

We run spiritual prayer meetings and workshop weekly or fortnightly throughout year except Jan-Feb & Jul-Aug for those who want to improve their faithful life. We lead Ignatian Contemplation Prayer, Lectio Divina, Centering Prayer, Rosary, Way of the Cross, Silence Prayer and Meditanz (Sacred Circle Dance). We also have a programme of "A day in Religious Life" and weekend Retreats for individuals and in groups.

SISTER HELEN ELIZABETH SHC *(priest)*
(Reverend Mother, assumed office 1 Jan 2016)

Sister Monica
Sister Phoebe Anne
Sister Edith
Sister Cecilia
Sister Maria Helen
Sister Etheldreda
Sister Catherine *(priest)*
Sister Maria Clara
Sister Pauline
Sister Angela
Sister Alma
Sister Theresa
Sister Grace
Sister Martha
Sister Prisca *(Novice Guardian)*

Novices: 3

Friends and Associates

FRIENDS are mostly Anglicans who desire to have a close

link with the community. They follow a simple Rule of Life, which includes praying for the Sisters and their work. Friends also form a network of prayer, fellowship and mutual support within Christ's ministry of wholeness and reconciliation. About one hundred members gather together for the annual meeting in May in the Motherhouse. The committee members meet bi-monthly at the convent in Seoul.

ASSOCIATES: Forty members have taken Life Vows and eleven will make Junior Vows in September 2017. Each one needs two years in the Formation period and then will renew vows annually for three years to be a full member. Each receives a grey uniform and a cross at Life Vows.

Other Addresses

St Anne's Nursing Home for Elderly People,
79 Jundeungsa Road, Onsuri, Kilsang, Kangwha, Inch'on, 23050 SOUTH KOREA Tel: 32 937 1935 Fax: 32 937 0696
Email: anna1981@kornet.net Website: www.oldanna.or.kr

St Bona House for Intellectually Handicapped People,
123-9 Keumgo Neam Road, Kadok, Chongwon, Chungbuk 28205, SOUTH KOREA Tel: 43 297 8348 Fax: 43 298 3156
Email: sralma@naver.com Website: www.bona.or.kr

Community Publication: *Holy Cross Newsletter*, published occasionally, in Korean. Sister Catherine SHC, *Holy Vocation* (booklet for the SHC 75th anniversary, 2000)

Community History

Jae Joung Lee, *Society of the Holy Cross 1925-1995*, Seoul, 1995 (in Korean).
Sisters Maria Helen & Catherine, *The SHC: the First 80 Years*, 2005
Sister Helen Elizabeth (ed), *Fragrance of the Holy Cross,* 2010 (story of Sister Mary Clare in Korean)

Guest and Retreat Facilities: The Community organizes Retreats and Quiet Days monthly for Associates and groups and individuals.

Community Wares: Vestments and altar lines. Wafers and wine for Holy Eucharist for all the parishes in Korea.

Bishop Visitor: Rt Revd Peter K Lee, Bishop of Seoul

Society of the Precious Blood (UK)

SPB

Founded 1905

Burnham Abbey
Lake End Road
Taplow, Maidenhead
Berkshire SL6 OPW
UK
Tel & Fax:
01628 604080
Emails:
General:
burnhamabbey@btinternet.com
Prayer requests:
intercessions@burnhamabbey.org
Hospitality:
hospitality@burnhamabbey.org

Website: www.burnhamabbey.org

Lauds 7.30 am

Eucharist 9.30 am

Angelus & Sext 12.00 noon

Vespers 5.30 pm

Compline 8.30 pm

Office Book
SPB Office Book

Registered Charity
No. 900512

We are a contemplative community whose particular work within the whole body of Christ is worship, thanksgiving and intercession. Within these ancient Abbey walls, which date back to 1266, we continue to live the Augustinian monastic tradition of prayer, silence, fellowship and solitude. The Eucharist is the centre of our life, where we find ourselves most deeply united with Christ, one another and all for whom we pray. The work of prayer is continued in the Divine Office, in the Watch before the Blessed Sacrament and in our whole life of work, reading, creating, and learning to live together. This life of prayer finds an outward expression in welcoming guests, who come seeking an opportunity for quiet and reflection in which to deepen their own spiritual lives, or to explore the possibility of a religious vocation.

Sister Victoria Mary SPB
(Reverend Mother, assumed office 6 August 2011)

Sister Margaret Mary
Sister Mary Bernard
Sister Dorothy Mary
Sister Jane Mary
Sister Mary Laurence
Sister Mary Philip
Sister Mary Benedict
Sister Miriam Mary
Sister Grace Mary

Companions and Oblates: Oblates are men and women who feel drawn by God to express the spirit of the Society, united with the Sisters in their life of worship, thanksgiving and intercession. They live out their dedication in their own situation and make a yearly Promise.

Men and women who desire to share in the prayer and work of the Society but cannot make as full a commitment to saying the Office may be admitted as Companions.

For information about living alongside the Community, please see the website.

Community History
Sister Felicity Mary SPB, *Mother Millicent Mary,* 1968.

Community Wares: A small shop for cards and rosaries.

Community Publications: *Newsletter,* yearly at Christmas. *Companions/Oblates Letter,* quarterly.

Guest and Retreat Facilities: Small guest wing with 3 single en suite rooms for individual (unconducted) retreats. Rooms available for Quiet Days or groups of up to 20.

Most convenient time to telephone: 10.30 am - 11.45 am; 3.30 pm - 4.30 pm; 7.00 pm - 8.00 pm

Bishop Visitor: Rt Revd Stephen Cottrell, Bishop of Chelmsford

Society of the Precious Blood (southern Africa)

SPB

Founded 1905

St Monica's House of Prayer
46 Green Street
West End
Kimberley, 8301
SOUTH AFRICA

Tel: 00275 38 331161

Email: sisterelainespb @gmail.com

Morning Prayer 7.00 am

Eucharist 8.30 am (Thu & Fri)

Midday Office 12 noon

Evening Prayer 5.00 pm

Compline 8.00 pm

Office Book
Daily Prayer & An Anglican Prayer Book 1989, CPSA

Five Sisters of the Society of the Precious Blood at Burnham Abbey went to Masite in Lesotho in 1957 to join with a community of African women, with the intention of forming a multi-cultural contemplative community dedicated to intercession. In 1966, this community at Masite became autonomous, although still maintaining strong ties of friendship with Burnham Abbey. In 1980, a House of Prayer was established in Kimberley in South Africa, which developed a more active branch of the Society. Sadly, due to diminishing numbers, health issues and finance, the Lesotho Priory was closed on 1 March 2014 and the sisters there dispersed. The Kimberley house continues its ministry.

SISTER ELAINE MARY SPB
(Prioress, assumed office 24 September 1997) *(at Kimberley)*

Sister Theresia Mary *(in Lesotho)*
Sister Lucia Mary *(in Lesotho)*
Sister Diana Mary *(in UK)*
Sister Camilla Mary *(at Kimberley)*

Oblates and Companions
The Community has thirteen oblates (in Lesotho, South Africa, Zambia, New Zealand and the UK), and eighty-six Companions and Associates (in Lesotho, South Africa and the UK). All renew their promises annually. Oblates are sent prayer material regularly. Companions and Associates receive quarterly letters and attend occasional quiet days.

Community Publication
Annual *Newsletter;* apply to the Prioress. No charge.

Community History and books
Sister Theresia Mary SPB, *Father Patrick Maekane MBK*, CPSA, 1987.
Evelyn Cresswell (Oblate SPB), *Keeping the Hours,* Cluster Pubs, Pietermaritzburg, 2007.

Guest and Retreat Facilities
Single room cottage.

Bishops Visitor
Rt Revd Adam Taaso, Bishop of Lesotho
Rt Revd Oswald P P Swartz, Bishop of Kimberley and Kuruman

Society of the Sacred Advent

SSA

Founded 1892

Symes Grove
Villas 30 & 31
333 Handford Road
Taigum
Qld 4018
AUSTRALIA
Tel: 07 3865 7618
or **07 3865 7604**

Email: eunice@ stmargarets.qld. edu.au

Quiet time
5.30 am - 6.00 am

Matins
6.30 am

Eucharist 7.00 am

Midday Prayer
12 noon

Evensong 5.00 pm

Compline 7.30 pm

Office Book
A Prayer Book for Australia; *The Daily Office SSF* for Midday Prayer.

Bishop Visitor
Rt Revd Godfrey Fryar, (retired bishop)

The Society of the Sacred Advent exists for the glory of God and for the service of His Church in preparation for the second coming of our Lord and Saviour Jesus Christ.

Members devote themselves to God in community under vows of poverty, chastity and obedience. Our life is a round of worship, prayer, silence and work. Our Patron Saint is John the Baptist who, by his life and death, pointed the way to Jesus. We would hope also to point the way to Jesus in our own time, to a world which has largely lost touch with spiritual realities and is caught up in despair, loneliness and fear. As part of our ministry, Sisters may be called to give addresses, conduct Retreats or Quiet Days, or to make themselves available for spiritual direction and parish work. The aim of the Community is to grow in the mind of Christ so as to manifest Him to others. The Society has two Schools, St Margaret's and St Aidan's. Each school is managed by the SSA Schools Pty Ltd.

SISTER EUNICE SSA
(Revd Mother, assumed office 21 March 2007)
Sister Sandra
Sister Gillian

Obituaries

20 Jun 2015 Sister June Ruth, aged 87, professed 31 years

Fellowship and Company

THE COMPANY/FELLOWSHIP OF THE SACRED ADVENT began in 1987. This group of men and women, clergy and lay, bound together in love for Jesus Christ and His Church in the spirit of St John the Baptist, seeks to proclaim the Advent challenge: 'Prepare the Way of the Lord.' Members have a Rule of Life and renew their promises annually.

Members of the Company/Fellowship are part of our extended Community family. The Sisters arrange Company/Fellowship meetings and mutual support with prayers, help, or spiritual guidance, as required.

Community History

Elizabeth Moores, *One Hundred Years of Ministry,* published for SSA, 1992.

Ray Geise, *Educating Girls since 1895,* Victory Press, Bribie Island, QLD, 2012.

Community Publication

There is a Newsletter, printed yearly. For a subscription, write to Sister Sandra SSA sandra@stmargarets.qld.edu.au No cost.

Society of the Sacred Cross

SSC

Founded 1914 (Chichester); to Wales in 1923

Tymawr Convent
Lydart
Monmouth
Gwent
NP25 4RN
UK

Tel: 01600 860244

Email:
tymawrconvent@btinternet.com

Website
www.tymawrconvent.org

Bishop Visitor
Rt Revd Dominic Walker OGS

Registered Charity:
No. 1135334

The community, part of the Anglican Church in Wales, lives a monastic, contemplative life of prayer based on silence, solitude and learning to live together, under vows of poverty, chastity and obedience, with a modern rule, Cistercian in spirit. At the heart of our corporate life is the Eucharist with the daily Office and other times of shared prayer spanning the day. All services are open to the public and we are often joined by members of the neighbourhood in addition to our visitors. Our common life includes study, recreation and work in the house and extensive grounds. It is possible for women and men, married or single, to experience our life of prayer by living alongside the community for periods longer than the usual guest stay. Hospitality is an important part of our life at Tymawr and guests are most welcome. We also organise and sponsor occasional lectures and programmes of study for those who wish to find or develop the life of the spirit in their own circumstances. The community is dedicated to the crucified and risen Lord as the focus of its life and the source of the power to live it.

SISTER GILLIAN MARY SSC
(Revd Mother, assumed office 2010)
SISTER VERONICA ANN SSC *(Assistant)*

Sister Lorna Francis	Sister Elizabeth
Sister Heylin Columba*	Sister Janet
Sister Rosalind Mary	Sister Katharine

* *Living the contemplative life away from Tymawr*

Companions, Oblates and Associates
There are 8 Companions; 40 Oblates, living in their own homes, each having a personal Rule sustaining their life of prayer; 111 Associates, women and men, who have a simple commitment.

Community Publication
Tymawr Newsletter, yearly at Advent. Write to the above address.

Community History
A Continuous Miracle: the history of the Society of the Sacred Cross. Copies can be obtained from Tymawr Convent.

Community Wares
Colour photographs cards of Tymawr available at 70p each (including envelope).

Morning Prayer
7.15 am

Terce
8.45 am

Eucharist
12.00 noon

Evening Prayer
5.15 pm

Silent Corporate Prayer
7.45 pm

Compline
8.15 pm

Guest and Retreat Facilities

The community offers facilities for individual guests and small groups. There are five rooms (one twin) in the guest wing of the main house for full board. Michaelgarth, the self-catering guest house, offers facilities for individuals and groups (five singles and two twin), and also for day groups. Individuals may have private retreats with guidance from a member of the community. The community occasionally organises retreats and study days. Please make all booking enquiries by e-mail if possible.

Most convenient time to telephone

10.00 am – 11.00 am; 6.30 pm – 7.30 pm.
Please be prepared to leave a clear message on the answer-phone, and use e-mail where possible.

Office Book

Celebrating Common Prayer, with additional SSC material.

Society of the Sacred Mission

SSM

Founded 1893

Office Book
Celebrating Common Prayer

Founded in 1893 by Father Herbert Kelly, the Society is a means of uniting the devotion of ordinary people, using it in the service of the Church. Members of the Society share a common life of prayer and fellowship in a variety of educational, pastoral and community activities in England, Australia, Japan, Lesotho, and South Africa.

PROVINCE OF EUROPE

JONATHAN EWER SSM
(Provincial, assumed office February 2014)

Frank Green
Andrew Muramatsu
Edmund Wheat
Robert Stretton
Mary Hartwell
Margaret Moakes
Anthony Purvis

Novices: 2

Associates:
Paul Golightly
Elizabeth Baker
Robin Baker
Joan Golightly

Obituaries

24 March 2016 Ralph Martin, aged 85, professed 55 years, Provincial 1973-1981

Bishops Visitor
Rt Revd
Stephen Conway,
Bishop of Ely
(PROVINCE OF EUROPE)

Rt Revd
Garry Weatherill,
Bishop of Ballarat
(SOUTHERN PROVINCE)

Right Revd Dino Gabriel,
Bishop of Natal
(SOUTHERN AFRICAN PROVINCE)

Community Publication:
for
SSM newsletter of the Province of Europe, contact: The Newsletter Secretary at St Michael's Priory.

Associates and Companions (applicable to all provinces)

ASSOCIATES: are men and women who share the life and work of a priory of the Society.

COMPANIONS: are men and women who support the aims of the Society without being closely related to any of its work. They consecrate their lives in loving response to a vocation to deepen their understanding of God's will, and to persevere more devotedly in commitments already made: baptism, marriage or ordination.

Addresses

Provincial & Administrator:

St Michael's Priory, The Well, Newport Road, Willen MK15 9AA, UK
Tel: 01908 241974 Email: ssmlondon@yahoo.co.uk

St Antony's Priory, Claypath, Durham DH1 1QT, UK Tel: 0191 384 3747
Email: info@stantonyspriory.co.uk

1 Linford Lane, Milton Keynes, Bucks MK15 9DL, UK Tel: 01908 663749

Community History

Herbert H Kelly SSM, *An Idea in the Working,* SSM Press, Kelham, 1908.

Alistair Mason, *SSM: History of the Society of the Sacred Mission,* Canterbury Press, Norwich, 1993.

Ralph Martin SSM, *Towards a New Day: a monk's story,* Darton, Longman & Todd, London, 2015.

AUSTRALIAN PROVINCE

CHRISTOPHER MYERS SSM
(Provincial, assumed office November 2009)

Society of the Sacred Mission
196 East Terrace
Adelaide 5000
SOUTH AUSTRALIA

Tel: 8 8227 0452

Email: ssm.s.province@esc.net.au

David Wells
Colin Griffiths
Margaret Dewey
Steven de Kleer
Gregory Stephens
Geoff Pridham
Lynne Rokkas
Des Benfield
Joyce Bleby Lewis
Iris Trengove
Sue Bellett
Catherine Pennington
Alexis Fraser
David McDougall
Bill Dahlberg
Ryan Bennett

Obituaries

24 May 2016 Dunstan McKee, aged 81, professed 58 years, Director 1972-1982

Community Publication

Missio (newsletter of the Southern Province). Contact: The Editor at the St John's Priory address.

Southern African Province

(re-founded September 2004)

Tanki Mofana SSM

(Provincial, assumed office January 2013)

Michael Lapsley	Moiloa Mokheseng	Tefo Rachaka
William Nkomo	Mosuoe Rahuoane	
Moeketsi Khomonngoe	Karabi Thulo	*Novices*: 2

Addresses

SSM Priory, PO Box 1579, Maseru 100, Lesotho
Tel: 22315979 Fax: 22325263 Email: ssmmaseru@tlmail.co.ls

33 Elgin Road, Sybrand Park, Cape Town, South Africa, 7700
Tel: 21 696 4866 Email: michaelssm@gmail.com

Community Publication: Michael Lapsley SSM, *Redeeming the Past: my journey from Freedom Fighter to Healer,* Orbis, 20

A group of SSM brethren assembled in front of the Kelham Rood at St John the Divine, Kennington, in London, UK

Society of St Francis

SSF

Founded 1919 (USA)
1921 (UK)

Minister General
Email: clark.berg@ s-s-f.org

Minister Provincial (European Province)
Email: ministerssf@ franciscans.org.uk

European Province Website: www. franciscans.org.uk

Office Book
The Daily Office SSF (revised edition 2010)

Bishop Protector
Rt Revd
Stephen Cottrell,
Bishop of Chelmsford

Community History
Petà Dunstan
This Poor Sort
DLT, London, 1997
£19.95 + £2 p&p

European Province SSF Registered Charity: No. 236464

The Society of St Francis has diverse origins in a number of Franciscan groups which drew together during the 1930s to found one Franciscan Society. SSF in its widest definition includes First Order Brothers, First Order Sisters (CSF), Second Order Sisters (OSC) and a Third Order (TSSF). The First Order shares a common life of prayer, fraternity and a commitment to issues of justice, peace and the integrity of creation. In its larger houses, this includes accommodation for short-term guests; in the city houses, the Brothers are engaged in a variety of ministries, chaplaincies and care for the poor and marginalised. They are also available for retreat work, counselling and sharing in the task of mission in parishes and schools. They also work in Europe and have houses in the Americas, Australasia, the Pacific, and Korea.

CHRISTOPHER JOHN SSF
(Minister General, assumed office 1 July 2017)

EUROPEAN PROVINCE
BENEDICT SSF
(Minister Provincial, assumed office June 2012, re-elected 2017)
PHILIP BARTHOLOMEW SSF *(Assistant Minister)*

Amos
Angelo
Anselm
Austin
Benjamin
Christian
Christopher Martin
Cristian Michael
David
David Jardine
Donald
Edmund
Eric Michael
Giles
Hugh
James Douglas
Jason Robert
John
Joseph Emmanuel
Julian
Kentigern John
Kevin
Malcolm
Martin John
Micael Christopher
Michael Jacob
Nicholas Alan
Peter
Raymond Christian
Reginald
Robert
Samuel
Thomas Anthony
Vincent

Novices: 1 *Postulants:* 1

Obituaries

17 Jan 2016 Damian, aged 74, professed 46 years, Minister Provincial 1991-2002

Companions: Companions are individual Christians who wish to associate themselves with the Society through prayer, friendship and in seeking to live the spirit of the Gospel in the way of St Francis. For more information about becoming a Companion contact: The Secretary for Companions at Hilfield Friary.

Addresses **All email addresses are @franciscans.org.uk**

The Friary, Alnmouth, Alnwick, Northumberland NE66 3NJ
Tel: 01665 830213 Fax: 01665 830580 Email: alnmouthssf

The Master's Lodge, 58 St Peter's Street, Canterbury, Kent CT1 2BE
Tel: 01227 479364 Email: canterburyssf

St Mary-at-the-Cross, Glasshampton, Shrawley, Worcestershire WR6 6TQ Tel: 01299 896345 Fax: 01299 896083 Email: glasshamptonssf

The Friary, Hilfield, Dorchester, Dorset DT2 7BE
Tel: 01300 341345 Fax: 01300 341293 Email: hilfieldssf

25 Karnac Road, Leeds LS8 5BL Tel: 0113 226 0647 Email: leedsssf

House of the Divine Compassion, 42 Balaam St, Plaistow, London E13 8AQ Tel: 020 7476 5189 Email: plaistowssf

85 Crofton Road, Plaistow, London E13 8QT
Tel: 020 7474 5863 Email: donaldssf

St Anthony's Friary, St Anthony's Vicarage, Enslin Gardens, Newcastle upon Tyne, NE6 3SRT Tel: 0191 276 0117 Email: newcastlessf

Anglican Chaplaincy, Via San Gabriele dell'Addolorata 12, 06081 Assisi (Pg), ITALY Bookings: passf@franciscans.org,uk

Community Wares: Hilfield Friary shop has on sale 'Freeland' cards, SSF publications and books of Franciscan spirituality and theology, as well as traidcraft goods. Alnmouth and Glasshampton also have small shops selling cards.

Guest and Retreat Facilities

HILFIELD: 8 bedrooms (2 twin-bedded) for men and women and 2 self-catering houses of 6 bedrooms each for the use of families and groups. Individually-guided retreats are available on request. There are facilities for day guests and for groups of up to 40. The brothers living at Hilfield are now joined by lay men and women, including families, who together comprise the Hilfield Friary Community, an intentional Franciscan community focussing on peace, justice and the integrity of creation. The Hilfield Peace and Environment Programme is an annual programme of courses & events which shares Franciscan insights on the care of creation and reconciliation *(www.hilfieldfriary.org.uk)*. The Friary is normally closed Sun pm - Tue am.

ALNMOUTH: The Friary has 12 rooms (including 1 twin-bedded) for men or women guests. Conducted retreats are held each year and individually-guided retreats are available on request. The recently-innovated chalet is available for families and groups in particular need referred by churches and social services. The Friary is closed for 24 hours from Sunday afternoon.

GLASSHAMPTON: This has a more contemplative ethos. The guest accommodation, available to both men and women, comprises five rooms. Groups can visit for the day, but may not exceed fifteen people. The friary is closed from noon on Mondays for 24 hours and at Christmas time.

Third Order SSF
see separate entry.

Community Publications
franciscan, three times a year - annual subscription is £9.00. Write to the Subscriptions Secretary at Hilfield Friary. Books available from Hilfield Friary book shop include: *The Daily Office SSF,* £10 + £2 p&p.

PROVINCE OF THE AMERICAS

San Damiano
573 Dolores Street
San Francisco
CA 94110, USA
Tel: 415 861 1372
Fax: 415 861 7952
Email:
desmondalbanssf@cloud.com

St Francis Friary
2449 Sichel Street
Los Angeles
CA 90031, USA
Tel: 323 222 7495

Minister Provincial
Tel: 415 298 8708
Fax: 415 861 7952
Email:
desmondalbanssf@cloud.com

The Province of the Americas of SSF was founded as the Order of St Francis in 1919 by Father Claude Crookston, who took the name Father Joseph. Under his leadership the community developed, based first in Wisconsin and then on Long Island, New York. The Order originally combined a monastic spirituality with a commitment to missions and evangelizing. In 1967, the OSF friars amalgamated with SSF in the UK and became the American Province of SSF.

Our lives are structured around our times together of formal prayer and the Eucharist, which give our lives a focus. Brothers engage in a wide variety of ministries: community organizing, missions, work in parishes and institutions, counselling and spiritual direction, study, the arts, serving the sick and infirm and people with AIDS, the homeless, workers in the sex industry, political work for the rights of people who are rejected by society. We come from a wide variety of backgrounds and cultural traditions. Living with each other can be difficult, but we work hard to find common ground and to communicate honestly with each other. God takes our imperfections and, in the mystery of Christ's body, makes us whole.

DESMOND ALBAN SSF
(Minister Provincial, assumed office 19 May 2017)

Ambrose-Christobal	Leo-Anthony
Antonio Sato	Robert Hugh
Clark Berge	
Ivanildo	*Novices:* 3
Jude	

Website
www.s-s-f.org

Office Book
SSF Office Book

Obituaries

6 Sep 2015	Derek, aged 83, professed 41 years
26 Jun 2016	Dunstan, aged 93, professed 61 years

Bishop Protector
Rt Revd Jon Bruno, Bishop of Los Angeles

Guest and Retreat Facilities
None at present. San Damiano sometimes has one small guest room available.

Community Publication
Clark Berge SSF, *The Vows Book: Anglican Teaching on the Vows of Obedience, Poverty and Chastity,*
Vest Pocket Publications, Mt Sinai, NY, 2014

The Province of the Divine Compassion

SSF friars went from England to Papua New Guinea in the late 1950s and the first Australian house was established in 1964. The first New Zealand house followed in 1970. In 1981, the Pacific Province was divided into two: Australia/New Zealand and the Pacific Islands. The latter was divided again in 2008 into Papua New Guinea and the Solomon Islands. In 1993 the first Koreans joined to form the Korean Franciscan Brotherhood, initially linked by covenant with SSF. They were received as members of SSF in 2010. Reflecting the geographic diversity of the province the name was changed to Province of the Divine Compassion in 2011.

Christopher John SSF
(Minister Provincial, assumed office April 2012)
Donald Campbell SSF *(Assistant Minister)*

Alfred BoonKong	Lawrence	Stephen
Bruce-Paul	Lionel	William
Cyril	Nathan-James	
Damian Kenneth	Noel-Thomas	*Novices:* 1
Daniel	Raphael	

Obituaries
29 Oct 2015 Brian, aged 90, professed 57 years, Minister Provincial ANZ 1981-1987, Minister General 1991-1997

Guest and Retreat Facilities
There is limited accommodation for short stay guests in the Brisbane, Stroud and Korea houses. In all cases, payment is by donation. Additionally, in Korea larger numbers can be accommodated at the nearby Diocesan Retreat House managed by the Brothers.

At Stroud, the old monastery of the Community of St Clare is available for accommodation. Contact: Friends of the Old Monastery: oldmonasterystroud@gmail.com

Community Wares
Holding Crosses (Stroud & Korea);
Candles (Korea)

The Hermitage
PO Box 46
Stroud
NSW 2425
Australia
Tel: 2 4994 5372
Email: ssfstrd@bigpond.com

The Friary
PO Box 6134
Buranda
Brisbane
QLD 4102
Australia
Tel: 7 3391 3915
Email: brisbane@franciscan.org.au

Website:
www.franciscandivinecompassion.org

The Friary, 1190 Handeokbalsan-gil, Nam-myeon
Chuncheon-si,
Gangwon-do 24468
Republic of Korea
Tel: 33 263 4662
Fax: 33 263 4048
Email:
ssfk1993@gmail.com

Website:
www.francis.or.kr

The community friary in Hamilton New Zealand was closed in 2016 and the remaining brother there is now living in a retirement village.

Office Book
The Daily Office SSF

Community Publication
Australia: *Franciscan Angles, (3 per year)*
Korea: *newsletter* in Korean (quarterly)
These are available on the relevant websites or by email. To subscribe to printed copies, please contact the Brisbane or Korea address as appropriate. In all cases, subscription is by donation.

Bishops Protector
Rt Revd John Stead, Bishop of Willochra *(Bishop Protector)*
Rt Revd Jim White, Assistant Bishop of Auckland *(Deputy Protector for New Zealand)*
Rt Revd Peter Lee, Bishop of Seoul *(Deputy Protector for Korea)*

Papua New Guinea Province

Oswald Dumbari SSF
(Minister Provincial, assumed office July 2012)

Anthony Kambuwa
Charles Iada
Clement Vulum
Collin Velei
Dominic Ombeda
Jerry Ross
Laurence Hauje
Nathaniel Gari
Sebastian Duna
Wallace Yovero
Worrick Marako
Novices: 4

Bishop Protector
Most Revd Clyde Mervin Igara, Archbishop of Papua New Guinea

Addresses in PNG
Saint Mary of the Angels Friary, Haruro, PO Box 78, Popondetta 241, Oro Province Tel: 329 7060 Email: ssfpngfrans@gmail.com
Saint Francis Friary, Koki, PO Box 1103, Port Moresby, NCD Tel & fax: 320 1499
Martyrs' House, PO Box 35, Popondetta, Oro Province Tel & fax: 3297 491 *(school)*
Ukaka Friary, PO Box 784, Alotau, Milne Bay Province

Province of the Solomon Islands

Samson Siho SSF
(Minister, assumed office 2015)

Amos Helo
Athanasius Faifu
Andrew Laukiara
Benjamin Tabugau
Christom Hou
Clifton Henry
Elliot Faga
Ellison Hoasipepe
Ellison Sero
Francis Ngofia
Gilford Maeta'a
Harry Belavalu
Hilton Togara
Hubert Tavato
John Kogudi
John Manedika
Jonah Manufakangasia
Jonas Balunga
Lent Fugui
Luke Manitara
Martin Aveva
Martin Tawea
Matthew Sikoboki
Patrick Paoni
Paul Tula
Rex Marau
Samson Amoni
Samson Siho
Selwyn Tione
Stephen Watson Hovu
Steven Siosi Amao
Thomas Peleba
Thompson Waketaku
Novices: 27

Obituaries

12 Jan 2017 Commins Romano, aged 68, professed 44 years

Bishop Protector: Rt Revd Samson Sahu, Bishop of Malaita

Addresses in the Solomon Islands

Patteson House, PO Box 519, Honiara, Guadalcanal Tel: 22386
Emails: honiarassf.bros@gmail.com ssffriars.solomons@gmail.com

Saint Francis Friary, PO Box 7, Auki, Malaita Province
Tel: 40054

Colin Baura Friary, PO Box 7, Busa, Auki, Malaita Province

St Bonaventure Friary, Kohimarama Theological College, PO Box 519, Honiara, Guadalcanal

La Verna Friary, Hautambu, PO Box 519, Honiara, Guadalcanal

Little Portion, Hautambu, PO Box 519, Honiara, Guadalcanal

Michael Davis Friary, PO Box 519, Honiara, Guadalcanal

Old Brothers' House, Hautambu, PO Box 519, Honiara, Guadalcanal

San Damiano Friary, Diocese of Hanuato'o, Kira Kira, Makira Ulawa Province

Holy Martyrs Friary, Luisalo, PO Box 50, Lata, Temotu Province

Society of St John the Divine

SSJD

Founded 1887

282 Alexandra Road
Pelham
Pietermaritzburg
SOUTH AFRICA
Tel: 033 346 1585

Emails:
maryevelyncoffee@gmail.com

hil64337@gmail.com

Angelus & Morning Prayer
8.15 am
followed by Midday Office

On Saints' Days, Eucharist
4.45 pm
followed by Angelus & Evening Prayer

Compline
7.30 pm

Prayer Time taken privately

The Society has never been a large community, with just sixty professions over a century, and has always worked in Natal. Originally the community ran schools and orphanages. In 1994, after the death of the older Sisters, the four of us who remained moved to a house that was more central in Durban.

We moved to Pennington in 2003 and then in 2015 to Pietermaritzburg. Our outside involvement includes being on the Board of Governors of our school, St John's Diocesan School for Girls in Pietermaritzburg, and all our Associates, Friends and Oblates worldwide.

Sister Mary Evelyn SSJD
Sister Sophia SSJD
Sister Hilary SSJD

Obituaries

4 Mar 2016 Sister Margaret Anne, aged 84, professed 40 years, Revd Mother 1994-99

Oblates and Associates

These are people who are linked with us and support us in prayer.

Oblates: There is one, non-resident, and she renews her oblation annually.

Associates: There are over a hundred, some overseas. They have a Rule of Life and renew their promises annually.

Friends: They have a Rule of Life and like the Associates and Oblates meet with the Sisters twice a year.

Community Publication

One newsletter is sent out each year to Oblates, Associates and Friends in Advent.

Community History and books

Sister Margaret Anne SSJD, *What the World Counts Weakness,* privately published 1987 (now out of print).

Sister Margaret Anne SSJD, *They Even Brought Babies,* privately published.

Bishop Visitor

Rt Revd Rubin Phillip

Office Book

An Anglican Prayer Book 1989 (South African) for Morning & Evening Prayer.

Our own SSJD book for Midday Office & Compline.

Society of St John the Evangelist (UK)

SSJE

Founded 1866

Email: superior@ ssje.org.uk

A Registered Charity.

The Society of Saint John the Evangelist is the oldest of the Anglican orders for men, founded at Cowley in Oxford in 1866 by Father Richard Meux Benson. From it grew the North American Congregation and we were also involved in the founding of several other Communities around the world both for men and women. SSJE worked as a Missionary Order in several countries, most notably India and South Africa. In 2012 the English Congregation closed its last House in London and went into retirement where they continue to live out their vows.

FATHER PETER HUCKLE SSJE
(Superior, assumed office 7 March 2002)
Father Peter Palmer
Brother James Simon

The Fellowship of St John: Email: superior@ssje.org.uk
Bishop Visitor: Rt Revd Dominic Walker OGS

Society of St John the Evangelist (North American Congregation)

SSJE

Founded 1866

**The Monastery
980 Memorial Drive
Cambridge
MA 02138
USA
Tel: 617 876 3037**

Email: monastery @ssje.org

The Society of St John the Evangelist was founded in the parish of Cowley in Oxford, England, by Richard Meux Benson in 1866. A branch house was established in Boston in 1870. The brothers of the N. American Congregation live at the monastery in Cambridge, Massachusetts, near Harvard Square, and at Emery House, a rural retreat sanctuary in West Newbury, Massachusetts. They gather throughout the day to pray the Daily Office, and live under a modern Rule of Life, adopted in 1997, which is available online at www.ssje.org. At profession, brothers take vows of poverty, celibacy and obedience.

SSJE's guesthouses offer hospitality to many. Young adults (ordinarily 21-34) may serve for a year as Monastic Interns. Guests may come individually or in groups for times of silent reflection and retreat. SSJE brothers lead retreats and programs in their own houses and in parishes and dioceses throughout North America. SSJE brothers also serve as preachers, teachers, spiritual directors and confessors. SSJE's ministry occasionally extends overseas to Europe, Israel/Palestine and Africa. Nearer to home, they are engaged in part-time ministries with students and young adults, homeless people, deaf people, Asian-Americans, and people in recovery (12-step programs).

The Brothers' web ministry (www.ssje.org) is an important resource for people all over the world. It includes: Brother Give Us A Word, a daily email of hope and inspiration; AdventWord, an Advent Calendar using social media; sermons preached by the Brothers; annual Lenten study material; and photographs of the Monastery.

Morning Prayer
6.00 am

Eucharist
7.45 am

Midday Prayer
12.30 pm

Evening Prayer
6.00 pm

Compline
8.30 pm

(The schedule varies slightly during the week. The complete schedule can be found on the community's website.)

Office Book
BCP of ECUSA, and the Book of Alternate Services of the Anglican Church of Canada

Website
www.ssje.org

Other address:
Emery House
21 Emery Lane
West Newbury
MA 01985
USA
Tel: 978 462 7940

Bishop Visitor
Rt Revd
Frank T. Griswold, III

BROTHER JAMES KOESTER SSJE
(*Superior, assumed office 2016*)

David Allen
John Oyama *(in Japan)*
Jonathan Maury
David Vryhof
Curtis Almquist
Mark Brown
Geoffrey Tristram
Robert L'Esperance
Luke Ditewig
Jim Woodrum
Nicholas Bartoli
Keith Nelson

Obituaries

26 Aug 2015 Eldridge Pendleton, aged 75, professed 26 years
11 Jan 2016 Bernard Russell, aged 93, professed 48 years
23 Sep 2016 John Goldring, aged 81, professed 37 years

Associates

The Fellowship of Saint John is composed of men and women throughout the world who desire to live their Christian life in special association with the Society of Saint John the Evangelist. They have a vital interest in the life and work of the community and support its life and ministries with their prayers, encouragement and gifts. The brothers of the Society welcome members of the Fellowship as partners in the gospel life, and pray for them by name during the Daily Office, following a regular cycle. Together they form an extended family, a company of friends abiding in Christ and seeking to bear a united witness to him as "the Way, the Truth and the Life", following the example of the beloved Disciple. For further information, or to join the Fellowship, visit the Society's website: www.ssje.org.

Community History

Eldridge Pendleton, *On the Kingdom: The life of Charles Chapman Grafton, Society of Saint John the Evangelist*, SSJE, 2014.

Community Publication: *Cowley*: a quarterly newsletter. Available online (www.ssje.org) or in printed form (contact monastery@ssje.org). For a subscription, write to SSJE at the Cambridge, Massachusetts, address. The suggested donation is US$20 annually.

Guest and Retreat Facilities

MONASTERY GUESTHOUSE in Cambridge, MA - 16 rooms.

EMERY HOUSE in West Newbury, MA - 6 hermitages, 3 rooms in main house.

At both houses: US$100 per night standard - US$50 for students; $125 individually guided - $65 for students; $135 program retreats - $65 for students (closed in August).

Society of St Margaret

(Duxbury)

SSM

Founded 1855
(US Convent founded 1873)

St Margaret's Convent
50 Harden Hill Road
PO Box C
Duxbury
MA 0233-0605
USA
Tel: 781 934 9477

Email: sisters@ssmbos.org

Website
www.ssmbos.org

Morning Prayer
6.00 am

Eucharist 7.30 am

Noon Office
12 noon

Evening Prayer
5.00 pm

Compline 7.30 pm

Office Book
BCP
of ECUSA

The Society of St Margaret is an Episcopal Religious Order of mission-focused sisters living an ancient tradition with a modern outlook. Our lives as Sisters are guided by the principle, "Love first, Love midst, Love last." We take vows of poverty, celibate chastity, and obedience; listening for the voice of God in all circumstances.

Our mission of hospitality calls us to welcome people to our houses for times of refreshment and renewal. Our mission of service calls us to move out beyond our dwelling places to serve those in need, to go where God leads and to share Christ's light. We strive to live a balanced life of active work and contemplative prayer, and are committed to partner with those who share our passion for a world of justice, mercy and peace.

The central work of the community is worship and prayer and the Eucharist provides the pattern for our daily lives. As Jesus took bread, blessed and broke it, so our lives are taken, blessed, broken, and given through our varied ministries. As we work with children, care for the elderly, and do parish work, we seek always to live as Christ's hands and heart in this world.

Sister Adele Marie SSM *(priest)*
(Mother Superior, assumed office March 2011)
Sister Carolyn SSM *(Assistant Superior)*

Sr Catherine Louise *(priest)*
Sister Marjorie Raphael
Sister Emily Louise
Sister Gloria
Sister Ann
Sister Claire Marie
Sister Mary Gabriel
Sister Adele
Sister Julian
Sister Christine
Sister Marie Thérèse
Sister Brigid
Sister Promise
Sister Sarah Margaret *(priest)*
Sister Kristina Frances
Sister Kethia

Associates

Associates of one Convent of the Society of St Margaret are Associates of all. They have a common Rule, which is flexible to circumstances. They include men and women, lay and ordained. No Associate of the Society may be an Associate of any other community.

Bishop Visitor: Rt Rev Alan Gates, Bp of Massachusetts.

Addresses of other houses:
Sisters of St Margaret, 375 Mount Vernon Street, Apt 511, Boston, MA 02125, USA
Tel: 617 533 7742
Email: srchristinessm@gmail.com

St Margaret's Convent, Port-au-Prince, HAITI
Mailing address: **St Margaret's Convent, Port-au-Prince, c/o Agape Flights, Inc., 100 Airport Avenue, Venice, FL 34285-3901, USA**
Tel: 011 509 3448 2609 Email: marietheresessm@yahoo.com

Neale House, 50 Fulton Street #2A, New York, NY 10038-1800, USA
Tel: 646 692 6621 Email: annwhitaker1942@gmail.com

Community Publication
Historic: *St Margaret's Quarterly*. Historical issues available free on our website or by mail. For information, contact convent@ssmbos.org.
Current: *St Margaret's Missive.* In addition, current Community news is shared via e-mail and Social Media. Those needing hard copies should contact us at convent@ssmbos.org.

Community Wares: Notecards: set of 12 for $26.00 US, plus $4 US for shipping and handling. Our website, www.ssmbos.org, has more information.

Community History Sister Catherine Louise SSM, *The House of my Pilgrimage: a History of the American House of the Society of Saint Margaret,* privately published, 1973; *The Planting of the Lord: The History of the Society of Saint Margaret in England, Scotland & the USA;* privately published, 1995. Contact convent@ssmbos.org to order. $6 US each, plus $4 US shipping and handling.

Guest and Retreat Facilities
In Duxbury, Massachusetts, guest facilities are available for small groups and individuals in two Guesthouses. The Farmhouse has 5 bedrooms and St. Marina's has 9 bedrooms: some bedrooms are double-bedded. Cost for individuals is $80.00 US per night, including meals. Group rates vary. Please contact convent@ssmbos.org for more information.

Society of St Margaret

(Hackney)

SSM

Founded 1855
(St Saviour's Priory 1866)

Website: www.stsaviourspriory.org.uk

St Saviour's Priory is one of the autonomous Houses which constitute the Society of St Margaret founded by John Mason Neale. Exploring contemporary ways of living the Religious life, the community seeks, through a balance of prayer and ministry, to respond to some of the needs that arise amongst the marginalised in East London. The Office is four-fold and the Eucharist is offered daily. The Sisters' outreach to the local community includes: working as staff members (lay or ordained) in various parishes; supporting issues of justice and racial equality; supporting the gay community; Sunday Stall and Drop in Centre; Dunloe Centre for the homeless and alcoholics; complementary therapy; individual spiritual direction and retreats; dance workshops; art work and design. The Sisters also share their community building and resources of worship and space with individuals and groups.

St Saviour's Priory
18 Queensbridge Road
London E2 8NS
UK
Tel: 020 7739 9976
Email: ssmpriory@aol.com

Leader of the community
020 7613 1464

Guest Bookings
020 7739 6775
Fax: 020 7739 1248

(Sisters are not available on Mondays)

Morning Prayer
7.15 am
(7.30 am Sun)
followed by
Eucharist
(12.15 pm on major feasts)

Midday Office
12.45 pm

Evening Prayer
5.00 pm

Night Prayer
8.30 pm

Office Book
Celebrating Common Prayer

Registered Charity
No 230927

THE REVD SISTER JUDITH BLACKBURN SSM *(priest)*
(Leader of the Community, assumed office 26 February 2014)
SISTER ANNA HUSTON & SISTER ELIZABETH CRAWFORD
(Assistant Leaders)

Sister June Atkinson
Sister Pauline (Mary) Hardcastle
Sister Enid Margaret Jealous
Sister Moira Jones
The Revd Sister Helen Loder SSM *(priest)*
Sister Pamela Radford

Obituaries

3 Dec 2015 Sister Frances (Claire) Carter, aged 89, professed 60 years

Associates and Friends

ASSOCIATES make a long term commitment to the Society of St Margaret, following a Rule of Life and helping the Community where possible. An Associate of one SSM house is an Associate of all the houses. There are regular quiet days for Associates who are kept in touch with community developments.

FRIENDS OF ST SAVIOUR'S PRIORY commit themselves to a year of mutual support and friendship and are invited to regular events throughout the year.

Community Publication: *The Orient*, yearly. Write to The Orient Secretary at St Saviour's Priory. Brochures about the Community are available at any time on request.

Community Wares

Cards, books and religious items for sale.

Community History

Memories of a Sister of S. Saviour's Priory, Mowbray, 1904.

A Hundred Years in Haggerston, published by St Saviour's Priory, 1966.

Sister Catherine Louise SSM, *The Planting of the Lord: The History of the Society of Saint Margaret in England, Scotland & the USA;* privately published, 1995.

Guest and Retreat Facilities

Six single rooms for individual guests. Excellent facilities for non-residential group meetings.

Most convenient time to telephone

10.30 am - 1.00 pm (Not Mondays).

Bishop Visitor

Rt Revd Jonathan Clark, Bishop of Croydon

Society of St Margaret

(Chiswick)

SSM

Founded 1855

St Mary's Convent & Nursing Home
Burlington Lane
Chiswick
London W4 2QE, UK
Tel: 020 8 994 4641
Fax: 020 8995 9697

Email: stmarysnh @gmail.com

Matins 8.00 am

Eucharist 10.00 am (9.00 am Tue & Sat)

Midday Office & Litany of the Holy Name 12.15 pm

Vespers 4.45 pm

Compline 6.15 pm

Office Book
'A Community Office' printed for St Margaret's Convent, East Grinstead.

Registered Charity: No. 231926

The Convent at Chiswick is one of the autonomous Convents that constitute the Society of St Margaret, founded by John Mason Neale. The Sisters' work is the worship of God, expressed in their life of prayer and service. At Chiswick they care for elderly people in a nursing home and have guests. There is a semi-autonomous house and a branch house in Sri Lanka. There are two Sisters in retirement flats in Uckfield who offer intercessory prayer, spiritual direction, pastoral support and other involvement in the life of the town and parish.

MOTHER JENNIFER ANNE SSM
(Mother Superior, assumed office 2 March 2015)
SISTER MARY CLARE SSM *(Assistant Superior)*
Sister Raphael Mary
Sister Rita Margaret
Sister Francis Anne
Sister Cynthia Clare
Sister Lucy
Sister Barbara
Sister Mary Paul
Sister Sarah

Associates: Associates observe a simple Rule, share in the life of prayer and dedication of the community, and are welcomed at all SSM convents.

Community Publication: The newsletter of St Margaret's Convent and St. Mary's Nursing Home is sent out if requested.

Community History
Sister Catherine Louise SSM, *The Planting of the Lord: The History of the Society of Saint Margaret in England, Scotland & the USA;* privately published, 1995.

Pamela Myers & Sheila White, *A Legacy of Care: St Mary's Convent and Nursing Home, Chiswick, 1896 to 2010,* St Mary's Convent, Chiswick, 2010.

Doing the Impossible: a short sketch of St Margaret's Convent, East Grinstead 1855-1980, privately published, 1984. Postscript 2000.

Most convenient time to telephone: 10am - 5pm.

Bishop Visitor
Rt Revd Dr Martin Warner, Bishop of Chichester

St Margaret's Convent
157 St Michael's Road
Polwatte
Colombo 3
SRI LANKA

Bishop Visitor
Rt Revd Dhiloraj Canagasaby, Bishop of Colombo

SEMI-AUTONOMOUS HOUSES OVERSEAS

The Sisters run a Retreat House, a Hostel for young women, a Home for elderly people, and are involved in parish work.

SISTER CHANDRANI SSM
(Sister Superior, assumed office 2006)
Sister Lucy Agnes
Sister Mary Christine

Novices: 1

Other address:
St John's Home, 133 Galle Rd, Moratuwa, SRI LANKA

Society of St Margaret

(Walsingham)

SSM

Founded 1855
(Walsingham Priory founded 1955)

The Priory of Our Lady
Bridewell Street
Walsingham
Norfolk
NR22 6ED
UK

Tel: 01328 820340 (Sisters & guests)

Tel: 01328 821647 (Admin)

Website:
www.ssmwalsingham.moonfruit.com

In January 1994, the Priory of Our Lady at Walsingham reverted to being an autonomous house of the Society of St Margaret. The Sisters are a Traditional Community whose daily life is centred on the Eucharist and the daily Office, from which flows their growing involvement in the ministry of healing, and reconciliation in the Shrine, the local parishes and the wider Church. They welcome guests for short periods of rest, relaxation and retreat, and are available to pilgrims and visitors. They also work in the local CofE Primary School, the Education Department, and Welcome Centre of the Shrine.

SISTER MARY ANGELA SSM
(Sister Administrator, appointed March 2015)
Sister Carol Elizabeth

Sister Mary Teresa
(St Mary's Convent and Nursing Home, Burlington Lane, Chiswick, London W4 2QE, UK)

Sister Alma Mary
(Courtenay House Care Home, Tittleshall, Norfolk PE32 2PF, UK)

Sister Columba
(St Margaret of Scotland House, 8 Cattofield, Aberdeen, AB25 3QL, UK)

Emails:
sisterangela@prioryofourlady.co.uk *(administration)*
bursar@prioryofourlady.co.uk *(bursar)*
Guests@prioryofourlady.co.uk

Bishop Visitor: Rt Revd Peter Wheatley

Readings & Morning Prayer 7.00 am

Mass 9.30 am
(Then Exposition of the Blessed Sacrament until 10.30 am Thu)

Exposition
10.30 am - 12 noon
(except Sun & Thu)

Midday Prayer
12.45 pm

Evening Prayer
5.00 pm

Night Prayer 8.00 pm
(7.30 pm Sun, Tue & Sat)

Office Book
The Divine Office

Associates
There are Associates, and Affiliated Parishes and Groups.

Community Publication
Newsletter bi-annually (Spring and Advent).

Community History & Books
Sister Catherine Louise SSM, *The Planting of the Lord: The History of the Society of Saint Margaret in England, Scotland & the USA;* privately published, 1995.
Sister Mary Angela SSM, *John Mason Neale and Mary*, CSWG Press, Crawley Down, RH10 4LH, UK, 2016.

Community Wares
Cards (re-cycled) and embroidered; books; Religious objects (statues, pictures, rosary purses etc).

Guest and Retreat Facilities: St Margaret's Cottage, (self-catering) for women and men, families and small groups. One single room (bed sit, en suite) on the ground floor, suitable for a retreatant, and three twin rooms upstairs.

Most convenient time to telephone: 10.30 am - 12.30 pm; 2.30 pm - 4.30 pm; 6.30 pm - 8.30 pm.

Registered Charity: No. 25515

Society of St Paul

SSP

Founded 1958

2567 Second Avenue
Unit 504
San Diego
CA 92103-6397
USA
Tel: 619 794 2095
Email: anbssp@societyofstpaul.com

Bishop Visitor
Rt Revd
James R Mathes,
Bishop of San Diego

The Society of St Paul began in Gresham, Oregon in 1958. Early ministry included nursing homes, a school, and commissary work in the Mid-East and Africa. In 1959, SSP was the first community for men to be recognized by the canons of ECUSA. The brothers live a life of prayer and are dedicated to works of mercy, charity and evangelism. In 1976, the order moved to Palm Desert, California, providing a retreat and conference center until 1996. In 2001, the brothers moved to St Paul's Cathedral in San Diego. In particular, we are involved at St Paul's Senior Homes and Services, the Uptown Faith Community Services, Inc., Dorcas House, a foster home for children whose parents are in prison in Tijuana, Mexico, and St Paul's Cathedral ministries.

THE REVD CANON BARNABAS HUNT SSP
(*Rector, assumed office 1989*)
THE REVD CANON ANDREW RANK SSP (*Associate Rector*)

Fellowship of St Paul
The Fellowship of St Paul, our extended family, is an association of Friends, Associates and Companions of the Society of St Paul, who live a Rule of Life centered on the Glory of God.

Society of the Sisters of Bethany

SSB

Founded 1866

7 Nelson Road
Southsea
Hampshire
PO5 2AR
UK
Tel: 02392 833498
Email: ssb@ sistersofbethany. org.uk

Website: www. sistersofbethany. org.uk

Mattins 7.00 am

Mass 7.45 am (8.00 am Sun; 9.30 am Wed & alternate Sats)

Terce 9.15 am

Midday Office 12 noon

Vespers 5.00 pm

Compline 8.00 pm

Office Book
Anglican Office book with adaptations

Bishop Visitor
Rt Revd Trevor Willmott, Bishop of Dover

Registered Charity:
No. 226582

The Sisters of Bethany (SSB) are the founding community of a wider Bethany family that includes Associates, Oblates and the Order of Companions of Martha and Mary (OCMM):

Associates are a body of close friends who live in their own homes and accept a simple Rule of Life.

Oblates are a recent development (2014), who also live in their own homes. They have adopted the Rule of Life used by the Sisters, modified appropriately to their own circumstances. Oblates and Sisters live by a spirituality derived from the Salesian Rule of the Visitation Order. They share times of study and ongoing formation.

The Sisters' online ministry using Facebook (**facebook.com@sisters.ofbethany**) engages with nearly 8,500 people, meeting them where they are and helping them see God in the 'everyday'. Each member of the Bethany family makes the offering of herself in the hidden life of prayer, praying daily for the unity of Christians and, by prayer and activity, seeking to share in Christ's mission reconciling the divided Churches of Christendom and the whole world.

The OCMM is a new monastic order (2010). The Sisters live in community under a Benedictine-inspired Rule and are linked to SSB by close ties of friendship, shared activity and prayer intentions under the patronage of the household of Bethany. **OCMM: St Joseph's House of Prayer, New Vicarage, Church Lane, Tunstall, Lancashire LA6 2RQ. Tel: 03330 119563**
Website: www.companionsmarthamary.org
Email: sistersocmm@gmail.com

MOTHER RITA-ELIZABETH SSB
(Reverend Mother, assumed office 22 October 2009)
SISTER MARY JOY SSB *(Assistant Superior)*

Sister Ruth Etheldreda	Sister Joanna Elizabeth
Sister Ann Patricia	Sister Elizabeth Pio
Sister Gwenyth	*Novices:* 1

Obituaries
22 Apr 2016 — Sister Katherine Maryel, aged 104, professed 63 years

Associates, Oblates, contacts
Associates' Sister: Sister Gwenyth
Oblates' Sister: Sister Elizabeth Pio
Companions of Martha & Mary: Amma Judith OCMM

Community Wares: Cards.

Community Publication: Associates' magazine, July and December

Guest and Retreat Facilities: Six guest rooms (one twin-bedded). Individual retreatants can be accommodated. Closed at Christmas.

Most convenient time to telephone: 9.30 - 11.45 am, 1 - 4 pm, 6 - 7.30 pm

Some other Communities

Asia

Devasevikaramaya
31 Kandy Road, Kurunegala, Sri Lanka Tel: 0094 372 221803
An order for women, founded by the first Bishop of Kurunegala, Rt Revd Lakdasa de Mel, in the 1950s.

The Order of Women, Church of South India
18, CSI Women's House, Infantry Road, Bengaluru, Karnataka 560001, India

Soon after the inauguration of the CSI in 1948, a Religious Order for women was organized under the initiative and leadership of Sister Carol Graham, a deaconess in the Anglican Church before 1948. The Order has both active and associate members. The former take a vow of celibacy, observe a rule of life and are engaged in some form of full-time Christian service. The Order is a member of the Diakonia World Federation. The Sisters are dispersed among the twenty-one dioceses of the CSI.

Europe

Society of the Franciscan Servants of Jesus and Mary (FSJM)
Posbury St Francis, Crediton, Devon, EX17 3QG, UK

Society of Our Lady of the Isles (SOLI)
Shetland Isles, UK
https://sites.google.com/site/societyofourladyoftheisles/

North America and the Caribbean

Order of the Teachers of the Children of God (OTCG)
5870 East 14th Street, Tucson, AZ 85711, USA

Society of Our Lady St Mary (SLSM)
Bethany Place, PO Box 762, Digby, Nova Scotia, BOV 1AO, Canada

Single Consecrated Life

One of the earliest ways of living the Religious life is for single people to take a vow of consecrated celibacy and to live in their own homes. This ancient form of commitment is also a contemporary one with people once again embracing this form of Religious life. Some may have an active ministry, others follow a contemplative lifestyle, some are solitaries, and others are widows or widowers.

In 2002, the Advisory Council (for Religious Communities in the Church of England) set up a Personal Vows group in response to enquiries from bishops and others to advise those who wish to take a vow of consecrated celibacy. In 2011 the Advisory Council approved a constitution for the network, and a leadership team was elected which now provides support for those who have professed this vow and arranges gatherings. In the Roman Catholic Church, this form of living the consecrated life was affirmed by Vatican II, which re-established the Order of Consecrated Virgins (OCV) and now an order of Widows is also emerging.

People exploring this call should be single, widowed, widowered or divorced, mature Christians (men or women) already committed to a life of prayer and willing to undertake a period of discernment before taking a temporary vow which may precede a life vow. An appropriate spiritual director and support from association with a Religious Community or through the Single Consecrated Life network is important to ensure adequate formation. We also have a group of Friends who support us in prayer.

The vow is received by a person's bishop. The bishop (or their appointee) becomes the 'guardian of the vow' and the act of consecration is registered with SCL for the Advisory Council.

BEVERLEY SMITH, CATHERINE WOOD,
HAZEL ADAMSON, SUE HARTLEY, *one vacancy*
(Group leadership of Deans)

Persons in Life Vows: 34
Persons in First Vows: 5
Seekers: 14

For further information contact:

Sue Hartley SCL,
272 New North Road, Ilford IG6 3BT, UK
Email: suemhartley@btinternet.com

Website: http://singleconsecratedlife-anglican.org.uk

Directory of dispersed celibate communities

In this section are communities that from their foundation have lived principally as dispersed communities. In other words, their members do not necessarily live a common life in community, although they do come together for chapter meetings and other occasions each year.

Like traditional communities, they do take vows that include celibacy.

Aspects of the life ... liturgy

SSM sisters in Duxbury

Oratory of the Good Shepherd

OGS

Founded 1913

Website
www.ogs.net

Bishop Visitor
Rt Revd Jack Nicholls

The Oratory of the Good Shepherd is a society of priests and laymen founded at Cambridge (UK), which now has provinces in North America, Australia, Southern Africa and Europe. Oratorians are bound together by a common Rule and discipline; members do not generally live together in community. The brethren are grouped in 'colleges' and meet regularly for prayer and support, and each province meets annually for retreat and chapter. Every three years, the General Chapter meets, presided over by the Superior of the whole Oratory, whose responsibility is to maintain the unity of the provinces.

Consecration of life in the Oratory has the twin purpose of fostering the individual brother's personal search for God in union with his brethren, and as a sign of the Kingdom. So through the apostolic work of the brethren, the Oratory seeks to make a contribution to the life and witness of the whole Church.

In common with traditional communities, the Oratory requires celibacy. Brothers are accountable to their brethren for their spending and are expected to live simply and with generosity. The ideal spiritual pattern includes daily Eucharist, Offices, and an hour of prayer. Study is also regarded as important in the life. During the time of probation which is for two years, the new brother is cared for and nurtured in the Oratory life by another brother of his College. The brother may then, with the consent of the province, make his first profession, which is renewed annually for at least five years, though with the hope of intention and perseverance for life. After five years, profession can be made for a longer period, and after ten years a brother may, with the consent of the whole Oratory, make his profession for life.

Companions and Associates

The Oratory has an extended family of Companions, with their own rule of life, and Associates. Companionship is open to men and women, lay or ordained, married or single.

Community History

George Tibbatts, *The Oratory of the Good Shepherd: The First Seventy-five Years,* The Almoner OGS, Windsor, 1988.

Obituaries

10 Jun 2016 Trevor Bulled, aged 67, professed 31 years
7 Feb 2017 John Salt, aged 75, professed 35 years, Bishop of St Helena 1999-2011

PETER HIBBERT OGS
(*Superior, assumed office August 2011*)
2 Blossom Road, Erdington, Birmingham, B24 0UD, UK
Tel: 0121 382 7286

The Community in Australia

KEITH DEAN-JONES OGS
(Provincial, assumed office 2011)
PO Box 377, Bundaberg, Queensland 4670, AUSTRALIA
Tel: (0) 26552 1310 Email: kdean-jones@ogs.net

Michael Boyle
Robert Braun
Michael Chiplin
Barry Greaves
Charles Helms
Ronald Henderson
Roger Kelly
Kenneth Mason
Kyle Penhaligon
Geoffrey Tisdall
Lindsay Urwin
Probationers: 1

The Community in North America

PHILIP HOBSON OGS
(Provincial, assumed office August 2005)
151 Glenlake Avenue, Toronto, Ontario, M6P 1E8, CANADA
Tel: (0) 416 604 4883 Email: phobson@ogs.net

David Brinton
Gregory Bufkin
William Derby
Carlson Gerdau
Michael Moyer
Bruce Myers
Walter Raymond
Edward Simonton
Probationers: 1

The Community in southern Africa

JABULANI NGIDI OGS
(Provincial, assumed office 2013)
16660 Luganda Road, Luganda, PO Box 846, Pinetown 3609, SOUTH AFRICA
Tel: +27 (0) 31-7060255 Email: jnigidi@ogs.net

James Mvuba
Thanda Ngcobo
Douglas Price
Barry Roberts
Thami Shange
Simphiwe Shange
Probationers: 0

The Community in Europe

DOMINIC WALKER OGS
(Provincial, assumed office July 2016)
2 St Vincent's Drive, Monmouth, NP25 5DS,UK
Tel: 01600 772151 Email: dwalker@ogs.net

Peter Baldwin
Michael Bartlett
Michael Bullock
Malcolm Crook
Peter Ford
Nicholas Gandy
David Johnson
Brian Lee
Christopher Powell
Peter Walker
Probationers: 2

Directory of acknowledged Communities

In this section are communities that are 'acknowledged' by the Church as living out a valid Christian witness, but whose members do not all take traditional Religious vows. Some communities expect their members to remain single whilst others may include members who are married: some have both members who remain celibate and those who do not. The specific vows they take therefore will vary according to their own particular Rule. However, communities in this section have an Episcopal Visitor or Protector. Some are linked to communities listed in section 1, others were founded without ties to traditional celibate orders. This section also includes some ashrams in dioceses in Asia.

In the Episcopal Church of the USA, these communities are referred to in the canons as 'Religious communities' - as distinct from those in section 1 of this *Year Book*, which are referred to as 'Religious orders'. However, this distinction is not used in other parts of the Anglican Communion where 'communities' is also used for those who take traditional vows.

Brotherhood of Saint Gregory

BSG

Founded 1969

Brotherhood of Saint Gregory
305 West Lafayette Avenue
Baltimore
MD 21217-3627
USA

Email:
Servant@ gregorians.org

Website
www. gregorians.org

We are always contactable by email or via our website.

Office Book
The Book of Common Prayer (1979)

The Brotherhood of Saint Gregory was founded on Holy Cross Day 1969, by Richard Thomas Biernacki, after consultation with many Episcopal and Roman Catholic Religious. The first brothers made their profession of vows in the chapel of the New York monastery of the Sisters of the Visitation (RC). Later that year, Bishop Horace Donegan of New York recognized the Brotherhood as a Religious Community of the Episcopal Church.

The community is open to clergy and laity, without regard to marital status. Gregorian Friars follow a common Rule, living individually, in small groups, or with their families, supporting themselves and the community through secular or church-related employment.

The Rule requires the Holy Eucharist, the four Offices of the Book of Common Prayer, meditation, theological study, Embertide reports, the tithe, and participation in Annual Convocation and Chapter.

The Postulancy program takes one year, the Novitiate two years, after which a novice may make First Profession of Annual Vows. Members are eligible for Life Profession after five years in Annual Vows.

Gregorian Friars minister in parishes as liturgists, musicians, clergy, artists, visitors to the sick, administrators, sextons, and teachers. A number serve the diocesan and national church. For those in secular work the 'servant theme' continues, and many are teachers, nurses, or administrators, sharing the common goal of the consecration of each brother's lifetime through prayer and service.

Community Publications
The Brotherhood produces a quarterly online newsletter titled *The Servant.*

Community Wares
There are a number of Brotherhood publications - please visit our website for further details.

Community History
Karekin Madteos Yarian BSG, *In Love and Service Bound: The First 40 years of the Brotherhood of Saint Gregory,* BSG, 2009.

Bishop Visitor
Rt Revd Rodney R Michel,
assisting Bishop of Pennsylvania

BROTHER RICHARD THOMAS BIERNACKI, BSG
(Minister General and founder, assumed office 14 September 1969)

The polity of the community includes seven regional Ministers Provincial as members of a leadership council.

Brother James Teets
Brother Luke Antony Nowicki
Brother William Francis Jones
Brother Tobias Stanislas Haller *(priest)*
Brother Edward Munro *(deacon)*
Brother Donovan Aidan Bowley
Brother Christopher Stephen Jenks
Brother Ciarán Anthony DellaFera
Brother Richard John Lorino
Brother Ronald Augustine Fox
Brother Maurice John Grove
Brother Virgilio Fortuna *(deacon)*
Brother Gordon John Stanley *(deacon)*
Brother Karekin Madteos Yarian
Brother William David Everett
Brother Thomas Bushnell
Brother Robert James McLaughlin
Brother Peter Budde
Brother John Henry Ernestine
Brother Francis Sebastian Medina
Brother Aelred Bernard Dean *(priest)*
Brother Joseph Basil Gauss
Brother Mark Andrew Jones *(priest)*
Brother Richard Matthias *(deacon)*
Brother William Henry Benefield
Brother Nathanael Deward Rahm
Brother Thomas Lawrence Greer
Brother Enoch John Valentine
Brother David Luke Henton
Brother David John Battrick *(priest)*
Brother Bo Alexander Armstrong
Brother Francis Jonathan Bullock
Brother James Patrick Hall
Brother Richard Edward Helmer *(priest)*
Brother Eric Shelley
Brother Larry Walter Reich

Novices: 4
Postulants: 2

Obituaries

29 Jan 2016 Brother Ron Fender, aged 61, professed 9 years

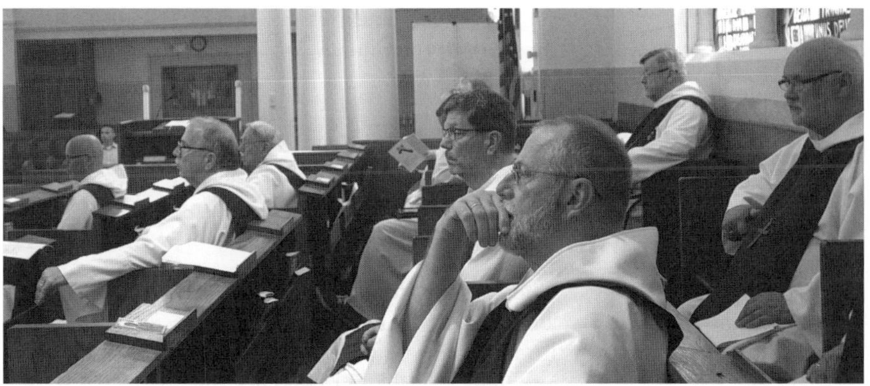

Gregorian friars in choir

Church Army

CA

Founded 1882

Acknowledged as
a mission community
2012

Church Army
Wilson Carlile Centre
50 Cavendish Street
Sheffield
S3 7RZ

Tel: 0300 123 2113

Email:
info
@churcharmy.org

Website
www.churcharmy.org

Daily prayers at 12 noon

Office Book
Through the Day with Church Army and our prayer diary – available on site or through our website.

Bishop Visitor:
Rt Revd Tim Thornton, Bishop of Truro

Registered Charity Nos.
No. 226226 and SC040457

Our vision is of a movement of Christ's disciples who are so set on fire by the love of Jesus that they go to the margins of society, beyond the reach of most of the Church, showing that love through both words and actions. It is for people like this that the Church Army Mission Community exists; to be a home for those with a passion for evangelism.

It is a family where they can be resourced and encouraged, a place where they can cry together and laugh together, celebrate God's goodness and stand with each other in the difficulties. It is not an organisation so much as a movement that focuses on relationships rather than rules. It is held together by a commitment to Christ, to the gospel and to holiness of life. Though coming from within the Anglican Church, it has an inclusive ethos and is open to those from other churches.

It is a vision of a community of love sustained by prayer and the grace of God. Our mission flows out from this Mission Community seeing transformed by Christ.

CANON MARK RUSSELL
(Community Leader, assumed office 2006)
CAPTAIN ANDREW CHADWICK *(Dean of Community)*

446 members

Community Publications
Shareit! A magazine that goes out to individual supporters and churches. It is full of real life stories of the work of the Church Army and our partners.

Church Army's daily prayer diary.

Community history
Videos and articles about the history of the Church Army can be found on our website here:
www.churcharmy.org

Guest and Retreat Facilities
20 single, 10 double rooms. No restrictions.
Rooms are available from £40* a night. (Some discounts available for churches and charities.)

Most convenient time to telephone:
9.00 am - 5.00 pm

Church Mission Society

CMS

Founded 1799

Acknowledged as a mission community 2008

CMS
Watlington Road
Oxford
OX4 6BZ

Tel: 01865 787400
Fax: 01865 776375

Email:
info@churchmissionsociety.org

Website: www.churchmissionsociety.org

Bishop Visitor
Rt Revd Dr Christopher Cocksworth, Bishop of Coventry

Registered Charity No.
No. 1131655
SC047163 (Scotland)
Company No. 6985330

We are a community of people set free to follow God's call in mission. Our vision is to see all God's people engaged in God's mission, bringing challenge, change, hope and freedom to the world. Our focus is to see both individual disciples and communities of disciples set free to play their part in the mission of God. Our common commitment is: to participate in mission, to learn from mission and to pray for mission. Church Mission Society has always had a significant community feel about it, being a membership Society, whose members associated together in order to promote and support evangelistic mission. A spread-out network of local members and associations quickly grew up. Some members even refer to CMS as their "family". A transforming community life was also part of CMS mission service, in mission compounds, mission schools and hospitals and the various CMS training colleges.

CMS had a major influence in forming what today is called the Anglican Communion, about two-thirds of whose Churches trace their origins to the missionary movement fostered by CMS or have had CMS contributions to their early growth and development. Over its 200-year existence, CMS has sent out about 10,000 people in mission. Community members make an affirmation, which they are encouraged to renew annually, including a commitment to participating in mission service, regular prayer, bible reading, study, reflection, supporting the Church's mission, and mutual encouragement. CMS supports people in mission in over forty countries in Africa, Asia, Europe (including the UK), the Middle East and Latin America.

Charles Clayton *(Chair of Trustees)*
The Reverend Canon Philip Mounstephen
(Community Leader/Executive Director, assumed office 2012)
Membership: 2,500+

Community Publications: CMS produces a quarterly newspaper, titled *The Call*, distributed free on request. Community members receive email updates. See the CMS website (churchmissionsociety.org) for news and information about its mission work and regular printed publications. It also produces an annual Members' Handbook: churchmissionsociety.org/handbook

Community Wares: Free resources for prayer, group study and seasons of the Christian year are available on churchmissionsociety.org

Community of the Gospel

CG

Founded 2007

PO Box 133
Waupaca
WI 54981
USA

Email: brdanjoe@ gmail.com

Website: www. communityofthegospel .org

Evening Prayer
7pm (Sat)

Office Book
BCP, The CG Prayer Book, or own choice.

Community Publication
The Belltower Newsletter; Quarterly, no cost, contact Br Daniel-Joseph Schroeder

Bishop Visitor
awaiting appointment in 2017

Chaplain
Father Tyrone Fowlkes

We are a non-residential Monastic Community whose members try to help each other become more Christ-like. We do this by living a monastic life of daily prayer, reflective study, and personal service in the secular world. We seek to demonstrate our faith in unique ways as best we can, while allowing our lives to be transformed by God. Although we are primarily a dispersed community (we live and work in various parts of the world), we travel together as one in spirit with Our Lord. We believe that our purpose is to awaken to God's wisdom and love, and to shape our lives following God's principles. The expression of our personal mission in life is a response to the love of God who made each of us in a unique way. We join together as the body of Christ to share our journey and our resources as we are able, and mutually to encourage each other's faith journey.

BROTHER DANIEL-JOSEPH SCHROEDER
(Guardian, assumed office 30 March 2007)
SISTER MARGARET BLACK *(Deputy Guardian)*

Br Daniel-Chad Hoffman
Br Gregory Thomas Schumacher
Br John Charles Westaway
Br Juan Charles Valles de Noriega
Br John Kneepkens
Sr Kathryn Elizabeth Scarborough
Sr Catherine Lo Prieno
Br Maximos Lee
Sr Rebecca Anne Cooper
Sr Julian Sky Welsh
Br John Huebner
Sr Laurie Sandblom
Sr Charity Aronson
Garth Wadleigh
Oblate Martha Thomas
Oblate Doug Webber
Oblate Louisa Young
Sr Mary-Katherine Wheeler
Michael Wraight
Br Thanasi Stama
Darryl Reed
Sr Dawna Clare Sutton
Rachel Diem
Oblate Anita Rockstroh
Oblate Donald Sutton
Bill Webb
Joanne Riley
Isaias Ginson

Novices: 4 *Postulants:* 4

Friends of the Community

These are people who wish to stay connected with the Community, but who do not wish to be engaged in a formal formation process. They prayer for us regularly, as we pray for them, and they are welcome to attend our annual Convocation.

Community of Hopeweavers

CoH

Founded 2007

Acknowledged as a community 2015

The Guardian
The Community of Hopeweavers
Tardis, Beacon Road
West End
Southampton
SO30 3BS
Tel: 02380 473680
Bookings: 07821 105245

Emails:
hopeweaverspace@gmail.com

Guardian:
hopeweaverfriend@btinternet.com

Website:
www.hopeweavers.co.uk

Community Publication
Free Friends e-mailing four times a year – please contact us hopeweaverfriend@btinternet.com

The Community of Hopeweavers is a dispersed fellowship of friends who seek God through stillness and silence, prayer, creativity, conversation and food, sharing the ups and downs of life wherever we are called to live and work. In 2015, we were welcomed as an Acknowledged Anglican Religious Community by the Advisory Council. We are very fortunate to be supported by our Visitor and our Warden. Through Quiet Days and other opportunities, we work together to offer a focus for all those who seek stillness as part of a Christian faith journey. We welcome you whatever your circumstances or beliefs. Our vision is to develop creative space within our everyday lives where we can make ourselves available to God. Many come to our quiet days and retreats in other places and find Hopeweavers to be a place of creative renewal as we seek to serve God where we are each called to be. Some choose to become Members of the Community of Hopeweavers, prayerfully supporting this ministry and living to our Rule of Life. Our Enquirers work alongside a Guide for a period of at least a year discerning whether membership is a helpful addition to an individual's discipleship journey.

Jacqui Lea
(Guardian, assumed office June 2007)

2015:
Kay Bowen
Debbie Bridger
Jackie Cooper
Harriet Dixon
Anna Evans
Jane Fisher
Dave Gibbs
Fi Gibbs
Emma Grove
Steve Grove
Judith Handford
Philippa Mills
Julia Mourant
Rachel Noel
Di Osborn
Jo Osborn
Helen Pain
Sue Phillips
Geoff Poulton
Sal Robinson
Joyce Seaman
Tony Seaman
Jann Sexton
Jay Shotter
Lou Shotter
Ann Spooner
Ange Whitmore
Helen Williams
Jeff Williams

2016:
Sunita Auger
Chris Duff
Judi Galbraigh
Jen Lambert
Paul Lambert
Gina McCausland
Anne Molyneux
Jane Thompson

Enquirers: 10

Community Wares: Prayer cards, prayer journals, greetings cards, art materials, items from other houses, e.g. prayer ropes from CSWG.

Midday Prayer
12 noon
(Mon, Tue, Thu)

Holy Communion
12 noon (Fri)

Other days and offices according to events and programme

Office Book
Hopeweavers Daily Office & Common Worship. Free download through our website.

Guest & Retreat Facilities: We are a dispersed non-residential community at this time. Guests are welcomed to our day programme of Quiet Days, Soul Days for Leaders and other events in a variety of locations. These include here in West End and also at Wolvesey Palace in Winchester, The Ascension Centre in Southampton, The Lodge Anchorage Park in Portsmouth, as examples. We also lead residential retreats in other places – such as Hilfield Friary. See website for details.

Most convenient time to telephone:
Any time – please leave a message. Prefer email contact whenever possible: hopeweaverfriend@btinternet.com

Bishop Visitor: Rt Revd Dr Jonathan Frost, Bishop of Southampton

Warden: The Venerable Caroline Baston

Community of St Anselm

CoSA

Founded 2015

Lambeth Palace
London SE1 7JU
UK
Tel: 0207 8981210
Email: stanselm@lambethpalace.org.uk

Twitter @ YearinGodsTime

Website: www.stanselm.org.uk

Morning Prayer (CW)
8.30 am

Eucharist 12.30 pm

Evening Prayer (BCP)
5.30 pm

The Community of St Anselm is an Acknowledged Religious Community in the Church of England, founded by Archbishop Justin Welby in 2015 as part of his first priority: the renewal of prayer and Religious life. We draw together Christians aged 20-35 from all over the world, and any branch of the Christian family tree, for a year of living a shared life of prayer, theological study and service to the poor. Members may be resident or non-resident, the latter shaping their lives at work or at home around the Community's Rule of Life and participating in Community meetings, retreats and other activities.

THE MOST REVEREND JUSTIN WELBY
(Abbot, assumed office, 3 September 2015)
REVD ANDERS LITZELL *(Prior)*

Up to 16 Resident Members and up to 40 Non-Resident Members in any academic year.
Community Members commit to a year of active membership, and so the membership (with the exception of the Core Team and Council) rotate from year to year.

Companions
The In God's Time Members from the previous years become Companions of the Community of St Anselm.

Bishop Visitor
Rt Revd Matthew Gunter, Bishop of Fond du Lac

Registered Charity No. 1161185

Community of Saints Barnabas & Cecilia

CSBC

Founded 1997

Revd Sister Sandra Sears CSBC
17 Sixth Street
Gladstone
South Australia
AUSTRALIA 5473

Tel:
Home **(61 8) 8662 2504**
Mobile **0400157709**

Emails:
comsbc@bigpond.com
personal: **srskscsbc@bigpond.com**

Website: www.communityofstsbarnabasandcecilia.com

Morning Prayer
8.00 am

Midday Office
12 noon

Evening Prayer
5.00 pm

Compline
personal choice

The Community of Ss Barnabas & Cecilia came into being in 1997, when the then Bishop of Willochra in South Australia, the Rt Revd David McCall, called Sisters Jean Johnson and Sandra Sears to Jamestown in the State's mid north to form Community.

Since then the Community house has moved twice - to Peterborough in 1998, and Gladstone in 2011. The community is open to men and women, (the double title reflects that) married and single, who are practising members of any Christian denomination. They live in their own environment, and are free to exercise their own gifts. This means that CSBC is dispersed throughout the three dioceses of S. Australia. The charism of the Community is 'Encouragement' - of gifts in each other, in our churches and in the wider community. Vows are renewed every year at our annual retreat. They are chastity, simplicity, and obedience to the Bishop under God. Our habit is a grey alb, navy blue scapular, and blue girdle (with three knots). Our cross has fluted tips redolent of the rose (St Barnabas) with a raised Celtic harp at its centre (St Cecilia).

BROTHER MARTYN ROBINSON CSBC
(Spokesperson, assumed office 5 April 2014 for 3-year term)

Revd Sr Sandra Sears
Revd Sr Sal Tatchell
Sr Sue Nirta
Revd Br John Edwards
Sr Riccarda Favorito
Sr Bev Driver
Sr Pauline Treloar
Sr Katherine Thorpe
Sr Cheryl Wiseman

Obituaries
2 May 2017 Sr Jeanne Frost, aged 79, in community 11 years

Community Publication: Quarterly newsletter. No subscription, but donation if possible.

Community Wares: Blank note cards and Christmas cards; Music (eg Southern Flinders Mass setting, various hymns and songs). Books: *Is There Room?* - a children's Christmas book. Parables, stories, liturgical resources – see website.

Office Book: A Prayer Book for Australia (APBA)
Taizé: Prayer for Each day

Community History: *In a Dry and Thirsty Land*, Anglican Diocese of Willochra, 2015. (A publication to celebrate the centenary of the Diocese.)

Guest & Retreat Facilities
Three double bedrooms (one with a double bed, the others with two singles). Cost - donation. The house is open depending on the movements of Revd Sr Sandra Sears.

Most convenient time to telephone:
0900 – 1700 (Central Standard Time GMT + 9:30 [+/- 1:00 Summer Time]. Mobile number preferred.

Friends
We have Friends of the Community who support us in prayer and in practice.

Bishop Visitor: Rt Revd John Stead, Bishop of the Diocese of Willochra

Chaplain: Fr Bill Goodes (Adelaide)

Community of St Denys

CSD

Founded 1879

contact address:
57 Archers Court
Castle Street
Salisbury
SP1 3WE
UK

Email: junewatt@ btinternet.com

Registered Charity
No 233026

The Community was founded for mission work at home and overseas. The remaining Sisters live in individual accommodation. The present dispersed community of men and women live with a Rule of Life based on the monastic virtues and a particular ministry towards encouragement in the practice of prayer and active service. There is a Board of Trustees responsible for financial matters.

MRS JUNE WATT, Oblate CSD
(Leader, assumed office October 2010, re-elected 2014)
REVD DAVID WALTERS, Oblate CSD *(Deputy Leader)*

Committed members: 16

among whom the professed sisters are:
Sister Margaret Mary Powell
Sister Frances Anne Cocker *(priest)*

Fellowship
CSD has a fellowship.

Community History
CSD: The Life & Work of St Denys', Warminster to 1979, published by CSD, 1979 *(out of print)*.

Community Publication
Annual *Newsletter*. Write to the Leader (address above).

Bishop Visitor
Rt Revd Nicholas Holtam, Bishop of Salisbury

Companions of St Luke, OSB

Founded 1992

Companions of St Luke, OSB
PO Box 861
Plaistow
NH 03865-0861
USA
Email:
csl91.membership @gmail.com

Website
www.csl-osb.org
"Opus Dei":
http://www.cslosb.rhcloud.com/

Office Book
BCP (ECUSA)

Community Publication
The Community has a quarterly newsletter called *Value Nothing Whatever Above Christ Himself*. It is available from our website: www.csl-osb.org

Bishop Visitor
Rt Revd
William Franklin,
Episcopal Diocesan of Western New York

The Companions of St Luke OSB is a Benedictine community as defined by the Canons of the Episcopal Church. As such, it incorporates vowed members and Oblates who may be married or partnered as well as celibates, those who live dispersed and those who are called to live in community. Our stability is in Christ and the Community, and our cloister is in the heart.

From our foundation, it has been the intention of the Companions to live the Benedictine life in a manner consistent with our time under the Benedictine Rule and our vows of Obedience, Stability, and Conversion of Life. Further, we are an intentional hybrid of 'Christian Community' and traditional monastic order, a dynamic tension that informs our commitment to "prefer nothing whatever to Christ, that He may bring us all together to everlasting life" [RB 72]. We are knit together with Christ and each other through our commitment to pray regular, daily Offices, spending time in contemplative prayer, and ongoing study. We live in the world, working to frame our secular lives around our love of God and our prayers.

BROTHER BASIL EDWARDS OSB
(Abbot, assumed office May 2014)
BROTHER DAVID GERNS OSB *(Prior)*

Br Matthias Smith
Sr Anna Grace Madden
Br Camillus Converse
Sr Martha Lamoy
Br Robert Cotton
Sr Mary Francis Deulen
Br Kenneth Maguire
Sr Helena Barrett
Br Stephen Francis Arnold
Sr Veronica Taylor
Br Dunstan Townsend
Br Steven Joseph Olderr
Sr Alison Joy Whybrow
Br Thomas Anthony Goddard
Sr Kate Maxwell
Sr Susanna Margaret Fronzato

Novices: 16 *Postulants:* 4

Obituaries: 31 Aug 2015 Br Luke Doucette, aged 79

Oblates and Companions: The Companions of St Luke has an Oblate program. Oblates are considered by this community to have a 'full and authentic' vocation with its own formation. Oblates sit with their vowed counterparts in the Office, have voice and seat in Chapter.

Community Publication: Brother David Gerns OSB (ed), *Reflections on Benedictine Life in the Modern World* - a small booklet of reflections on Benedictine Life in a dispersed community by members of the Companions of St Luke. It is available upon request from csl91membership @gmail.

Company of Mission Priests

CMP

Founded 1940

Warden's address:

St Mary Magdalene's Vicarage
Wilson Street
Sunderland
SR4 6HJ
Tel & Fax: 0191 565 6318
Email: frskelsmm @btinternet.com

Website : www. missionpriests.com

Associates
Laymen closely associated with the Company in life and work may be admitted as Associates.

Community Publication:
Occasional Newsletter

Office Book:
The Divine Office (Vincentian calendar)

Bishop Visitor
Rt Revd Dr Martin Warner, Bishop of Chichester

The Company of Mission Priests is a dispersed community of male priests of the Anglican Communion who, wishing to consecrate themselves wholly to the Church's mission, keep themselves free from the attachments of marriage and the family, and endeavour to strengthen and encourage each other by mutual prayer and fellowship, sharing the vision of Saint Vincent de Paul of a priesthood dedicated to service, and living in a manner prescribed by our Constitution, and with a Vincentian rule of life. For many years the company, although serving also in Guyana and Madagascar, was best known for its work in staffing 'needy' parishes in England with two, three, or more priests who lived together in a clergy house. Although this is rarely possible nowadays, because of the shortage of priests, we encourage our members who work in proximity to meet as often as practicable in order to maintain some elements of common life. The whole company meets in General Chapter once a year, and the Regional Chapters more frequently.

We were among the founding members, in the year 2000, of the Vincentians in Partnership, which works in accordance with the principles established by St Vincent de Paul, to support and empower those who are poor, oppressed, or excluded.

FATHER BERESFORD SKELTON CMP
(Warden, assumed office 2012)

Michael Whitehead
Anthony Yates
Allan Buik
Peter Brown
Michael Shields
David Beater
Michael Gobbett
Ian Rutherford
Andrew Collins Jones
Tim Pike
Philip North
Mark McIntyre
Alan Watson
Simon Atkinson
Robert Martin
Kevin Palmer
Andrew Welsby
Derek Lloyd
James Hill
Benjamin Eadon
Andrew Horsfall
Adrian Ling
Simon Sayer
Alan Paterson
Ben Kerridge

Probationers: 2 *Aspirants:* 2

Obituaries

15 Nov 2015 John Cuthbert, aged 81, in community 43 years

24 Apr 2017 Roger Davison, aged 97, in community 40 years

Contemplative Fire

CF

Founded 2004

Contemplative Fire Registered Office: The Circle 33 Rockingham Lane Sheffield S1 4FW Tel: 0114 230 7706 *or* **07896 342 907**

Email: info @contemplativefire. org

Website: www. contemplativefire.org

Office Book
Each local CF community develops its own liturgical pattern and provision, with a variety of resources drawn upon.

Community Wares
Cards, CDs, DVDs, booklets, small cherry wood trefoil.

Bishop Accompanier/ Visitor:
Rt Revd Paul Bayes
Bishop of Liverpool

Senior Accompanier:
Sister Rosemary SLG

Registered Charity No: 1106392

Contemplative Fire is a network community having a Trinitarian rhythm of life of prayer, study and action, or being, knowing, doing. *Contemplative Fire: Creating a community of Christ* at the edge was established in the Oxford Diocese in 2004 by Philip Roderick as one of the Diocese's "Cutting Edge Ministries". It then became one of the first generation of the national initiative, Fresh Expressions of Church. *Contemplative Fire* was welcomed as an Acknowledged Community in November 2013.

The call and charism of *Contemplative Fire* seeks to hold in creative tension contemplation and engagement, the hidden and the apostolic. *Contemplative Fire* is increasingly geographically dispersed. Companions on the Way are those who are drawn to become "members" of *Contemplative Fire.* Currently, we have 115 Companions in the UK, (33 in Canada, Maui in Hawaii and California).

As a whole community rhythm we currently have, for those who are able to attend, an annual *Contemplative Fire* retreat, a Community Weekend and four Wisdom on the Way days each year. In addition, there are opportunities for Companions at local, regional or national level, to facilitate, attend events, and design, or receive online, *Contemplative Fire* resources on different aspects of prayer and contemplative discipleship.

Leadership of CF
is via an emergent shared leadership core group
Members/Companions on the Way: 115 UK, 33 non UK

Community Books

Philip Roderick, *Travelling Light, Dwelling Deep: A Guide for the Contemplative Fire Community,* Contemplative Fire, 2006.

Philip Roderick, 'Dynamic Tradition: Fuelling the Fire' in Louise Nelstrop and Martin Percy (eds), *Evaluating Fresh Expressions,* Canterbury Press, Norwich, 2008.

Tessa Holland & Philip Roderick, 'Contemplative Fire: Creating a Community of Christ at the Edge' in Steven Croft and Ian Mobsby (eds), *Fresh Expressions in the Sacramental Tradition,* Canterbury Press, Norwich, 2009.

Tessa Holland, 'A Rhythm of Life: Critical Reflections' & Philip Roderick, 'Connected Solitude: Re-Imagining the Skete', both in Graham Cray, Ian Mobsby and Aaron Kennedy (eds), *New Monasticism as Fresh Expression of Church,* Canterbury Press, Norwich, 2010.

Little Sisters of Saint Clare

LSSC

Founded 2002

Mother Guardian, LSSC
400 NW Gilman Blvd #2511
Issaquah
WA 98027-011411
USA

Tel: 253 569 4759

Email: lsscmotherguardian@gmail.com

Website: www.stclarelittlesisters.org

Most convenient time to telephone:
(Pacific Time, USA)
3:30 pm to 7:30 pm
(Mon-Fri)
10 am - 4.00 pm (Sat)

Office Book
Episcopal BCP

Bishop Visitor
Rt Revd Greg Rickel, Bishop of Olympia

The Little Sisters of St. Clare is a Community of faithful women who seek to live a contemplative life of prayer, study, and service, in the tradition of St Clare and St Francis. As a Community, our beliefs are seen in our actions, our worship, and in our commitment to a common life. We actively serve in the world through guiding children and youth; caring for the poor, the ill, and the marginalized; nurturing the environment; and healing the wounded.

We are not cloistered but live independently, valuing our proximity to each other. We gather two or three times a year for Community worship and celebration. We gather each month for Franciscan study and prayer, most typically in small Chapters located throughout Western Washington. As individuals, our faith is rooted in our baptismal covenant; we express our response to God's call in a lifestyle which interprets monastic traditions in a contemporary way. We guide our lives by the vows of simplicity, fidelity, and purity. We demonstrate our Franciscan roots in an attitude of respect and love for all creation, including deep care and consideration for each other. We are single, married, and in committed relationships.

Sister DedraAnn Bracher, LSSC
(Mother Guardian, assumed office October 2015)
Sister Brigid Kaufmann, LSSC *(Deputy Guardian)*

Sisters:
Sr Maria Elizabeth Bracher
Sr Grace Teresa Grant
Sr Judith Ann Kenyon
Sr Dorothy-Anne Kiest
Sr Kathryn-Mary Little
Sr Patrice Hilda O'Brien
Sr Julian Ortung
Sr Mary-Olivia M. Stalter
Sr Mary-Louise Sulonen
Sr Mary Agnes Staples
Sr Marie-Elise Trailov
Sr Karen-Anne Williamson

Companions:
Tovi Andrews
Nancy Jones
Patricia Roberts
Laura Carroll

Novices: 1
Deacon Lani Hubbard

Associates LSSC: 8

Companions and Associates: In addition to vowed Sisters, we have two other membership levels: Companion and Associate. Generally, Companions seek to journey with the Sisters, are invited to Chapter meetings, and live in Western Washington. Associates can live world-wide.

Community Book: We have self-published a little book called *Holy Weavings - A Tapestry of Reflections* by LSSC. We offer this for a donation of $15 to cover costs and shipping. We also are in the process of copyrighting and publishing a set of Franciscan formation and reflection materials.

Order of Anglican Cistercians

OCist

Founded 2010

Chepynge Saint Bernard
47 Park Road
Chipping Norton
Oxfordshire
OX7 5PA
UK

Email:
ocist@talktalk.net

Website:
www.ocista.webs.com

Vigils *(at dawn)*

Lauds

Midday Office

Vespers

Compline

The Order of Anglican Cistercians consists of uncloistered and dispersed professed men of eighteen years or over; laity who are confirmed and communicant Anglicans, and priests. The Order is open to celibate, single or married men who live within the jurisdiction of an Anglican diocese in Great Britain. Our way of life is lived according to our Rule, and in substantial conformity with that mapped out in the *Rule of Saint Benedict* and thus we are part of the Benedictine family. Our lives are dedicated to seeking union with God through Jesus Christ, whilst living a dispersed and uncloistered form of monasticism. The day is balanced between the *Opus Dei*, work, reading and study. We aspire to a life-long desire to seek God through silence, contemplation, *Lectio* and the daily Offices. We live under the three vows of Stability, Conversion of Character, and Obedience, and we aim to live this out by the grace of God.

Brother Geoff van der Weegen OCist
(Prior, elected 12 May 2010)
Brother Philip Barratt OCist *(Sub-Prior)*
Brother Aelred Partridge
Brother Andrew Law

Novices: 2 *Postulants:* 0

Office Book
Benedictine Daily Prayer Book (Anglican Cistercian Calendar)

Bishop Visitor
Rt Revd Tony Robinson, Bishop of Wakefield

Order of the Community of the Paraclete

OCP

Founded 1971
Reformed at Chapter of Pentecost 1991

Ordinary People Living Extraordinary Lives

Community of the Paraclete@ St. Dunstan's Episcopal Church 722 N. 145th Street Shoreline WA 98133 USA

Website
www.theparacletians.org

1st Friday of the month: informal gathering 12 noon - 3 pm

3rd Friday of the month: Eucharist, Office, study group & lunch 12 noon - 3 pm

Members of the community remain in contact and/or ministry throughout the month.

The Community of the Paraclete is an apostolic community offering an authentic Religious life of prayer and service. We were recognized by the Episcopal Church in 1992. The Paracletians are self-supporting women and men, lay and ordained, who have committed themselves to live under the Paracletian Rule and constitution. Our vision: we are a network of Paracletian communities learning how to grow spiritually and exercising our gifts in ministry. We stand with and serve anyone who is broken in mind, body or spirit. See our website for current ministries.

Brother Marvin Taylor OCP
(Minister, assumed office June 2016)
Email: *brmarvintaylor@hotmail.com*
Brother John Ryan OCP *(Vice-Minister)*
Email: *rjhbro@mac.com*
Sister Susanne Chambers *(Treasurer)*
Email: *mom4435web@gmail.com*
Brother Carle Griffin *(Secretary)*
Email: *griffin@seanet.com*

Br Richard Buhrer
Br Douglas Campbell
Sr Ann Case
Sr Barrie Gyllenswan
Br Timothy Nelson
Sr Suzanne Waldron

Associates 3; *Friends* 10; *Companions* 23

Obituaries

2015 Sr Patricia Ann Harrison
2015 Sr Martha Simpson
2015 Companion Ronald G Lehman

Friends, Associates and Companions

Friend: any baptized Christian, with the approval of chapter.

Associate: confirmed Episcopalian, active member of an Episcopal parish, or church in communion with the Episcopal Church or the Episcopal See of Canterbury; six months' attendance at local chapter, and the approval of chapter.

Companion: Any person who is a benefactor of the Order.

Other Addresses: Members are in the states of Arizona, Florida and Washington, USA.

Community Publication: *Paracletian Presence*, free

Office Book: Book of Common Prayer

Bishop Visitor: Rt Revd Nedi Rivera

The Order of Mission

TOM

Founded 2003
Acknowledged as a Religious community 2013

Postal address: **c/o St Thomas Crookes Nairn Street Sheffield S10 1UL**

Tel: c/o 0114 2671090

Email: admin @missionorder.org

Website: www.missionorder.org

Registered Charity No.: 1100206

The Order of Mission (TOM) is a dispersed global covenant community of Missional Leaders. We take vows to live in Simplicity, Purity and Accountability and make a commitment to live according to the TOM Rule that focuses on:
1 Prayer – daily rhythm of prayer.
2 Pattern – lifeshapes, a set of practical tools grounded in biblical insights, to help us live out the vows and our mission.
3 People – fellowship and accountability with other TOM members.
4 Purpose – missional zeal in our daily lives.
We are a family on mission committed to hearing the call of God in our lives and responding in obedience and faith. TOM has a global membership. Each region is served by a small team of Guardians headed by a Chair.

REVD KELD DAHLMANN
(Senior Guardian, assumed office March 2015)

Revd Canon Mick Woodhead *(UK)*, Revd Eric Taylor *(USA)*, Revd Malcolm Potts *(Australia)*, Revd Thomas Willer *(Scandanavia)* - *(Regional Chairs of Guardians)*

Permanent Members 242 (122 in UK)
Temporary Members 272 (63 in UK)
Explorers 63 (26 in UK)

Associates: Associate members are those who support the value, calling and work of the Order and seek to live according to the pattern of the community but do not feel called to take vows to become either Permanent or Temporary Members. Associates 87 (68 in UK)

Bishop Visitor: Most Revd John Sentamu, Abp of York

The Sisters of Jesus

Founded 2000

34 Eaton Road
Bowdon
Altrincham
Cheshire
WA14 3EH
Tel: 0161 233 0630 (evenings)

E-mail:
(Foundation Sister)
susangabriel@btinternet.com

Website:
www.sistersofjesus.org.uk

Bishop Visitor
Rt Revd Richard Blackburn, Suffragan Bishop of Warrington

Registered Charity No.:
The Gettalife Project. Charity number 1131341.
See the Sisters of Jesus website for more information and the website www.gettalife.org.uk

The core of our vocation is the call to the Religious Life, not living in community but in the midst of everyday circumstances. It is to have our first priority a search for the reality of the living God as Ignatius of Loyola put it, to 'know God in all things' and to live out a life of kinship based on this call of our shared life in Christ and therefore Sisters of him and of each other.

The first vows were taken by the Foundation Sister before Bishop Christopher Mayfield, the Bishop of Manchester, on the festival of St Michael and All Angels, 2000. The Foundation Sister took permanent vows in 2007. The Community was acknowledged by the Advisory Council in July 2011. At present this dispersed community comprises 3 core Sisters, 2 of whom are in Permanent Vows, 1 Affiliated Sister and 2 people exploring.

Revd Dr Susan Gabriel Talbot
(Foundation Sister)
Helen Oakley & Claire Sherman *(Co-Leaders)*

Novices: 1 *Explorers:* 2

Office book
We have developed our own liturgies for Morning and Evening worship as well as our use of the traditonal Compline liturgy.

Associates and Friends: It is possible to join as an Affiliated Sister or Friend should that be appropriate for the candidate and according to our Constitution. There are guidelines for an Affiliated Sister which can be discussed with the Foundation Sister.

Guest and Retreat Facilities: It is possible to stay for a time of quiet at the main house,which is a period terrace with one guest room. The 24 hour or 48 hour stay would be as the Foundation Sister's guest. It can be directed or just 'time-out' (women only). Costs, depending on circumstance, but full board for 24 hours £25-30. £15 for a day with soup, bread and cheese lunch.

Sisters of Saint Gregory

SSG

Founded 1987 as the Companion Sisterhood of Saint Gregory by the Brotherhood of Saint Gregory. Achieved autonomy in 1999 as The Sisters of Saint Gregory.

Contact address for the Treasurer, who receives and routes all communications:

Sr Susanna Bede Caroselli, SSG
545 Dogwood Road
Mechanicsburg
PA 17055
Tel: (717) 697 7040

Email: SCAROSEL@messiah.edu

Website: www.sistersofsaintgregory.org

Office Book
Book of Common Prayer (1979)

The Sisters of Saint Gregory is a women's community canonically recognized by the Episcopal Church. The community is comprised of lay and clergy, young and old, regardless of marital status. Called together by God to the vowed life in the world, we live intentionally dispersed, some individually and some with our families, supporting ourselves and the community through secular or church-related employment performed in a spirit of service. Sisters are also encouraged to serve their parishes and dioceses and other church-sponsored or civic outreach programs. We follow a Rule of Life that requires the Daily Offices in the *Book of Common Prayer*, prayer and meditation, the Holy Eucharist, Embertide reports, a tithe, and participation in an annual convocation and chapter for retreat, business, fellowship and worship. The formation program includes a one-year postulancy and two-year novitiate with spiritual and theological study. After five years in annual vows, a Sister may elect to make life profession.

SISTER LAURIE JOSEPH NIBLICK, SSG
(Leader, assumed office 2013)
SISTER MARY CATHERINE ROBERTSON, SSG *(deacon)*
(Administrator)
Sister Lillian-Marie DiMicco
Sister Helen Bernice Lovell
Sister Susanna Bede Caroselli
Sister Carin Bridgit Delfs *(priest)*
Sister Connie Jo McCarroll *(deacon)*
Sister Eugenia Theresa Wilson *(deacon)*
Sister Michael Julian Davidson
Sister Mary Ann Rhodes *(deacon)*

Novices: 1 *Postulants:* 0

Bishop Visitor
Rt Rev. Laura J. Ahrens,
Bishop Suffragan of
Connecticut

Society of the Community of Celebration

SCC

Founded 1973

809 Franklin Avenue
Aliquippa
PA 15001-3302
USA
Tel: 724 375 1510

Email: mail@communityofcelebration.com

Website: communityofcelebration.com

Morning Prayer
8.00 am

Noonday Prayer
12.30 pm

Evening Prayer
5.30 pm

Conventual **Eucharist** is celebrated on Sat evenings at 5.30 pm, and Saints' days as applicable. Service of Taizé worship Apr – Oct, 1st Sun of the month at 7.30 pm

Office Book
Book of Common Prayer

The Community of Celebration is a life-vowed, contemporary residential community whose roots stretch back to the renewal of the Church of the Redeemer, Houston, Texas, in the 1960s. Today the Community resides in Aliquippa (near Pittsburgh), Pennsylvania. Members are women and men, single and married, lay and ordained. Following the *Rule of St Benedict*, members live a rhythm of prayer, work, study, and recreation.

Our ministry is to be a Christian presence among the poor, responding to the needs around us by offering safe, affordable housing; serving with neighborhood organizations concerned with the revitalization of Aliquippa, and providing hospitality, retreats, sabbaticals, and conferences. We provide various chaplaincies, supply clergy, liturgical consultants, worship leadership and speakers for conferences.

BILL FARRA
(Primary Guardian, assumed office 1995)
JAMES VON MINDEN *(Assistant Guardian)*

Joe Beckey
Revd Phil Bradshaw
Margaret Bradshaw
Mimi Farra
Revd Steven McKeown

Obituaries

28 Apr 2015 May McKeown, professed 30 years

Companions: Companions of the Community of Celebration follow the Rule of Life for Companions.

Other address: UK branch house, c/o Revd Phil Bradshaw, 35 Cavendish Road, Redhill, Surrey RH1 4AL, UK **Website:** ccct.co.uk

Guest Facilities: We offer a chapel, meeting and dining spaces, and overnight accommodation for 11-13 people (one guesthouse can be self-catering for 4-5 people). We welcome individual retreatants and groups, men and women. For further information contact Celebration's hospitality director by mail, telephone or email.

Most convenient time to telephone:
9.00 am - 12.00 pm Eastern Time (Mon-Fri)

Community Wares: Music and worship resources, including CDs, songbooks, liturgical music, children's music, *A Pilgrim's Way* study manual (English & Spanish) - see website store.

Bishop Visitor: Rt Revd C. Christopher Epting

Community Publication: *News from Celebration* - once a year. Contact Bill Farra for a free subscription.

Community books

W Graham Pulkingham, *Gathered for Power*, Hodder & Stoughton, London, 1972
Michael Harper, *A New Way of Living,* Hodder & Stoughton, London, 1972
W Graham Pulkingham, *They Left their Nets,* Hodder & Stoughton, London, 1973
Betty Pulkingham, *Mustard Seeds,* Hodder & Stoughton, London, 1977
Faith Lees with Jeanne Hinton, *Love is our Home,* Hodder & Stoughton, London, 1978
Maggie Durran, *The Wind at the Door,* Kingsway Publications/Celebration, 1986
David Janzen, *Fire, Salt, and Peace,* Shalom Mission Communities, 1996
Phil Bradshaw, *Following the Spirit,* O Books, 2010
Betty Pulkingham, *This is my story, this is my song,* WestBow Press, 2011

Society of St Luke

SSL

Founded 1994

32b Beeston Common
Sheringham
NR26 8ES
Tel: 01263 825623

Emails:
ssluke@btinternet.com

andrewssl@me.com

Morning Prayer & Eucharist 8.30 am

Midday Prayer & Meditation 12.15 pm

Evening Prayer 5.00 pm

Night Prayer 9.00 pm

Office Book
Common Worship

Registered Charity No.: 1107317

The Society of St. Luke was established by the Christian Deaf Community (CDC) of the Middle East. CDC is an Anglican Religious Community within the Province of Jerusalem. Initially SSL focused upon the two schools for deaf youngsters situated in Beirut (Lebanon) and Salt (Jordan.) Times have changed since those roots were set down. The Society today, while remembering the schools in prayer and where possible giving financial support to them, has broadened its mission. It became a charity in 2004 with its primary aims of providing 'prayer for the suffering world' and 'relief and support to those who come for help and counsel.' These aims reflect the Anglican Church's mission of 'care and prayer'.

FATHER ANDREW LANE SSL
(Superior, assumed office 18 October 1994)

Sister Julie Wiseman
Sister Penny Daniels
Sister Ashley Williams
Novices: 1

Associates: 24 Associates (Oblates) who take vows of Simplicity and to keep the Aims of the Society.

Other address: The Rectory, 131 Mounts Road, Greenhithe, Kent, DA9 9ND

Community Publication
Newsletter at the Feast of St Luke, Christmas & Easter. Contact the Community; donations invited.

Community Wares: Crafts, marmalade & pickles.

Most convenient time to telephone:
Any time as answer phone is available.

Bishop Visitor
Rt Revd Graham James, Bishop of Norwich

Society of Saint Anna the Prophet

SSAP

Founded 2005

SSAP Chapter House
1655 Rainier Falls Drive NE
Atlanta, GA 30329
USA

Mailing Address:
SSAP, PO Box 15118
Atlanta, GA 3033
USA

Email *(superior)*:
nancyjuliabaxter@gmail.com

Website:
annasisters.org

at the Chapter House:
Community Prayers
12.30 pm Mon-Fri
Rosary 11.30 am Thu

Holy Eucharist:
Mon-Thu (in elder care facilities); each Anna worships in her own parish on Sunday.

Office Book
St Helena Breviary
(The Offices are scheduled during retreats and quiet days.)

The SSAP is a vowed religious community of elder women in the Episcopal Church USA. Their mission is Godly aging and ministry with the old and young, particularly those who are not able to participate in a parish. The Society has formed six congregations of elders in senior living communities, celebrating Holy Eucharist and offering pastoral care. In addition to the corporate ministries of the Society, individual ministries within Episcopal parishes and in the workplace fulfill the sisters' call to serve old and young. Several of the Annas are care-giving grandmothers. Some are retired and focus on a more contemplative life. A few are living in care.

The SSAP is a *dispersed* community and sisters are single, widowed, married, and partnered. Their ages range from 56 to 91. Embracing vows of **simplicity, creativity, and balance**, the Annas are committed to their own Godly aging and the challenge of being a prophetic presence as elders in the Church and in the world. Each Anna creates a personal *regula* which structures her day-to-day spiritual disciplines. Leadership of the Society is vested in a council of six sisters. Episcopal women over 50 may apply for a provisional year of discernment.

Community Wares
None at present. We do knit prayer shawls which are given as gifts to elders in care.

Community History
A history of our first ten years is currently being written. There is a brief history entitled *Beginnings*.

Guest Facilities
The Chapter House has four bedrooms for brief overnight stays by out of town Annas.
Overnight hospitality may be offered to members of other religious communities (women only) if space is available. Donations accepted.

Most convenient time to telephone
Communication by email or post is preferred; however, phone calls may be received between 6.00 pm – 8.00 pm (Eastern Standard Time) at 404 373 4666

Bishop Visitor
Rt Revd Anne Hodges-Copple,
Suffragan Bishop of North Carolina

REVD NAN BAXTER
(Founder and Superior, assumed office 2 February 2005)
KATHERINE MITCHELL
(Assistant Superior)

Life Vows:
Julia Bottin
Peggy Courtright
Alice Davidson
Maggi Ewing
Revd Eloise Hally
Revd Ruth Healy
Revd Katharine Hilliard-Yntema
Marilyn Hughes
Revd Lori Lowe
Adair Maller
Katherine Mitchell
Revd Mary Moore
Jane Moser
Laura Pittard
Eleanor Pritchett
Revd Lily Anne Rein
Revd Katherine Roberts
Linda Claire Snyder

Annual Vows:
Sally Addis
Elizabeth Allan
Gwen Bottoms
Marjorie Chandley
Revd Cynthia Hizer
Joyce Hunn
Revd Patricia Merchant
Ann Ottesen
Revd Joan Pritcher
Revd Barbara Ryder
Karen Swenson
Lynn Tesh
Revd Carolynne Williams

Novices: 5   *Provisionals:* 1

Obituaries
28 Apr 2015   Mary Ann Neale, aged 81, professed 5 years

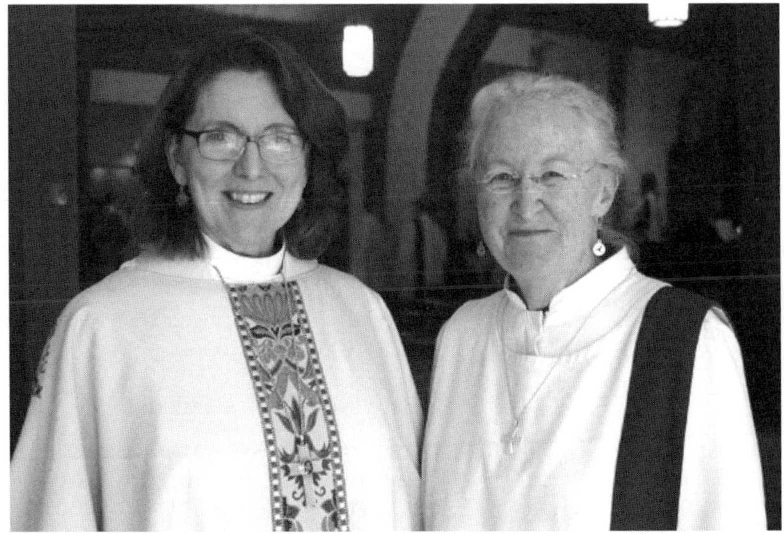

Bishop Anne with the superior

The Third Order, Society of Saint Francis

The Third Order of the Society of Saint Francis consists of men and women, ordained and lay, single or in committed relationships, who believe that God is calling them to live out their Franciscan vocation in the world, living in their own homes and following ordinary professions. Like the First Order Friars and Sisters and Second Order Nuns, The Third Order members, (called Tertiaries) encourage one another in living and witnessing to Christ through a Rule of Life that includes prayer, study and work. The Third Order is worldwide, with a Minister General, and five Ministers Provincial to cover their respective Provinces.

TSSF

Founded:

1920s
Americas

1930s
Europe

1975
Africa

1959
Australia / Asia Pacific

1962
Aoteoroa-New Zealand

Bishop Protector General
The Rt Revd
J. Jon Bruno, DD,
Episcopal Diocesan of
Los Angeles, CA,
USA

KENNETH E. NORIAN TSSF
(Minister General, assumed office September 2011, election for successor pending Fall 2017)
45 Malone Street, Hicksville, NY 11801, USA
Tel: +1 917 416 9579 Email: ken@tssf.org
AVERIL SWANTON TSSF *(Assistant Minister General)*
11, The Grange, Fleming Way, Exeter EX2 4SB, UK
Tel: +44 1392 430355

Statistics for the whole community

	Professed	*Novices*
Americas	415	37
Europe	1772	94
Asia Pacific	323	70
Africa	109	34
Pacific	184	51
Total	**2803**	**286**

Office Book
Each of the five Provinces has different norms regarding the Offices used. Common to all is the 'The Community of Obedience'. Members are encouraged to use this in the context of Morning and Evening Prayer. This may be from:
Provincial Books of Common Prayer; Daily Office SSF;
CSF Office Book

PROVINCE OF THE AMERICAS

REVD TOM JOHNSON TSSF *(Minister Provincial)*
214 Leafwood Way, Folsom, CA, USA
Tel: +1 916 987 1711
Email: tjohnsonret@gmail.com

Website of Province: www.tssf.org

Statistics of Province
Professed: 415; *Novices:* 37; *Postulants:* 37

Associates of the Society of Saint Francis
Welcomes men and women, lay or clergy, single or in committed relationships, young and old, to join us as Associates in our diverse Franciscan family.

Provincial Publication
The Franciscan Times. Available online at www.tssf.org/archives.shtml

Bishop Protector: Rt Revd David C. Rice

PROVINCE OF EUROPE

JAMIE HACKER HUGHES TSSF *(Minister Provincial)*
St Paul's Vicarage, Lorrimore Square, London SE17 3QU UK
Tel: +44 07515 895214
Email: ministertssf@franciscans.org.uk

Provincial Secretary: MARTIN ALLEN, 25 Broadmead, Hitchin, Herts SG4 9LU, UK
Tel : +44 1462 432761 Email: martin.allen5@ntlworld.com

Website of Province: www.tssf.org.uk

Statistics of Province: *Professed:* 1772; *Novices:* 94

Provincial Publication
The Little Portion (twice yearly), also available on TSSF Website.
Contact: editor@tssf.org.uk
Third Order News (three times a year); Contact: ton@tssf.org.uk

Bishop Protector: Rt Revd Stephen Cottrell, Bishop of Chelmsford

PROVINCE OF ASIA PACIFIC

RT REVD GODFREY FRYER TSSF *(Minister Provincial)*
9 Stonebridge Place, Aspley, QLD 4034, Australia.
Tel: +61 (0)7 31226541
Email: provincial.minister@tssf.org.au

Website of Province: www.tssf.org.au

Statistics of Province:
Professed: 323 *Novices:* 70

Provincial Publication: *Quarterly Newsletter* - available on request from the website www.tssf.org.au/Newsletter/

Community History: Denis Woodbridge TSSF, *Franciscan Gold: A history of the Third Order of the Society of St Francis in the Province of Australia, Papua New Guinea and East Asia: Our first fifty years: 1959-2009.* Available from the Provincial Secretary.

Bishop Protector: Rt Revd Garry Weatherill, Bishop of Ballarat

Province of Africa

Revd Dr Michael Twum-Darko TSSF *(Minister Provincial)*
2A Avenue de Mist, Rondebosch, 7700, Cape Town, South Africa
+27 21 671 6199
Email: mtdarko@gmail.co

Provincial Secretary: Veronica Mary Roberts
37 Mon Repos Crescent, Welgelegen, 7500 Western Cape, South Africa

Website: www.tssf.org.za

Statistics of Province

Professed	*Novices*
109	34

Bishop Protector: Most Revd Daniel Yinka Saro, Ghana

Provincial Publication
Pax et Bonum (published three times a year). Available free of charge from provincial Publications Officer: Alan Rogers TSSF Email: alanrs@telkomsa.co.za
Or the Newsletter Editor: The Rev Stewart Lane TSSF
Email: stewartlane36@yahoo.co.uk

Pacific Province

(formerly New Zealand Province)

Revd Margaret Smith TSSF *(Minister Provincial)*
692 Cornwall Road, RD 7 Masterton 5887, New Zealand
Tel: 06 370 2539
Email: mptssf@gmail.com

Website of Province: www.franciscanthirdorder.godzone.net.nz

Statistics of Province

	Professed	*Novices*
New Zealand	97	18
Melanesia	87	33
TOTAL	**184**	**51**

Provincial Publication: *TAU* Available from the Provincial Secretary:
Helene Young Email: kosmic.edu-k@clear.net.nz

Community History: Booklets by Chris Barfoot:
Beginnings of the Third Order in New Zealand 1956-74;
Peace and Joy : Part 2 of the History of the Third Order, Society of St Francis in New Zealand

Bishops Protector
Rt Revd Philip Richardson, Archbishop and Bishop of Taranaki
Rt Revd Alfred Karibongi *(for Melanesia)*

The Worker Sisters and Brothers of the Holy Spirit

WSHS & WBHS

Founded 1972 (Sisters) & 1979 (Brothers)

Contacts:

Sr Deborah WSHS
(Canadian Director)
Email: strdeborah @hotmail.com

Sr Christine WSHS,
(American Director)
Email: casturges @gmail.com

Sr Lucia WSHS
(Director of Admissions)
Email: Abw1nurse @aol.com

Website: www. workersisters.org & www. workerbrothers.org

The Worker Sisters and Brothers of the Holy Spirit is a Covenant Community which seeks to respond to God's call through the power of the Holy Spirit, participate in Jesus Christ's vision of unity, become his holy people, show forth Fruit, and in obedience to his command, go forth into the world. It offers women and men, regardless of marital status, a path for individual spiritual growth through a life commitment to a Rule which provides an opportunity to experience prayer, worship, becoming, discovery, belonging, relating, commitment and mission.

Membership is made up of:

First Order: Sisters - Lay Workers and Lay Sisters;
Second Order: Brothers - Lay Workers and Lay Brothers;
Third Order: Clergy Sisters and Clergy Brothers;
Companions: Lay and Clergy Persons;
Friends: Lay and Clergy Persons

The first three Orders are bound together under a Life Commitment to a common Rule which is Benedictine in orientation. Companions make a Life commitment to a Rule of Life. Friends share in the prayer and spiritual journey of the community. Members do not live together, yet are not separated by geographical boundaries.

Our Community currently supports a Brother in Haiti by providing water purification tablets for his people. This is an ongoing project since the earthquake in Haiti.

SISTER DEBORAH WSHS *(Canadian Director)*
SISTER CHRISTINE WSHS *(American Director)*
(Co-Directors, assumed office April 2010)

Members: 134
Novices: 1 *Postulants:* 2

Companions and Friends

COMPANIONS make a Life of Commitment to a Rule of Life. FRIENDS share in the prayer and spiritual journey of the Community.

Office Book: Book of Common Prayer

Community Ecclesiastical Visitors

CANADA: Rt Revd Peter DeC Fenty, Friend WSHS/ WBHS, Diocese of Toronto, Ontario, Canada

USA & HAITI: Rt Revd Barry Howe, Friend WSHS/ WBHS, Diocese of West Missouri, USA *(retired)*

ASHRAMS & OTHER COMMUNITIES

BETHEL ASHRAM

Warickadu, Kuttapuzha P.O., Tiruvalla, Pathanamthitta District, Kerala, INDIA Tel: 09562 335401

The Ashram is a part of Madhya (Central) Kerala Diocese, CSI. Located in Warickad, since 1926 the Ashram has run a school, looked after orphans and run a dispensary. Today its ministry includes a small geriatric care ward, a retirement home for monastic sisters of the Church of South India, and a boarding school. It is also used as a place of retreat for the diocese.

CHRISTA KULU ASHRAM

Tirupattur, Vellore, Tamil Nadu 635602, INDIA

The Christu Kula Ashram was among the earliest Christian Ashrams, starting in 1921. It aimed to promote equality between Europeans and Indians, and to give an Indian presentation of Christian life and worship. It is in Vellore Diocese, CSI, and is linked to the National Missionary Society of India.

CHRISTA PREMA SEVA ASHRAM

Shivajinagar, Pune - 411 005, INDIA Tel: 20 553 9276

Founded as the Ashram for the Christa Seva Sangha in 1922 by Jack Winslow to create a community of Indian and British members living in equality, the original community ceased in the early 1960s. Some members of this group were influential in the formation of the Third Order SSF *(see entry elsewhere)*. The Ashram is now the focus of a non-celibate community.

CHRISTA SEVAKEE ASHRAM

Karkala, Karnataka, INDIA

Started in 1950 in Karnataka (Southern) Diocese, CSI, this Ashram runs a home for aged men and two homes for aged women, altogether caring for fifty elderly people, who are deserted, poor or without relatives. This Ashram is also functioning as a self-employment training centre, a centre for retreats and conferences, and as a short-term stay home for deserted women or women in distress.

COMMUNITY OF ST STEPHEN

4 Rajput Road, Delhi 110 054, INDIA Tel: 11 2396 5437

St Stephen's Community, for women, began as St Stephen's Home in 1871 and formally became a community in 1886. In the 1940s, it came to consist of those Indian and English women who wished to live together as a community under a simple rule of prayer and life.

CHRISTAVASHRAM

Manganam P.O., Kottyam District, Kerala 686 018, INDIA
Email: christavashram@gmail.com
Website: manganam.tripod.com/ashram/index.html

Christavashram (Society of St Thomas) is an active Christian community for service, founded in 1934. It is in Madhya (Central) Kerala Diocese, CSI. The Community consists of 120 people, including members, staff and children of the Kerala Balagram, staff and trainees of the Gurukul Ecumenical Institute and Peace Centre staying in the campus, and 30 Associate members living outside

Some other communities

This section includes communities, either monastic or acknowledged, that whilst not Anglican in ecclesiastical allegiance are in communion with Anglicans.

There is also here a community in the USA, inter-denominational in its origins, which includes Lutherans as well as Anglicans, as the ELCA is now in full communion with the Episcopal Church of the United States.

Aspects of the life ...
meeting together

Worker Sisters and Brothers
of the Holy Spriit

Community of Ss Barnabas and Cecilia

Mar Thoma Syrian Church

Mar Thoma Dayarya

Plachery PO (Kalayanad), Punalur 691 331, Kerala, India Tel: 475 2222 281

Mar Thoma Sanyasini Samaoham

Elanthor P.O., Pathanamthitta District, India Tel: 468 2361972

Christa Panthi Ashram

Darsani P.O., Sihora - 483 225, India Tel: 07624 260260

Christa Panthi Ashram, Sihora, was established in 1942 under the leadership of Revd K T Thomas, Mr John Varghese and Mr M P Mathew, who both later became ordained. Today there are more than forty members, including permanent workers and volunteers. In addition to Gospel work, the activities of the Ashram include hospital work, village schools, a home for the destitute, agricultural work and a rural development programme.

Christu Kulu Ashram

Mahadeva P.O., Satna, Madhya Pradesh 485 001, India
Tel: 7672 225508

Christu Mitra Ashram

P.B. No. 3, Ankola P.O., North Kanara, Karnataka - 531 314, India
Tel: 8388 230392 or 8388 230287
Started in 1940, an ashrams of the Mar Thoma Evangelistic Association.

Christu Dasa Ashram

Olive Mount P.O., Palakkad - 678 702, India Tel: 492 272974

Started in 1928 as an Ashram with celibate members, it is located in the north-eastern part of Kerala near the Tamil Nadu border.

Santhigiri Ashram

Holistic Healing and Meditation Centre, 11/488, Edathala North, Aluva,
Kerala - 683 564, India
Tel: 484 2639014
Email: santhigiriasram@yahoo.co.uk

Suvartha Premi Samithi

Kenchora, Ranthi P.O., Pithorragarh, Uttarharakand, India
Tel: 596 1222033

Revd A K George and two lady workers went to Tejam and Munsiari on the border of Tibet and started work among the Bothi community. The Bhotias used to trade with Tibet until the 1949 invasion by China. The missionaries hoped to reach Tibet with the help of the Bhotias. Some from the Bhotia community accepted the Gospel and congregations have been founded at Munsiari and Tejam. At present, two groups are working here.

Communities in Churches who have signed the Porvoo agreement

Porvoo created a community of Churches, the members of which have signed an agreement to "share a common life in mission and service". Anglicans in the British Isles and Iberia are currently members, with Lutherans from Denmark, Estonia, Finland, Iceland, Lithuania, Norway and Sweden.

There are a number of established Religious communities in the Church of Sweden, entries for which can be found in the following pages with the addresses of others below.

Community of the Holy Trinity Founded 1993
Mount Foundation, 795 91 Rättvik, Sweden Tel. 0248 79 7170

Mary Magdalene Sisters
Henriksdalsringen 9, 4th floor, 131 32 Nacka, Sweden Tel. 08 714 7751

Östanbäcks Kloster
SE– 733 96 Sala, Sweden Tel: +46 224 25088, 251 80, 251 88

Sankt Sigfrid Sisters
Sjöborgen, Old Växjövägen 5, 360 44 Ingelstad , Sweden Tel 0470 30128

The Risen Saviour sisterhood
Overselo Abbey Farm, 640 61 Stallarholmen, Sweden Tel: 0152 41116

Congregation of Daughters of Mary of the Evangelical Way of Mary

Founded 1958

The establishment of the Evangelical Way of Mary is a work of God. He found an instrument that was willing to listen and obey, so that he could speak, act and create. Her name was Paulina Mariadotter (Gunvor Paulina Norrman 1903-1985). She belonged to the Evangelical-Lutheran Church of Sweden. As a young woman, Paulina Mariadotter dedicated herself to Christian social work. She became aware of the need of the single woman and she received a message from God: "Jesus Christ both can and wants to deliver the single woman's energy of life to the Service of His Love's Life."

Paulina Mariadotter lived this message in her own life and other women came and experienced that this was something from God. God could create "a new congregation, religious life in the midst of the world". Our mission is to live and pray for unity. We also have a mission to make the Lord's Mother Mary known, loved and honoured also in the Evangelical-Lutheran part of the Church of Christ.

Mariadöttrarna
Mariagården vid Vallby Kyrka
SE - 745 98
Enköping
SWEDEN
Tel & Fax:
0046 (0)171 811 47

"Quiet Time" for sisters only
6.30 am

Prayer at noon
9.30 am

Vespers
3.00 pm

Compline
9.00 pm

The Holy Communion
Wed 9.00 am
Fri 5.30 pm
Sun 10.00 am

Guest & Retreat Facilities
To live with us in our open home, we welcome women. In groups that visit over the day, we welcome both men and women.

Most convenient time to telephone:
10.00 am – 12 noon,
4.00 pm – 6.30 pm

The spiritual content for the Evangelical Way of Mary was received between 1938 and 1949. As Birgitta Laghé (Doctor of Theology) sums up: "The vision of the designation 'the Visitation' (1949) constitutes the foundation for both the Lutheran and the Roman Catholic branches of the Daughters of Mary." In 1958, the first sisters gave their perpetual vows and received the blessing by a priest. In connection with this the sisters began using a habit. There is also a branch in the Roman Catholic Church, the Daughters of Mary OSB at Vadstena, Sweden. The movement into the Roman Catholic Church was taken in deep unity in 1988.

The Lord's Mother Mary is the Mother of the Congregation. The possibility for the Daughters of Mary to live without a visible Mother is that each sister has devoted herself to the vocation so that gives the engagement for her to subject herself by her own free will to what the Lord had spoken about the Evangelical Way of Mary. We are 23 sisters, ranging in age from 27 to 93 years old, with 1 novice. We are of four nationalities: Swedish, Danish, Finnish and German.

Obituaries
14 Sep 2016 Sr Birgitte, aged 86, professed 49 years

Bishop Visitor & Chaplain
Bishop: Ragnar Persenius Chaplain: Bertil Murray

Other Address
Mariadöttrarna, Mariagarden, Østerskovvej 38, Kollund, DK-6340 Krusaa, DENMARK
Tel & Fax: 0045 74678898

Community History
Birgitta Laghé, *Den Evangeliska Mariavägen till enhet: En studie i Paulina Mariadotters spiritualitet*, Artos & Norma bokförlag, 2004. Summary (English): *The Evangelical Way of Mary to Unity: a study of the spirituality of Paulina Mariadotter.*

Yvonne MariaWerner (editor), *Nuns and Sisters in the Nordic countries after the Reformation: a female counter-culture in modern society*, The authors and the Swedish Institute of Mission Research, printed by X-O Graf, Uppsala, 2004.

Mariadöttrarna, P*aulina Mariadotter HERRENS Redskap*, Verbum förlag, 1990. This biography by the sisters is translated into German, Danish and Finnish.

Sisters of the Holy Spirit in Alsike kloster

Helgeandssystrarna

Founded 1965

Alsike Kloster
SE - 741 92
Knivsta
SWEDEN
Tel: 46 (0) 1838 3002
Emails:
systrarna@ alsikekloster.org
or
syster.marianne @gmail.com

Website:
www.alsikekloster.org

Lauds 7.00 am

Terce 9.00 am

Midday prayer
12 noon

None 3.00 pm

Vespers 6.00 pm

Compline/Vigils
8.00 pm

Office Book
adjusted
Benedictine Office

The monastic family of the Holy Spirit Sisters at Alsike Kloster is one of the fruits of the re-awakening of monastic life which started in the first half of the 20th century in the Reformation churches in Europe. This movement touched the Swedish Church in the 1940s-1950s.

In 1948, Sister Marianne Nordström was invited by the Order of the Holy Paraclete to test her vocation. Having returned to Sweden in 1954, she and Sister Ella Persson started a common life in the Diocese of Stockholm, moving to Uppsala in 1956 on the invitation of the then Dean, Olof Herrlin (later Bishop of Visby) to take up work among the university students. In 1964 the community moved to Alsike, twenty kilometres south of Uppsala, continuing their life of prayer and hospitality in the old schoolhouse close to the parish church. During this period novices came and went. In 1983, Sister Karin Johansson was received as a postulant and made her final profession in 1995. By then, Archbishop Gunnar Weman had succeeded Bishop Herrlin as Visitor, and the community, having become involved in refugee work since 1978, was declared the Sanctuary of the diocese by him. The years of crisis in the Swedish Church brought them into contact with the Evangelical Lutheran Church of Kenya, where they have found a response for their way of life and a new hope of growth. There are now plans to erect a kind of monastic village for work with refugee children, students and mission.

SISTER MARIANNE NORDSTRÖM
(Prioress, assumed office 1965)
Sister Karin Johansson

Obituaries
Feb 2016 Sister Ella Persson, aged 92, prof. 61 years

Community Publication
Meddelande till S:t Nicolai Vänkrets (twice a year)

Guest & Retreat Facilities
According to plans for the "monastic village", there will be five rooms, free of charge.
Most convenient time to telephone: between Offices.

Oblates and Friends
The community has Oblates and 'Friends of St Nicolas'.

Bishop Visitor: Rt Revd Göran Beijer

Chaplain: Rt Revd Gunnar Weman

Sisters of Saint Francis

Helige Franciskus Systraskap

Founded 1979

Klaradals kloster
Lindåsvägen 22
SE 443 45 Sjövik
SWEDEN
Tel:+46 302 43260

Email:
porten@ klaradalskloster.se

Lauds
6.45 am

Sext
12 noon

Vespers
5.30 pm

Compline
8.30 pm

Mass
Tuesday 6.30 pm
Thursday 8.00 am
Friday 8.00 am

Helige Franciskus Systraskap (Sisters of Saint Francis) is a community in the Swedish Lutheran Church. We follow an adapted version of the Catholic Rule for the Third Order Regular of St Francis.

Our convent is situated 40 kilometres north east of Göteborg. Our life has its center in prayer, community life and meeting others either in our guest house, in the village or when invited to parishes, prayer groups, networks and other gatherings.

SISTER LENA PETTERSSON
(Leader, assumed office 15 January 2017)
Sister Hanna Söderberg
Sister Inger Johnson
Sister Gundega Petrevica

Guest & Retreat Facilities
Five rooms.
For organized retreats we welcome both men and women, otherwise women only.
We take guests in periods, normally two weeks per month.
Guests leave a gift for food and lodging.

Most convenient time to telephone
Weekdays 9.30 am -11.30 am

Bishop Visitor
Rt Revd Biörn Fjärstedt (retired bishop of Visby)

Brothers of Saint John the Evangelist (OSB)

EFSJ

Founded 1972

**PO Box 782
Freeland
WA 98249
USA
Tel: 360 320 1186
Email:
efsj@whidbey.com**

Website: www.
brothersofsaintjohn
.org

Most convenient time to telephone: 10 am - 12 noon, 2 pm - 3 pm

Morning Prayer
8.45 am

Noonday Prayer
12 noon

Vespers 5.30 pm

Office book: BCP

Bishop Visitor
Rt Revd Brian Thom,
Diocese of Idaho

The community strives to promote interest, study and understanding of the vocation to the Religious life, and to sustain a Religious community on South Whidbey Island, WA. This monastic community is guided by the venerable *Rule of St Benedict.*

The Ecumenical Fellowship of Saint John was founded in Los Angeles in the spring of 1972 by five men - clergy and lay - from the Episcopal, Lutheran and Roman Catholic Communions of the Church. On Saint John's Day 1973, four of the founding group (two Lutherans and two Roman Catholics) made Promises of Commitment at Saint John's Episcopal Church in Los Angeles. After some years in Fallbrook, San Diego County, the Community moved to Whidbey Island in 1990. In 2000, we were blessed with the gift of 10 secluded and wooded acres, with an additional 10 added in 2013, donated by Judith P Yeakel of Langley. Here the monastic house was built, and blessed on Holy Cross Day 2003. The 'Called to Common Mission' declaration of ELCA and TEC made it easy for Lutherans and Episcopalians to become one. We were officially recognised as a canonical Religious community at the Diocesan Convention 2010.

BROTHER RICHARD TUSSEY EFSJ
(Superior, assumed office December 1973)
BROTHER DAVID MCCLELLAN EFSJ *(Prior)*

Sister Julian of Norwich DiBase Obl/OSB
Brother Aidan Shirbroun Obl/OSB
Brother Thomas Langler Obl/OSB
Sister Frideswide Dorman Obl/OSB
Sister Hildegard Babson Obl/OSB
Sister Agnes Steele Obl/OSB
Brother Columba Johnson Obl/OSB

Associates: We currently have one Associate.

Community Publication: *Benedicite.* Contact us via email or post; no charge other than freewill offering.

Community Wares: "Tanglewood Treats": jam, pecan pie, etc. (Tanglewood is the name of our monastery.)

Guest and Retreat Facilities: No overnight guests at present. We do have a building fund.

Remembering and thanksgiving

Aspects of the life ... light in the darkness

Brother Brian SSF
(1925-2015)

Brian was brought up in Bristol (UK) before studying theology at King's College London. Whilst there, he got to know the SSF house in Cable Street, London, and was inspired by the poverty of the friars and the incarnational ministry which flowed from that. After ordination and serving a curacy at St Agnes Church in Bristol, he joined SSF, being professed in 1958. Soon after, he was sent to New Guinea, where SSF had only recently begun to minister. His thirteen years in PNG were some of the most formative for him. He lived very simply, refusing any "white man's privileges" and was able to guide others, including novices, and, through his work as Principal of St Francis Evangelists' College, he trained local men to be evangelists in their villages.

Brian wanted to withdraw from active ministry and experience a deeper life of prayer, but there always seemed to be a greater need. Finally, the chance for this came. The Community of St Clare in Stroud, NSW, in Australia needed a chaplain. Brian went in 1979 to live with one or two other brothers in the nearby hermitage. Brian's unfussed patience provided a lifeline of stability through the Clare community's challenges.

He was then elected Minister Provincial (1981-87) of the newly formed ANZ Province, and later served as Minister General (1991-97). He used a former 'junk room' at the end of the hermitage corridor as an office and from there ran the international affairs of SSF, writing numerous aerogrammes in his rather indecipherable hand. He would then from time to time wander off with his bag in hand, to journey to somewhere in the world. He enjoyed the chance to travel and meet people although probably not the formal meetings. However, he was able to indulge his great love of cricket and somehow it usually seemed that wherever Brian was there just happened to be a test match.

The final period in his life was spent in New Zealand. For five years he lived in a small hut at St Isaac's Retreat in Opononi in Northland. It could be a temptation in such a life to be withdrawn from others' concerns, but Brian found a deep awareness of the needs of those living around him and the effects of rural poverty. In 2005 he moved south to the friary at Hamilton. A man of prayer, always faithful to the Office and daily Eucharist he was a well-known sight in the surrounding village as he made his way from friary to chapel and back again three times a day. He died just ten days after a final move to a Rest Home aged 90.

SSF's Principles speak of becoming "emptied of self" and "surrendered to God" and becoming "effective instruments of [God's] mighty working." Brian was such a person, emptied of self, and he bore the fruits of a life dedicated to seeking God above all else.

Sister Mary Bernard OSB (1924-2016)

Joan Ethel Taylor was born in Peckham in 1924. From an early age she loved reading and was encouraged by a local bookshop owner to read in his shop after school. She won a scholarship to Oxford to read history at St Hugh's, but changed to theology in her second year. It was in Oxford that she became an Anglican.

After graduating she taught in Coventry and became sacristan at St John's, one of the Anglo-Catholic churches in the city. During the school holidays, after making a retreat, she would think nothing of cycling into Wales, sleeping under hedges and in barns.

She entered Burford Priory in 1960 and was professed in 1963. As a bookish Oxford theology graduate she was set to work in the kitchen – and there she remained until the Brothers took over in 1991 – famous for her 'cholesterol bombs' from the frying pan! She grabbed what time she could for study, writing poetry and delighted in the time allocated for 'gardening'. One respite from the kitchen came when she was allowed to attend the annual Benedictine History Symposium, and later, after being elected Conventual Prioress in 1984, the Free Association of Benedictine Nuns and the General Assembly of the Union of Monastic Superiors.

She took the brave decision to open the novitiate to men and received the first two postulants in October 1987. Before retiring from office in 1996 she had received the Simple Vows of six men and the Solemn Vows of three.

Her long 'retirement' gave ample time to indulge her passion for gardening, her succession of feline familiars and her great gift of friendship. Many of her friendships dated from teenage and university years, others were with former colleagues and pupils, many from her time as 'Mother', as well as many newer ones and, of course, her family – all well represented at her funeral, following her death on 4 January 2016 aged 91.

Brother Damian SSF (1941-2016)

Brother Damian (Roger James Kirkpatrick) was professed as a Franciscan friar in 1969. He was a vivacious brother, a man of considerable energy and great warmth. During his community life at various times he held most of the positions of authority: Guardian, Provincial Secretary, Novice Guardian, Provincial minister and of course with his accountancy training he was bound to become Provincial Bursar. He served his fellow Religious on the Advisory Council and was important in the creation of the Anglican Religious Communities Development Trust.

Damian was at home in the larger more conventual friary as well as the smaller urban house. It was whilst living in Belfast that he responded to the call to ordination in 1986. He had a huge pastoral heart and many sought him out for spiritual direction and counsel. He was tireless in making visits to friends, Family, schools, prisons and parishes; he clocked up many miles (and penalty points!). No journey was as simple as getting from A to B without zigzagging around the country to fit in as many people and appointments as possible en route. Damian touched the lives of an incredible range of people, of all age groups, and eventually welcomed 'Sister Death' at the age of 74 years on 17 January 2016.

Brother Ron Fender BSG (1954-2016)

Brother Ron Fender died on 29 January 2016 of a massive heart attack on the train as he was beginning his journey home to the US state of Tennessee, after the Brotherhood's Winter Convocation at Alvernia Retreat Center, Wappingers Fall, in Upstate New York. Attendees at his funeral numbered in the hundreds as people converged from far and near to pay their respects to the man known as 'The Saint of Chattanooga'. He was sixty-one and in the ninth year of his profession as a Gregorian friar.

Ron served as Outreach Manager at the Chattanooga Community kitchen for ten years, during which time he also developed a program of permanent supportive housing focused upon end-of-life care. He was a tireless advocate and was simply unconditionally present for anyone in need. He was a beloved parishioner at Saint Paul's, where he served as a lay reader and outreach ministry volunteer. Ron was a frequent speaker before community organizations and a guest preacher in local churches, always sharing his love of Christ and his firm belief in showing that love through service. He made his first vows in the Brotherhood in 2006 and his life profession in 2011. He lived his vocation as a friar through his tireless work with the homeless.

Most of all, Ron saw the observation of our Rule of Life as a great opportunity to deepen his spiritual life while growing into a more faithful Christian person. He loved the brothers of our order and experienced the return of that love in the great respect all held for him. He spent the last week of his life with his brothers and who among us could want for more?

Ron's joyful, humble and generous spirit touched people from all walks of life and inspired many others to engage in similar works of mercy. His impact on those most vulnerable will live on forever. "Well done, good and faithful servant! Come and share your master's happiness!" Amen and AMEN!

Father Ralph Martin SSM (1930-2016)

Don Martin was a Canadian priest who came to SSM in Britain to test his vocation in 1957. He was an intelligent and well-educated man yet modest and reticent. He soon established himself as a special presence in the community with his capacity for friendship and integrity and later his abilities as a teacher and guide. He was professed in 1960 with the name Ralph at a time when SSM was thriving both as a worldwide Religious community and as a provider of theological education for ordinands. Within a few years came the rapid social change of the 1960s, which affected religion and theology profoundly. Both vocations to the Religious Life and candidates for the priesthood shrank dramatically in number and SSM could not be the same again. Ralph described these years in his autobiographical book (*Towards a New Day*) as 'an earthquake, which shattered the foundations of society'.

Ralph was the man to whom the community in Britain turned to find a new vision for the brethren who remained in the Society, serving as Provincial 1973-1981. He did so with quiet determination, gathering a widely-diverse group of associates as well as brothers to create a new type of Religious house in Willen, where professed brethren lived alongside families and friends. In doing this he changed profoundly the possibilities of Religious life and was a pioneer of developments which have followed more widely among other community groups in the decades since.

He spent much of the 1980s and 1990s as a pilgrim for SSM through several continents, taking roles in Japan, Ghana, Italy, Lesotho and Australia, until in his seventies he returned to Britain for the final years of his ministry.

He died on Maundy Thursday 2016, after fifty-five years in profession, aged 85.

Sister Gladys (Moyo) CZM (1964–2016)

Sister Gladys was called home in the 21st year of her Final profession, and 23 days before her 52nd birthday. Indeed, called to higher glory, after a life well lived as a true monastic. A brave, strong, vigilant, focused, and destined woman of virtue. She left memories to cherish for those she worked, lived with, and met. She was a bundle of joy and loved peace.

She attended school to finish high school at St Columbus (Anglican) High school Bulawayo. On 27 August 1984, she joined the CZM Religious community, and walked through the journey to final profession on 9 September 1995. She gained a qualification in Nutrition at Range House College Harare, hence her love to create delicious meals with very little. For five years, she served as the matron at St Agnes

Children's home, Gokwe, a role she executed with diligence, satisfaction, and love from the heart. At the end of her term, she moved from the mother house briefly to St James' branch house, Bulawayo, stayed there for a year, and came back to the mother house. She was later sent to St Patrick's Mission branch house, Gweru, in the Diocese of Central Zimbabwe. She took a different role, working in the St Patrick's (Boarding) High School kitchen. This gave her a greater opportunity to mix/interact with people of all ages and levels, with whom she shared her gifts of joy, happiness, above all counsel. She had such sense of humour and a word of hope and encouragement for everyone and every situation.

In her everyday, busy schedule, she found joy in offering voluntary service at the Diocesan Centre at St Patrick's Mission, experimenting with food to make delicious meals for the many visitors who passed through the centre. Her input will be greatly missed by the diocesan clergy family and their wives. "What could be better than being served food by a happy, and cheerful, smiling person?", said Bishop Ishmael Mukwanda (Diocese of Central Zimbabwe) at her interment.

Her heart was always on serving the Church. She so loved music, so she was a member of the local church choir and was always singing with joy all times.

On 8th July 2016, she lost in a very brief (seven weeks) fight to cancer, that she endured with grace, joy, and bravery. "Ok, I am going." And so she peacefully rested.

Sister Mary Gundulf OSB
1943 – 2017

Sister Mary Gundulf was the only child of two geography teachers. Her father, to whom she was devoted, died when she was nine. She attended Girton College, Cambridge and took her degree in English Literature.

Sister Mary Gundulf entered Malling Abbey in 1969 and was professed on All Saint's Day 1974. She was a very thoughtful, private person and strongly introverted. Discussions and meetings were not her favourite activities! She was happiest and most creative in her gardening and in her writing; she had several books published. She worked in the Abbey Guest House (being known for her welcoming smile), and in the laundry and buttery.

After Christmas 2016 she became ill and was told she had advanced cancer of the pancreas. After a spell in hospital she returned to the Abbey. The illness, like her severe scoliosis, was borne with quiet fortitude and a lack of fuss. She died surrounded by her sisters on 4 March 2017, just one day short of her 48th anniversary in this community.

Organizations

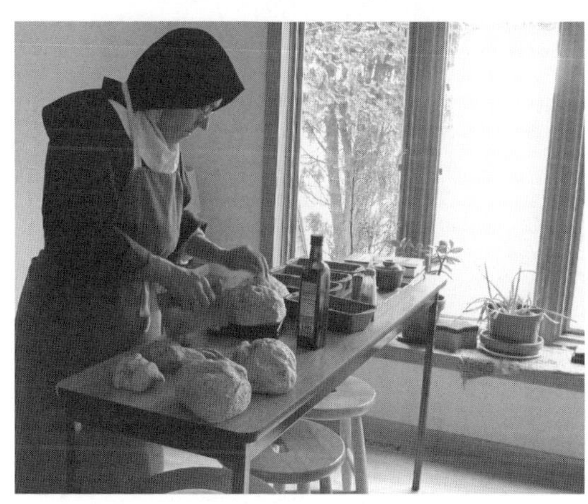

Aspects of the life ... wearing an apron!

Sisters of Jesus Way (top) and OJN (left)

Australia

Advisory Council for Anglican Religious Life in Australia

The Council consists of:

Rt Revd Garry Weatherill, Bishop of Ballarat *(Chair)*

The Committee also includes several other bishops

The Brother Robin BSB
Sister Sue Nirta CSBC
Sister Linda Mary CSC
Sr Carol Francis CHN
Brother Wayne LBF
Fr Keith Dean-Jones OGS
Sister Raphael OSB
Sister Juliana SI *(Secretary)*
Sister Eunice SSA
Br Christopher John SSF
Father Christopher SSM

Website: www.anglicanconsecratedlife.org

New Zealand

Conference of Anglican Religious Orders in Aotearoa New Zealand (CAROANZ)

Membership consists of: Rt Revd Victoria Matthews *(Chair)* with representatives of: Associates of the Holy Cross; CSN; SLG; Associates of Southern Star Abbey, Kopua; Order of St Stephen; First Order SSF; Third Order SSF; Urban Vision.

Europe

Advisory Council on the Relations of Bishops & Religious Communities (commonly called 'The Advisory Council')

Rt Revd David Walker, Bishop of Manchester *(Chair)*
Rt Revd Jonathan Clark, Bishop of Croydon
Rt Revd Tony Robinson, Bishop of Wakefield
Rt Revd Tim Dakin, Bishop of Winchester

Communities' representatives (elected Mar 2016 for 5-year term):

Sister Alison Fry OSB
Sister Anita Cook CSC
Sister Heather Francis OHP
Sister Joyce Yarrow CSF
Sister Margaret Theresa SLG
Sister Mary Julian CHC
Sister Mary Stephen Packwood OSB
Father Peter Allan CR
Brother Philip Bartholomew SSF
Brother Stuart Burns OSB

Co-opted:
Mark Berry *(Church Mission Society)*
Dr Petà Dunstan *(Trustee of ARCDT)*
Revd Ian Mobsby *(representing new and emerging communities)*
Revd Tim Watson *(Chemin Neuf)*

ARC representative: Dom Simon Jarrett OSB
Conference of Religious Observer: Abbot Richard Yeo OSB
Hon. Secretary: Father Colin CSWG Email: father.colin@cswg.org.uk

Conference of the Leaders of Anglican Religious Communities (CLARC)

The Conference meets in full once a year.
Hon. Secretary: Father Colin CSWG Email: father.colin@cswg.org.uk

General Synod of the Church of England

Representatives of Lay Religious

Sister Catherine SLG (Elected 2015)
Brother Thomas Quin OSB (Elected 2010, re-elected 2015))

Representatives of Ordained Religious

Revd Sister Anita Cook CSC (Elected 2015)
Revd Thomas Seville CR (Elected 2005, re-elected 2010 & 2015)

Anglican Religious Communities in England (ARC)

ARC supports members of Religious Communities in the Church of England. At present its membership is the entire body of professed members of communities recognised by the Advisory Council *(see above)*. It has held occasional conferences when members can come together both to hear speakers on topics relevant to their way of life and to meet and share experiences together. A news letter is sent out three times a year to all houses. ARC represents Anglican Religious Life on various bodies, including the Vocations Forum of the Ministry Division of the CofE, The Advisory Council and the *Year Book* editorial committee. Some limited support is also given to groups of common interest within ARC who may wish to meet. Its activities are coordinated by a committee with members elected from Leaders, Novice Guardians, General Synod representatives and the professed membership. The committee usually meets three times a year.

Following a successful conference in 2015 open to members of Recognised, Acknowledged and Emerging Communites as well as others interested in the Religous Life, it was agreed that another conference would be held in 2017. These meetings are generating interest for the future development of ARC.

Prior Simon OSB & Sister Sue CSF *(representing Leaders)*
Sister Catherine SLG *(representing General Synod Representatives)*
Brother Ian OSB *(Chair and representing Novice Guardians)*
Sister Catherine CHN, Sister Helen OHP, Sister Jane ASSP,
& Sister Louise SJW *(representing professed members)*
Sister Chris James CSF *(co-opted, Treasurer)*, Brother Michael OGS *(Observer)*
Jean Orpwood *(Secretary)*

More information about ARC may be obtained from:
The Anglican Religious Communities, c/o The Secretary to the House of Bishops, Church House, Great Smith Street, London SW1P 3AZ

Email: info@arcie.org.uk Website: www.arlifeorg.com

Conference of Anglican Religious Orders in the Americas (CAROA)

The purpose of CAROA is to provide opportunities for mutual support and sharing among its member communities and co-ordinate their common interests and activities, to engage in dialogue with other groups, to present a coherent understanding of the Religious Life to the Church and to speak as an advocate for the Religious Orders to the Church. CAROA is incorporated as a non-profit organization in both Canada and the USA.

Sister Faith Margaret CHS (*President*)
Father David Bryan Hoopes OHC (*Vice-President*)
Sister Margaret Hayward CSC (*Secretary-Treasurer*)
The Revd Dr Donald Anderson (*General Secretary*)
PO Box 99, Little Britain, Ontario K0M 2C0, CANADA
Tel: 705 786 3330 Email: dwa@nexicom.net

House of Bishops Standing Committee on Religious Orders in the Anglican Church of Canada

The Committee usually meets twice a year, during the House of Bishops' meeting. Its rôle is consultative and supportive.

Rt Revd Linda Nicholls, Bishop of Huron *(chair)*
Most Revd Fred J Hiltz, Archbishop & Primate of Canada *(ex officio)*
Rt Revd Michael Bird, Bishop of Niagara
Rt Revd Logan Mcmenamie, Bishop of Brirish Columbia
Rt Revd Bruce Myers OGS, Bishop of Quebec
The Superiors of CSC, OHC, SSJD & SSJE
Revd Dr Donald W Anderson, General Secretary of CAROA
The Ven Paul Feheley, Principal Secretary to the Primate (*Secretary*)

General Synod of the Anglican Church of Canada

Religious Synod members:

Sister Elizabeth Rolfe-Thomas SSJD
Sister Heather Broadwell CSC

National Association for Episcopal Christian Communities (NAECC)

The NAECC is an inclusive association that shares and communicates the fruits of the Gospel, realized in community, with the church and the world. It is primarily a forum for those who are living or exploring new or continuing models of religious commitment within the context of community.

Bill Farra SCC *(President)*
Masud Ibn Syedullah TSSF *(Secretary)*
James Mahoney *(Treasurer)*

Website: naecc.us

Glossary and Indices

Aspects of the life ... sharing laughter

Sisters from three communities (OHP, CSC, CSF)

Glossary

Aspirant

A person who hopes to become a Religious and has been in touch with a particular community, but has not yet begun to live with them.

Celibacy

The commitment to remain unmarried and to refrain from sexual relationships. It is part of the vow of chastity traditionally taken by Religious. Chastity is a commitment to sexual integrity, a term applicable to fidelity in marriage as well as to celibacy in Religious Life.

Chapter

The council or meeting of Religious to deliberate and make decisions about the community. In some orders, this may consist of all the professed members of the community; in others, the Chapter is a group of members elected by the community as a whole to be their representatives.

Clothing

The ceremony in which a postulant of a community formally becomes a novice, and begins the period of formation in the mind, work and spirit of the community. It follows the initial stage of being a postulant when the prospective member first lives alongside the community. The clothing or novicing ceremony is characterised by the Religious 'receiving' the habit, or common attire, of the community.

Contemplative

A Religious whose life is concentrated on prayer inside the monastery or convent rather than on social work or ministry outside the house. Some communities were founded with the specific intention of leading a contemplative lifestyle together. Others may have a single member or small group living such a vocation within a larger community oriented to outside work.

Enclosed

This term is applied to Religious who stay within a particular convent or monastery - the 'enclosure' - to pursue more effectively a life of prayer. They would usually only leave the enclosure for medical treatment or other exceptional reasons. This rule is intended to help the enclosed Religious be more easily protected from the distractions and attentions of the outside world.

Eremitic

The eremitic Religious is one who lives the life of a hermit, that is, largely on his or her own. Hermits usually live singly, but may live in an eremitic community, where they meet together for prayer on some occasions during each day.

Evangelical Counsels

A collective name for the three vows of poverty, chastity and obedience.

Habit

The distinctive clothing of a community. In some communities, the habit is worn at all times, in others only at certain times or for certain activities. In some communities, the habit is rarely worn, except perhaps for formal occasions.

Novice

A member of a community who is in the formation stage of the Religious Life, when she or he learns the mind, work and spirit of the particular community whilst living among its members.

Oblate
Someone associated closely with a community, but who will be living a modified form of the Rule, which allows him or her to live outside the Religious house. Oblates are so-called because they make an oblation (or offering) of obedience to the community instead of taking the profession vows. In some communities, oblates remain celibate, in others they are allowed to be married. A few oblates live within a community house and then they are usually termed intern(al) oblates. The term oblate is more usually associated with Benedictine communities.

Office/Daily Office/Divine Office
The round of liturgical services of prayer and worship, which mark the rhythm of the daily routine in Religious Life. Religious communities may use the services laid down by the Church or may have their own particular Office book. The Offices may be called Morning, Midday, Evening and Night Prayer, or may be referred to by traditional names, such as Mattins, Lauds, Terce, Sext, None, Vespers and Compline.

Postulant
Someone who is in the first stage of living the Religious life. The postulancy usually begins when the aspirant begins to live in community and ends when he or she becomes a novice and 'receives the habit'. Postulants sometimes wear a distinctive dress or else may wear secular clothes.

Profession
The ceremony at which a Religious makes promises (or vows) to live the Religious Life with integrity and fidelity to the Rule. The profession of these vows may be for a limited period or for life. The usual pattern is to make a 'first' or simple profession in which the vows are made to the community. After three or more years a Life Profession may be made, which is to the Church and so the vows are usually received by a bishop. In the Anglican Communion, Life Professed Religious can usually be secularized only by the Archbishop or Presiding Bishop of a Province.

Religious (as in 'a Religious')
The general term for a person living the Religious life.

Rule
The written text containing the principles and values by which the members of a community try to live. The Rule is not simply a set of regulations, although it may contain such, but is an attempt to capture the spirit and charism of a community in written form. Some communities follow traditional Rules, such as those of St Benedict or St Augustine, others have written their own.

Tertiary/Third Order
This term is usually associated with Franciscan communities, but is used by others too. A Third Order is made up of tertiaries, people who take vows, but modified so that they are able to live in their own homes and have their own jobs. They may also marry and have children. They have a Rule of Life and are linked to other tertiaries through regular meetings. In the Franciscan family, the Third Order complements both the First Order of celibate friars and sisters and the Second Order of contemplative Religious.

Vows
The promises made by a Religious at profession. They may be poverty, chastity and obedience. In some communities, they are obedience, stability and conversion of life.

Index by location

Index of Community Wares & Services for Sale

CHURCH LINEN & NEEDLEWORK, EMBROIDERY & VESTMENTS

CRAFTS & RELIGIOUS ARTEFACTS

Index of Communities by Initials

Index by dedication/patron saint